CITY AT THE EDGE OF FOREVER

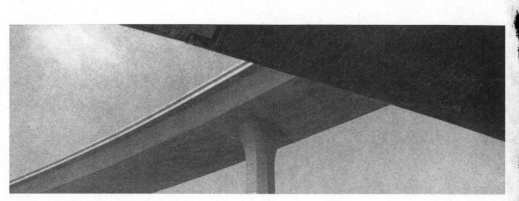

UNTITLED #2 (FREEWAYS) I 1994 I PLATINUM PRINT I 2 ¼ X 6 ¾ INCHES (5.7 X 17.1 CM)

CITY AT THE EDGE OF FOREVER

LOS ANGELES REIMAGINED

PETER LUNENFELD

VIKING

VIKING
An imprint of Penguin Random House LLC
penguinrandomhouse.com

Grateful acknowledgment is made to the Arthur Lee Estate for permission to reprint
lyrics to "You Set the Scene."

All images © Catherine Opie, Courtesy Regen Projects,
Los Angeles and Lehmann Maupin, New York, Hong Kong, and Seoul

Library of Congress Cataloging-in-Publication Data

Names: Lunenfeld, Peter, author.
Title: City at the edge of forever : Los Angeles reimagined / Peter
    Lunenfeld.
Other titles: Los Angeles reimagined
Description: New York : Viking, [2020] | Includes bibliographical
    references and index.
Identifiers: LCCN 2020013210 (print) | LCCN 2020013211 (ebook) |
    ISBN 9780525561934 (hardcover) | ISBN 9780525561941 (ebook)
Subjects: LCSH: Los Angeles (Calif.)—Social life and customs—20th
    century. | Los Angeles (Calif.)—Civilization—20th century. |
    Los Angeles (Calif.)—History—20th century. | Popular
    culture—California—Los Angeles—History—20th century.
Classification: LCC F869.L85 L86 2020 (print) | LCC F869.L85 (ebook) |
    DDC 979.4/94—dc23
LC record available at https://lccn.loc.gov/2020013210
LC ebook record available at https://lccn.loc.gov/2020013211

Printed in the United States of America
10 9 8 7 6 5 4 3 2 1

DESIGNED BY MEIGHAN CAVANAUGH

For Maud and Kyra and George

The legends may not be true, but they're definitely real.

CONTENTS

CITY AT THE EDGE OF FOREVER

Introduction WELCOME TO LA

UNTITLED #1 (FREEWAYS) | 1994 | PLATINUM PRINT | 2 ¼ X 6 ¾ INCHES (5.7 X 17.1 CM)

When I got off the plane at LAX three decades ago, I knew exactly two people in Los Angeles. One was a college buddy writing spec scripts for *Star Trek: The Next Generation*, the other a family friend working for the *National Enquirer* on the Michael Jackson–and–Bubbles beat (Bubbles was then Michael's boon companion, and a chimpanzee). I had moved west for grad school, and for the first six months I couldn't tell what I thought about my new hometown. I bought a Volkswagen with an underpowered diesel engine from two Germans who needed to fly back to Berlin the next day. They started at two thousand dollars and settled for the five hundred bucks I had on hand. Two weeks later, I was the third car in the queue to make a left on yellow—okay, when I was ready to turn, it was red—and an LAPD motor-

> A place belongs forever to whoever claims it hardest, remembers it most obsessively, wrenches it from itself, shapes it, renders it, loves it so radically that he remakes it in his own image.
>
> —Joan Didion, *The White Album*

cycle cop pulled me over. He looked straight out of central casting. Peering at my New York State driver's license through mirrored sunglasses and over a luxurious mustache, he said unsmilingly, "Welcome to LA. You'll learn." He was right.

I learned that Los Angeles fascinated me on every level, from the way the last bit of sunlight flares out on a summer night behind the Santa Monica Mountains to how people on the West Coast wear their learning more lightly than I was used to. I learned the ways that constant good weather alters the psyche. I learned that the place I'd moved to, hoping it would have so little history that I might have a chance to make some myself, instead rewarded constant digging and curiosity. I learned that the Formosa Café, a bar on Santa Monica Boulevard, still had a floor safe under one of the tables, installed by famed gangster Benjamin "Bugsy" Siegel. I learned that there'd been a utopian socialist commune in the Antelope Valley desert near Palmdale a century ago, and that there are cloistered nuns just below the Hollywood sign. I learned that the novelist John Rechy penned one of the first great novels about male hustlers out of his experiences in downtown's Pershing Square, and that the anarcho-communist Flores Magón brothers fomented rebellion in their native Mexico from Edendale, a long-forgotten neighborhood now absorbed into Silver Lake and Echo Park. I learned that Southern California has a wealth of architectural intelligence deployed on single-family homes and an anemic system of public parks, and that these two facts are not coincidental. I learned that San Francisco's Summer of Love could have taken place in Los Angeles if the cops and the sheriffs hadn't railroaded the city's best musicians out of town in the midsixties. I learned that John McLaughlin, one of the great hard-edged LA abstractionists of the 1950s, created such uniformly sized paintings because he bought his canvases prestretched from the art department at Sears.

At forty, I learned how to surf.

I learned that the more I thought about what made Los Angeles unique, the more unique it became to me. I co-organized a conference on how space itself can be scripted and ended up leading bus tours of the city that tried to decipher those scripts. I taught a seminar on rebranding Los Angeles. I spent a year at the Huntington Library going through the archives looking for tissue that would connect everything I was learning. I came to realize that the only way to understand the city, at least for me, was to weave stories about it and, like Scheherazade, to keep weaving as if my life depended on it.

The stories that follow reimagine Los Angeles, creating a series of internal connections between the disparate, but also around common themes. Each chapter is a narrative unto itself, but there are threads that connect one essay to another. Characters return in different guises, landscapes get retraced, familiar locales take on new attributes, correlations build. The web works of Los Angeles–based artist Pae White have been an inspiration. White would search her grandmother's garden in Pasadena for the largest, most labyrinthine spiderwebs she could find, slide colored paper behind them, spray them with fixative, and frame the results in a spare, modernist style. Like alchemy, White's simple process transmutes nature into culture and reminds us that nothing stands in isolation, that connection is the way of the world.

The old line about Hollywood-the-Industry—scratch the phony tinsel and you'll find real tinsel underneath—has tended to apply to too much writing about Los Angeles–the–Place. LA is a real place, after all, not just a back lot, with real stories that are more complex, contradictory, and compelling than anything that ever made it to the screen. These are the stories that follow, and they are for the people who live in the city, but also those who don't but are drawn to its legends.

A story about a story told by Aimee Semple McPherson might be just the right way to finish here. Sister Aimee, as she was known, was the most famous woman in 1920s America, and without doubt the most famous resident of Los Angeles not working in the movie business. A white Pentecostal preacher who lost her first husband while evangelizing in China, who spoke in tongues, faith-healed the sick, and rode a motorcycle onstage to preach the gospel, Sister Aimee was a hellion who enraged the more genteel elements of the city, as well as other pastors, when she preached racial harmony on the radio and fed the poor of all colors and nationalities from her Angelus Temple, just below Sunset Boulevard with a grand view of Echo Park Lake.

One day in 1926, she disappeared while visiting Venice Beach. Her mother hired divers to search for her body, her followers were devastated, and the city went through one of its longest periods of true mystery. Five weeks later, the miraculous occurred. Sister Aimee popped up in Mexico, having escaped from a trio of kidnappers— "Steve, Jake, and Mexicali Rose." She returned to be greeted by some thirty thousand jubilant Angelenos, unfazed by the fact that her desert captivity had left her neither bloody nor bowed and accepting of the fact that the hunky (and married) engineer of her radio show had disappeared and reappeared at about the same time, witnesses claiming they'd seen him and Sister Aimee canoodling in Northern California. No amount of shaming by the city's power elite and her fellow preachers, not even a grand jury inquiry, was able to rattle Sister Aimee. "That's my story and I'm sticking to it," she said.

So, too, is it with my stories about what is now as much my city as it was Sister Aimee's. And I'm sticking to them.

1 THE ALCHEMICAL CITY

UNTITLED #2 (FREEWAYS) | 1994 | PLATINUM PRINT | 2 ¼ X 6 ¾ INCHES (5.7 X 17.1 CM)

Drive-By Punditry, Location Scouts, and a User's Guide to Elemental Los Angeles

here it is. Take it." So William Mulholland addressed the thirty thousand flag-waving people who'd hiked, driven, and arrived on horseback at the terminus of the Los Angeles Aqueduct. Deep in the dusty San Fernando Valley on November 5, 1913, the band played "Yankee Doodle" as the sluice gates opened and millions of gallons of water flowed down from the Owens River, more than two hundred miles away. Mulholland had engineered the marvel of the age, irrigating the Valley and quenching the city's thirst. His great public work performed an alchemical transformation on the landscape, transmuting a town into a metropolis as the arid desert around it blossomed into lush farmland. There is no question that Mulholland made the twentieth century possible in the City of Angels. A man of few words, Mulholland managed to be both laconic and ambiguous: "There it is. Take it." What is the "it" to which he referred? Many commenters take "it" as a simple description of the water, while others see "it" as a ceremonial offering of a marvel of infrastructure. There is, however, another way to understand "it" as something less material and more mythic: "it" was the future, the tomorrow that Los Angeles lives in the twenty-first century.

Like so many drawn to the edge of the Pacific Ocean, William Mulholland came in search of a new world, and so he created one. The place that he made possible is crowned by a road that snakes atop the Santa Monica Mountains and the Hollywood Hills. Just above the Hollywood Bowl, there's a vantage point from which, on a clear day, Hollywood, downtown, the Valley, the surrounding mountains, and even the Pacific Ocean are all visible simultaneously—one of the few places where Los Angeles coheres as a whole. This road is appropriately named Mulholland Drive, and when you look out from that point, you see, manifested in the city's present, the future toward which its greatest engineer pointed in the past.

Los Angeles County had a population of 3,530 in 1850, which grew to just over a half million people when Mulholland opened the aqueduct and to more than ten million today, with so many layers of history accumulating so quickly that the kinds of narrative arcs we use to explain the trajectories of older cities simply do not apply. The city expanded out of the historic downtown core to colonize sprawling Valley suburbs. Sleepy beach towns outgrew their origins to emerge as economic dynamos. Newcomers never stopped coming, scaling the hills, building houses on stilts, gridding out the desert, carving cul-de-sacs from the sagebrush. As it flourished, Los Angeles fostered a uniquely creative spirit, its cultures reflecting a horizontal city rather than a vertical one, the width of new frontiers offering the opportunity to escape from top-down cultural hierarchies. In Los Angeles, all was change and novelty for a century, and the city's history was seen to be of little use to its future. There would be no end to it: Los Angeles, the city fated to be eternally at the edge of forever.

But it turns out that the city's fate was not eternal. The result of all of Los Angeles's building and moving and wanting and failing and trying again is that even the edge of forever has developed a history, and the task of the present is to make that history legible. Treating Southern California as an ever-refreshing Etch A Sketch, a tabula rasa that could never be filled, freed generations to explore their own possibilities, but all of that worked better when history was thinner on the ground. Now those looking to build new and improved futures need to be familiar with what worked, what didn't, what was prohibited from being tried in the first place, and why.

Getting to the point of such knowledge, much less wisdom, requires more than purely political or social history. Carey McWilliams, Reyner Banham, and Mike Davis understood this and are responsible for the three most important and influential studies of Los Angeles. McWilliams was a civil rights lawyer and journalist who went on to become editor of *The Nation*. He wrote *Southern California: An Island on the Land* in 1946 to distill and disseminate some of the best reportage about the region. He concentrated on Southern California's explosive growth and the discombobulating, and sometimes amusing, social effects all this newness and change brought about. McWilliams also presaged contemporary views of LA as the premier polyglot, hybridized cultural space in the United States. In the seventies, Banham arrived in LA as precisely the sort of person—a British architectural historian and critic—one would expect to hate everything about the city. But his *Los Angeles: The Architecture of Four Ecologies* became a classic specifically because it embraces the freeways, decentralization, and neophilia that set LA up in opposition to accepted standards of urbanism. Another two decades on, in 1990, Southern California–born Davis published his searing *City of Quartz: Excavating the Future in Los Angeles*. A Marxist, organizer, and urban theorist, Davis countered the twentieth century's real estate boosterism with a far bleaker portrait of how the city's working classes, and especially people of color, had been exploited and abused by racism, redlining, economic disenfranchisement, punitive policing, and even targeted environmental degradation. Davis juxtaposed sunshine and noir—boosters versus detractors—and showed a generation just how and why Los Angeles erupted during the civil unrest of 1992, which took place just two years after his book was first published.

When I moved to LA from New York decades ago, with the understanding that I was trading one great city for another, these three were among the first books I read. Despite their brilliance, however, they didn't fully evoke the spirit of the city as I was experiencing it. We import a word from German to describe the "spirit of the times": "zeitgeist." Less familiar may be a more recent neologism to describe the "spirit of the place": "platzgeist." Film scouts are perforce experts in platzgeist. Their job is to convey not just the visuals of a place but the ineffable relationships among natural geography and built environment, the quality of the light, the ambient soundscape, the people who live there, the ones just passing through. The interaction of these characteristics may not be comprehensive, but it is comprehensible. A vintner speaks of a wine's terroir, the specific attributes of taste, smell, and mouthfeel that can only come from a specific place. Similarly, a platzgeist should evoke a sensation similar to déjà vu, even if one has never been to that place or if what's being described took place a century ago.

The spirit of a place is not static, and a platzgeist evolves as a place sloughs off attributes and attitudes assigned to it over time and adopts new ones, especially as its population swells and changes composition. Cities have the most complex platzgeists because they are where the most compelling culture is made. It's not that forests and deserts don't command attention; it's that they are most interesting for what humans observe, rather than create, there. The platzgeist of a village can be charming, but it's parochial, and while the platzgeist of a suburb can make for fascinating sociology, it will rarely inspire passion. The British historian Sir Peter Hall is admirably direct:

"Every great burst of human creativity in history is an urban phenomenon." What makes charting a platzgeist for Los Angeles in the
twentieth century so elusive is that during those dizzying hundred
years the city didn't just expand in population; it exploded into global significance. There are many reasons for this, demographic, economic, and political, but I would argue that Los Angeles's eruption
into worldwide prominence follows its ramp-up of the arts, architecture, design, cuisines, music, theater, and literary cultures, not to
mention technical and scientific accomplishments, at a speed and
with a reach unprecedented in human history.

In 1927 Don Ryan, a journalist turned studio hack turned occasional novelist, presciently claimed that Los Angeles is the "city
with the aspirations for the Los Angelicization of the world." The
rest of the world has inherited ideas about automobile-dependent
urban, suburban, and exurban development from Los Angeles, and
while you won't find mini-malls (an LA invention) in historic city
centers, you will find them popping up on their peripheries all
across the globe, the architectural equivalents of invasive, non-
native plants. But the propensity for blending the inside and the
outside, for eschewing the formal for the casual, and the city's willingness to reinvent, to strive for limitlessness, and to embrace pleasure, all of this and more made Los Angeles a center of gravity in
global culture.

That this explosion of influence took place during the ceaselessly
recorded and endlessly commented-upon twentieth century means
Los Angeles's cultural triumphs had to compete with other stories
about the city, which almost instantly calcified into stereotypes.
Hollywood is an industry named after a place, after all, and that
industry has long attracted people who would never have moved

west were it not for the film business. Their attitudes about Southern California transmuted into myth, because myth is precisely
what popular entertainment hopes to produce. The vision of Los
Angeles as a dream factory, where everything is shiny and soul-
crushingly empty, reworks Hollywood as Moloch, the Canaanite
god who devours his own children. Even LA-born Eve Babitz, who
cleverly chronicled the city in the sixties and seventies, recapit-
ulates the usual conventions. Here is composer Igor Stravinsky's
goddaughter, a woman who famously played chess against Marcel
Duchamp during his first retrospective in the United States in Pasadena (he was clothed, she was nude; both understood the power of
the photo op), kissing off her hometown with the quip that "people
with brains went to New York and people with faces came to Los
Angeles."

But people with brains (often from New York) kept streaming
west regardless. In the thirties, Dorothy Parker traded Manhattan's
legendary Algonquin Round Table for Hollywood's writers' table,
snagging two Academy Award nominations for screenwriting along
the way to ever-greater consumption of alcohol and a place on the
blacklist for her leftist politics. Parker is reputed to have dismissed
her new hometown of LA as "seventy-two suburbs in search of a
city," a nasty little dig that resonated for generations of Angelenos
in her wake. Three decades later, Babitz herself was among them,
haunting the same bars as her idol—from the Garden of Allah to
the Chateau Marmont—though the younger woman quaffed tequila,
while Parker preferred the Scotch that ended up killing her.

Parker's scorn is emblematic of the way that LA and its narratives
about itself have come to be defined by a specific kind of intelligence,
that of the bitter screenwriter. Bitterness is the eternal condition of

the screenwriter—witness the old (self-loathing and misogynistic) joke about starlets so dumb they sleep with the writer. Witness also that Irving Thalberg, the boy wonder producer of MGM's storied years and inspiration for F. Scott Fitzgerald's *The Last Tycoon*, once said that "the most important person in the motion picture process is the writer, and we must do everything in our power to prevent them from realizing it." No wonder the writers were bitter. And is it any surprise that resentment about Hollywood-the-Industry curdled into bile about Los Angeles–the–Place? Herman Mankiewicz, who'd already moved west, wrote a famous one-line telegram to playwright Ben Hecht, who hadn't yet: "Millions are to be grabbed out here and your only competition is idiots." Within a few years, Mankiewicz and Hecht had penned two of the most iconic scripts of Hollywood's Golden Age—*Citizen Kane* (1941) and *His Girl Friday* (1940). But while Hollywood's film colony embraced these two fast-talking New York–born sons of Jewish immigrants as masters of story structure and dialogue, they were "outsiders" to the midwestern transplants who made up the vast majority of Southern California's population. These were people looking for second acts in the sun after lives spent toiling on farms and populating prairie towns. Those affected by tuberculosis and other ailments sought relief in what was advertised as "the Sanatorium of the World." During the Depression, they were joined by "Okies" from Texas, Arkansas, Oklahoma, and points south fleeing the Dust Bowl. This pairing of older "lungers" and the desperate and displaced young became known colloquially as the "Folks." The Folks may have liked the movies, but they tended to view "movie people" with suspicion, bordering on and occasionally crossing over into overt anti-Semitism. Their preachers would attack Hollywood-the-Industry (code then as now for Jews) on multiple, often contradictory fronts—as the locus of money-grubbing capitalists and simultaneously as a haven for godless communists. Hollywood-the-Industry, in return, publicly thanked the Folks for buying tickets and writing fan letters, while privately mocking them as rubes and snake handlers.

But over time the Folks changed, even if the bitter screenwriters refused to acknowledge any difference. The Folks were an uprooted people with little to lose, and their willingness to try something—anything—different made twentieth-century Southern California as early as the teens and twenties a hotbed of both innovation and quackery. For everyone who decided that the meat and potatoes of their youth could be improved by adding more vegetables and fruit, there were others willing to embrace a raw-food diet. For every seeker who embraced the serious study of Eastern practices like yoga and Buddhism, there were a hundred more flirting with cults and gurus running the gamut from the inane to the insane. In the pages that follow, you'll see how the Folks seeded the ground that allowed for the emergence of figures like Jack Parsons, a rocket scientist who was also a warlock; Jim Baker, the Hollywood restaurateur who rebranded himself "Father Yod" and established a love cult; and even Angelyne, famous for being famous long before anybody struggled to keep up with the Kardashians, and who saw her quest for celebrity as a spiritual gift to the world.

One of the first writers to crystallize what made the Folks and their city unique was Nathanael West. West moved to Los Angeles to become a screenwriter, but success eluded him, and for the most part he toiled in B pictures. He channeled his disappointments into his fourth book (the first three had sold poorly) and, in 1939, ended up publishing *The Day of the Locust*, the first truly great novel of and from Southern California. His book was both the exemplar and the sturdiest of the bitter-screenwriter narratives of Los Angeles. West's city is filled with the flamboyantly freakish, desperate to be part of the dream factory but forever relegated to the sidelines. They seethe with envy that explodes first into a riot and finally into a terrifying conflagration. Horace McCoy's existentially bleak *They Shoot Horses, Don't They?* of 1934, F. Scott Fitzgerald's dissipated Pat Hobby stories for *Esquire* in the 1940s (while he was hacking away for the studio system and pining for Paris), Bruce Wagner's millennium-era cell-phone trilogy—*I'm Losing You, I'll Let You Go,* and *Still Holding*—all these fictions are driven by a screenwriter's rage about Hollywood that burns through the very landscape of Southern California.

This scorched-earth rendition of the city by those actually living and working in Hollywood would be powerful enough, but over the decades the city also found itself being defined, and dismissed, by out-of-towners, usually Londoners and New Yorkers. From Evelyn Waugh and his mordant meditation on death in the sun, *The Loved One* (1948), to Norman Mailer's overwrought Hollywood novel *Deer Park* (1955) and equal parts brilliant and contemptuous "Superman Goes to the Supermarket," for *Gentlemen's Quarterly,* about Los Angeles's 1960 Democratic presidential convention, out-of-town writers after World War II practiced what I think of as drive-by confirmations of their preconceptions. So many people have "seen" Los Angeles as a backdrop to Hollywood's entertainments that it builds a false familiarity, preconditioning them to feel that the moment they get off the plane, it's time to comment about a place they think they already know, even though they don't.

Drive-by punditry was only rarely redeemed, and usually only by virtue of the acerbic wit of intelligences like Waugh and Mailer, who were indeed writing about a city which, at that point, lived up to well-trodden legends about freeways, sprawl, movie stars, and New Age nonsense. But that old understanding of the region doesn't allow room for those who are now emerging from or moving to Los Angeles wanting to be chefs or social-change agents or high-tech entrepreneurs, not "settling" for these careers after failing to secure a foothold in the entertainment-industrial complex. These people realize that a city known for too long for excluding voices from its culture and politics is striving to include them at every level. Los Angeles continues to live at the edge of forever, but it now has the capacity to take in its past as well as the future, and its new cohort deserves new stories.

Moving beyond a series of anecdotes, facts, images, icons, sonic traces, and other pieces of evidence requires a framework, a conceptual map to overlay on the physical geographies of the city. The coordinates for this particular mapping draw from the ante- or even anti-modern system known as alchemy, which, when remembered at all, is regarded as the infant cousin of chemistry, and mostly for its promise to transform lead into gold. What goes unremembered is that alchemy was both an experimental protoscience and a spiritual system, simultaneously pursuing both exoteric and esoteric ends. Those esoteric goals, too, had to do with transformation and purification, but of the soul, not of the base elements. The esoteric alchemists were intent on improving the state of man, to make man more like God, or at least the angels.

There were good reasons for the alchemists to shield their works and ideas behind allegorical screens. Had they been able to realize their ultimate extrinsic goal—the transformation of base into precious metals—they would have found themselves quite quickly either imprisoned or at work for the royal exchequer, just as the miller's daughter who can spin straw into gold in "Rumpelstiltskin" finds herself at the mercy of a greedy king. The alchemists' intrinsic goals— stripping Adam's stain from the human soul and making of man a divinity—strayed close to, and often over, the line of Christian heresy.

A system that on the one hand tried to construct technological practices to make something out of nothing, and that on the other was about the spiritual purification of the individual, is a compelling lens through which to look at Los Angeles: a desert made to flower, empty housing lots built to sell, a place that has never met a self-improvement scheme it couldn't transform into a cult or a gluten-free-downward-dog-facing-juicing-soft-tissue-massaging way of life.

Even more relevant are the ways in which alchemy embraces correspondence as opposed to causation. Correspondence allows us to build networks of discrete details and deploy them in space and over time to weave necessary narratives. In alchemy, correspondences are meaningful rather than coincidental. Correspondence relates the intrinsic to the extrinsic, the macro to the micro, the elements to the planets, the vices to the virtues. One of the aphorisms of alchemy is "as above, so below," an attractive concept to anyone trying to map culture to geography over time.

Alchemy's theory of the elements turns out to have yet more arcane correspondence to Los Angeles. Alchemists accepted the four classical elements of earth, air, fire, and water but subsumed them all to a fifth, the Aristotelian quintessence of the aether. The stories of Southern California during the twentieth century can be arranged under these broad rubrics in order to construct an elemental narra-tive of the region. As much as the world and even the region sees Los Angeles–the–Place as driven by Hollywood-the-Industry, there was only a short time in the 1920s when show business was the dominant economic player. Before then, it was earth and fire, and since then, air and water.

Start with earth, here corresponding to land. The Tongva were the first people of the land they called Yaa. Like the other Indige-nous peoples up and down the Pacific coast, they were almost de-stroyed by their encounter with Europeans. Spain's priests seeded missions up and down Alta California's coast through the middle of the eighteenth century, creating feudal, even slave-like conditions for the Tongva, the Chumash, and other native peoples. When El Pueblo de Nuestra Señora la Reina de los Ángeles was founded in 1781, the *pobladores*—forty-four original settlers and four soldiers—included those of Indigenous, mixed African Mexican, and Euro-pean heritage, a reminder that the population of Los Angeles has never been homogeneous. Their *pueblo* was under the rule of the original Californios, beneficiaries of land grants from the Spanish king. As the Californio grandees had displaced the priests, so they were later overrun by governors authorized by the newly indepen-dent Mexican nation. Cattle was king in this era, no matter who ruled, with grazing taking precedence over growing. Spanish-speaking rule ended as the forces of Yankee Manifest Destiny took control after 1848's Treaty of Guadalupe Hidalgo ended the brutal Mexican-American War. By that time, the city's name was stripped down to "Los Angeles" and, as the decades passed, even further, to "L.A." or, my preference, "LA."

The incoming Yankees and the remaining Californios continued ranching after 1848, but the one-two punch of devastating droughts in the 1860s, which killed off entire herds, and the advent of refrigerated boxcars in the 1870s shifted the calculus. Because the region's harvests could now be shipped by rail across the continent, Los Angeles's farm sector experienced phenomenal growth, eventually emerging as the single most productive agricultural county in the United States. But Yankees did more than ranch and farm. They transmuted earth into the commodity we call real estate. The land that had been stolen, and then granted and grazed, was now to be divided and subdivided, parceled into ever more remote, inaccessible, or even unbuildable plots. Southern California's real estate business was not solely about selling space, but instead the manufacturing and dissemination—nationally and then globally—of a dream. The boom-and-bust cycles in local housing date back more than a century and a half, and the fever for land never wanes in Southern California.

Earth was the dominant element until the second decade of the twentieth century, when fire supplanted it, or rather the combustion that occurs when oil is extracted from the ground, refined, and then pumped into car engines that mobilized an ever-exploding population, allowing them to reach out and grab all that land, if only as a small piece of paradise in front of which they could park their Ford. By the late 1920s, the economy was all about fire, with the energy industry pumping oil all across the region, local wildcatter Edward Doheny reputed to be richer than Rockefeller, and the Southland's automobile culture defining the landscape. The wealth that oil generated built downtown Los Angeles into a commercial hub at the very same time it contributed to the explosion of suburban development fed by automobiles. The oil wealth drew new

populations, created whole new industries, and contributed to burgeoning scandal and corruption, from the local Julian Pete swindles
of small investors in the twenties ("Pete" was short for "petroleum")
to the national scandal of the naval fuel reserves at Teapot Dome,
which nearly brought down President Warren G. Harding's administration. Oil had been central to the transformation of agricultural
land into automobile-centric suburban development, and oil was
just as essential to the infrastructure of the next element to ascend
to preeminence. I speak here of air, or, better yet, aerospace.

By the 1930s, the economy took to the skies, as the region's
weather was conducive to both flying and the manufacturing of aircraft. With the onset of the Second World War, Southern California's aeronautics sector was remade into an arsenal of democracy,
designing and producing more than 40 percent of all U.S. military
aircraft during the conflict. At the height of wartime production,
Douglas Aircraft alone built more than one hundred B-17 bombers,
A-20 attack bombers, and C-47 cargo planes *every single week*.
Companies like Douglas, Lockheed, and Hughes manufactured the
planes that won the war, and hired the people who populated the
valleys where their plants were located. The war effort was vora-
cious and demanded workers of all kinds, welcoming the very "Okies"
who a decade earlier had been illegally arrested at the state border
during the Depression, and making space for African American workers on production lines. Air's ascendancy was linked to conflict, and
even on the home front it was hardly an era of harmonious relationships. The war years saw the infamous mass internment or, more
accurately, incarceration of Japanese and Japanese American residents; attacks on Mexican American zoot-suiters; and, a decade later,

the brutal deportation of more than a million Mexican "guest workers," known as *braceros*.

During the Cold War, Southern California shifted from air to the airless regions beyond the atmosphere and created aerospace, the dominant industry until the start of the 1990s. If planes had been central to aviation, it was now satellites, rockets, and computerized central command systems that were being integrated into a vast, interlocking, security-obsessed system of defense and war-making capability.

The aerospace era saw an epochal transfer of wealth from Washington to Southern California, with the Department of Defense pouring more than $40 billion into the state (half a trillion in contemporary dollars). This arms-driven largesse was like a rain of gold, creating a giddy sense of prosperity for those parts of the region's population able, by virtue of their race, class, and gender, to partake in it. The defense industries built up the South Bay, and especially Orange County, into new regional centers, leaving enough cash to spread around to their children, the rising teenage demographic. Those kids used that money and the leisure time that accompanied it to create a youth-lifestyle capitalism that became the envy of the world, with surfboards, hot rods, skateboards, tennis courts, and suburban pools the seeming birthright of every Anglo kid lucky enough to grow up under the California sun.

This is not to say that everyone participated in this beach-party fantasia. Southern California was simultaneously the site of tremendous oppression of minority groups. It was also a place of riot and resistance, most famously in the African American communities during Watts in 1965; the Chicano civil rights movement and antiwar protests later in the 1960s; then, most recently, the South LA uprising in 1992, at the end of aerospace's regional dominance. That era saw Southern California's peak of influence on the national scene, with not one but two presidents of the United States hailing from the region: Richard Nixon, a native, and Ronald Reagan, who hightailed it out of the Midwest for Hollywood when he was twenty-six. Nixon and Reagan were conservatives, obsessed with strong defense. They practiced a military pump-priming, spending lavishly and promoting growth, at least in Southern California, where they funded the secret labs and immense factories of the region that produced the United States' high-tech space weaponry. The culture of secrecy that made the aerospace industry possible has also rendered it virtually invisible within the region's historical memory. The number of Southern Californians who even remember the reign of aerospace dwindles with every passing year.

A similar invisibility affects the fourth element of this alchemical mapping: water. It's been said that fish are the last to notice water because it surrounds them. Angelenos are not that different, as only a very few would even recognize the acronyms POLA or POLB. These are the abbreviations for the combined ports of Los Angeles and Long Beach, and the waters of these ports are the largest and busiest in the United States and the most important in the Western Hemisphere. Sixty percent of the Chinese-made goods that Americans consume float into POLA and POLB on their way to Walmarts and Targets from Minneapolis to Memphis—more than half a trillion dollars in trade.

The ports have been important for a century, but it's only since the early 1990s that they have been central to neoliberal globalization and to the so-called China effect, which drives the price for consumer goods to an asymptote that occasionally approaches zero. The era of water has coincided not only with the globalization of Los Angeles's trade but also with the globalization of its demographics. In this period Southern California found itself at the center of not only global trade but also global migration, with an influx of new national and ethnic populations, from Thais to Iranians to Salvadoreans, and continued border crossing by Mexican migrants, creating a thoroughly hybridized region in the twenty-first century. Perhaps because of all this change, driven by so many global factors, this era of water is not well understood, the ports the least visible of the four major historically important Southern California sectors, a blip in comparison to the attention generated by Hollywood.

Regardless of the realities of culture and commerce, we continue to build narratives of Los Angeles around the screenscapes of entertainment. This I put forward as the fifth element, the aether, or quintessence, of Hollywood the dream factory, which floats above while subsuming the other four elements of earth, fire, air, and water in the imagination. The alchemical elements regularly combine and recombine, with earth and water here, air and fire there, the quintessence of Hollywood in all its glamour and pathos serving as foil to those living the real rather than the fantasy. Understanding Los Angeles, however, requires going beyond the screen, in order to weave all these elements into the narrative tapestry of the city, reworking its cartography to create correspondences between people and places over time, and drafting an alchemist's map of Los Angeles.

Over a decade ago, I strayed into alchemy, not from a sense of belief but rather because I was interested in that period before science definitively split from the mystical, before the moment when physics renounced metaphysics. I live around the corner from a place that now sells vape juice but used to be a wondrous shop called Objets d'Art & Spirit. It sold charms and oils to questing Hollywood types. Potions for Passion, Fast Luck, and Success in the Arts sold out fast, as you might expect, but Knowledge usually languished on the shelf. Funny thing, though: when I stopped in just before the shop shuttered to get some Knowledge, it was fresh out, but I did manage to find Wisdom. When I asked the difference between Knowledge and Wisdom, the woman behind the counter said that Knowledge is red and Wisdom is green. An alchemical map of a Los Angeles reimagined transmutes the elements, diagramming a connectionist platzgeist built from correspondences, from stories that bridge the gulf between knowledge and wisdom, positioning itself between the red and the green.

2 GIDGET ON THE COUCH

UNTITLED #3 (FREEWAYS) I 1994 I PLATINUM PRINT I 2 ¼ X 6 ¾ INCHES (5.7 X 17.1 CM)

Freud, Dora (No, Not That Dora), and the Secret Austro-Hungarian Roots of Surfing

While sports, life, and style have been around for a while, the "sports lifestyle" as a distinct market is just more than a half century old. Like much else of cultural import in the years since World War II, this niche is the product of the human laboratory we call California, and specifically of its coastline. Surfing is enjoying one of its periodic peaks in the general consciousness, which makes it appropriate to look back to the moment when the sport broke free of its cult status and became the urtext of athleticism as consumer commodity. The publication of *Gidget: The Little Girl with Big Ideas* in 1957 did not just introduce us to the barely fictionalized account of a girl's summer in Malibu; it started a chain reaction that introduced surfing to the rest of the country and spread it to the world at large. The novel was an international

If all American literature comes from *Huckleberry Finn*,
all American surf culture comes from *Gidget*.

—Tim Appelo

If I had a couple bucks to buy a book, I wouldn't.
I'd buy some beer.

—Malibu surfer in *Life* magazine, right after *Gidget* came out

bestseller, was licensed for three hit movies, and was later made into numerous television shows, a comic book, and even a *Gidget* fortune-telling game. Within just a few years of the novel's release, the Beach Boys, woodies, hangin' ten, and board shorts were as popular in Kansas as they were in California and Hawaii.

The key thing to remember is that since 1957, surfing as something that you *buy* has completely overshadowed surfing as something that you *do*. I would hazard that no other activity has ever generated as many products among people who neither know how to do it nor follow those who do. The market's archetypal surfer might be blond, vacant-eyed, and deracinated, but there are deeper stories beneath surfing's glossy surface. Like Los Angeles, surfing often seems to be outside the realm of history, existing in a permanent present. In this story, though, noir can eclipse sunshine; high culture butts heads with low commerce; utopia inspires and disappoints in equal measure for local and émigré alike; and the surf shops of Huntington Beach end up owing an unacknowledged debt to Viennese coffeehouses.

Before Gidget the transmedia phenomenon, there was a real girl named Kathy Kohner who learned to surf Malibu in the summer of 1955. From her house in Brentwood, it was a trip of fewer than ten miles, but one that took her out of American suburbia and into one of the fifties' emergent youth subcultures, though nobody called them that then, just outliers from the norm. California was full of outliers—bikers in San Bernardino, Beats in San Francisco, lowriders from East LA, and surfers paddling what looked like planks spread out from Oceanside near San Diego to Santa Cruz up north. But the most visible of all, at least after Gidget, were the ones in Malibu. Malibu was then seventeen miles of unincorporated land, just north of Los Angeles and over the hill from the rapidly filling suburbs of the San Fernando Valley. Kathy's mother (an exceedingly minor player in our Papa-centric tale) was insistent that her movie-loving fifteen-year-old get out into the sunshine, forcing her to go to the beach every weekend with two older male cousins.

Bored and curious in a classically adolescent way, Kathy wandered from one side of the Malibu pier to the other and for the first time saw a collection of great-looking young men riding the waves. She walked up to one, started asking him questions, and wondered if she was bothering him. He responded, "You're breathing, aren't you?" Unlike the beach bunnies who were already hopping along the shore, Kathy decided that she wanted to join the men in the water and brought sandwiches with her to trade for time on their boards. The "boys" all had nicknames—from the Big Kahuna to Tubesteak to Da Cat (more on him later). Kathy—just under five feet tall and ninety-five pounds when wet—was a girl and, evidently to the rest of the surfers, midget-sized: hence, Girl-Midget or Gidget, a fusion that reeks of both schoolyard taunts and what Sigmund Freud called "condensation." Eventually, Kathy/Gidget bought a board and taught herself to surf.

It was at the point that Kathy decided to commit her experiences to paper that things became more complicated. She told her father that she wanted to write a book about her experiences, but he convinced her that he himself should write it. On the one hand, this made a certain amount of sense, as Frederick Kohner was a professional writer, and an accomplished one at that. Born in Teplitz-Schönau, the Czech spa town that inspired Henrik Ibsen's play *An Enemy of the People*, Frederick got his PhD in Vienna and then moved to Berlin to work in film. His brother had left for Los Angeles in 1921, so when the Nazis made Berlin increasingly inhospitable for Jews in all fields, Frederick followed in 1933. The newcomer gained steady work and even received an Oscar nomination for co-authoring *Mad About Music* in 1938. Frederick would be all but invisible today (with the exception of his Internet Movie Database entry) had it not been for his daughter, Kathy, and the new friends she made the summer of her sophomore year in high school.

Freud, that famous son of Vienna, never made it out west, and the closest he ever came to New World beach culture was a day trip to Brooklyn's Coney Island in 1911, but we might start with him, because *Gidget: The Little Girl with Big Ideas* is a title that in and of itself sounds like one of the great doctor's case studies.

Frederick began to listen in on his daughter's phone calls with her friends—with Kathy's permission, but not theirs—in order to "get the language right." After the success of the novel, there was a magazine photo shoot of Kathy on the phone, as her father— omnipresent pipe in mouth—lurks in the doorway, bathed in shadows, looking for all the world like a voyeur or stalker straight out of the Alfred Hitchcock canon. In other words, Frederick, having stolen his daughter's life, sold it as a transmedia property via his agent to publishing, film, and television.

In addition to the Gidget sequels with her name in the title, Frederick wrote other novels about precocious young girls, *Cher Papa* and *Kiki of Montparnasse* among them. In the original, Frederick is both prurient and ambivalent about his fictional daughter's sexual awakening. On the one hand there is much fifties-era talk of breasts "that would put Jayne Mansfield to shame." On the other hand, Gidget doesn't know the meaning of the word "orgy." She has to look it up "in my old man's *Funk & Wagnall's*," manages to trace its etymology back to Pythagoras, and yet inexplicably never figures out its sexual meaning. *Gidget* was released within weeks of *Lolita*. It must have been something in the air.

Gidget is very much the outsider's book, a girl watching boys being watched by her émigré father. In the novel, Gidget's dad is a professor of German literature at USC, and a certain *Mitteleuropean* gloss pervades the description of Gidget's life. There are sabbaticals in Berlin, side trips to Switzerland and Venice, and "that bitchen Mondsee in Austria." Gidget reads Françoise Sagan's famed French sexual-coming-of-age novel *A Certain Smile* three times, all the while listening to early rocker Fats Domino. Gidget's brother-in-law is a psychoanalyst, a "disciple of Freud and Rorschach" with a Beverly Hills practice specializing in children. Freudian language pervades the novel—"I guess you would call this fetishism or something," as Gidget says. Relocate *Jules et Jim* from Paris to LA, and they're Moondoggie and the Big Kahuna, with Sandra Dee subbing in for Jeanne Moreau.

Like fellow icons Captain Kirk of the starship *Enterprise* and the Thing from the Fantastic Four, Gidget is Jewish, but nobody knows this. To complicate matters even further, Gidget is the obvious inspiration for Malibu Barbie. Ruth Handler, the Jewish cofounder of Mattel, named Barbie after her own daughter, Barbara. This lineage means that Malibu Barbie, the ultimate California blonde, is a double-secret-crypto-Jew.

As Gidget moved from the page to the screen—from the "real" Kathy Kohner to Sandra Dee (herself "really" Alexandra Zuck) to Sally Field to the many other actresses who have played her—she followed the great American trajectory of willful forgetting of ethnic and regional roots. No more talk of the Mondsee and *Mitteleuropa*— the cinematic and televisual Gidgets came from bland American families and generic WASP moms and dads. Within half a decade, her deracinated status as commodity was complete. Writer Deanne Stillman claims that Kathy Kohner is a feminist heroine, and in the novel she is. The book concludes with Gidget riding a wave by herself for the first time. "I was so jazzed up that I didn't care whether I would break my neck or ever see Jeff again—or the great Kahuna. I stood, high like on a mountain peak, and dove down, but I stood it."

Standing on the board ("getting up") and angling down the face of the wave is the first lurching movement into the ranks of real surfers. The literary Gidget gives voice to the physicality of surfing and the terrifying joys peculiar to all gravity-driven thrills. But by the time the novel was adapted for films and television, seeing "Jeff again" regained its supremacy, and Gidget the inspiration became Gidget as played by a succession of Hollywood actresses, using

Malibu as a backdrop for the expected Hollywood dyad of girl meeting boy. But before she moved on, Kathy/Gidget left an indelible mark on the place where she was named. As surf journalist Paul Gross has written, "Malibu is the exact spot on earth where ancient surfing became modern surfing," and Gidget announced this to the world. This transformation has always been seen as one moving from Hawaii to California, but it was, as we have seen from the Kohner family saga, at least touched by the historical flow of refugees from Europe's near annihilation in the first half of the twentieth century.

Of the surfers that Gidget hung with that fabled summer, none was more ambivalent about the transformation of Malibu than the mysterious and gifted Miki Dora, who was likewise a child of that move from Europe to California. Dora was the master of the Malibu waves, an innovative iconoclast, a true rebel in a sea of poseurs, "a Kerouac in shorts," as the *London Times* put it in his obituary. Born Miklos Sandor Dora in Budapest, he had more aliases than a master thief, which later in life he became. He was Miki Dora, but sometimes Mickey Dora, occasionally Dickey Mora, and for a while he took his stepfather's last name and became Mickey Chapin. Then there were the nicknames—the Black Prince or the Gypsy Darling for his dark good looks; Malibu Mickey, King 'Bu, the Fiasco Kid; and most famous of all, Da Cat for his feline grace on a board.

Before we get any deeper into the stories about Dora, and they are legion, often unverified and unverifiable, we should make clear the one thing that all who saw and knew Dora agreed upon. Dora was an artist, a man who lived only for the moment of being and being seen on the wave. He was the master of small- to medium-wave surfing, a graceful longboarder in complete sync with the elements, famed for his light stance on the board and ultranimble footwork. Off the water, he was omnipotent yet inscrutable, wearing trench coats or top hats down to the water, shooting rockets off the pier, painting swastikas on his board (less fascist impulse than a last-ditch effort to *épater les bourgeois*), driving the fastest cars, dating Hollywood starlets, and never, *never* holding down a real job. Others of his generation might have been surfing bigger waves or winning more contests, but Dora was about style above all else. Dora's friends, fans, and even enemies imitated him on the water and off. He virtually created the concept of the haole soul surfer, California's version of Hawaii's aloha spirit.

Dora's father was a Royal Calvary officer in Budapest who met a beauty from Los Angeles and moved with her to Hollywood. The father opened a restaurant on Sunset Boulevard called Little Hungary, and there young Miklos met regulars Billy Wilder, Michael Korda, and Greta Garbo. These were émigrés who hungered for the culture that had disappeared along with the rest of the Austro-Hungarian Empire. Miki's exposure to these film colonials meant that Hollywood and its parties were as open to him as the waters on the coast.

Young Miki, like the sport that became his life, was a hybrid. After his mother divorced his father, she married a different sort of man. Miki's new stepfather was surf pioneer Gard Chapin, a roughneck rebel who never fit into polite society. If Miki's biological father connected him to Hollywood, Chapin's obsession with the development of surfboards brought the young Miki into the high-tech world of California's industrial design, including visits to Charles and Ray Eames's studio. The legacy of Miki Dora's two patriarchs, the Hungarian hussar and the surfing Okie, influenced the entire course of his life. Dora might have been born to ride waves, but he never shared the sunny obliviousness of postwar California teens. Instead, along with his boards and wax, he brought European nihilism to the beach.

Dora started surfing when virtually no one did. He and a few others had the waves to themselves. The late forties and early fifties were to Dora an unrecapturable Eden, a mythic space of freedom that a ninety-five-pound girl-midget destroyed. Yet Dora was also willing to cash in—as an extra in the awful beach-party films shot in Malibu, happily grabbing a free trip to Hawaii to stunt double for *Ride the Wild Surf*, teaching actress Sally Field how to handle herself on a board when she was television's first Gidget. Dora was the prototype for the new sports lifestyle icon of independence, the extreme outlaw who decries selling out at the very moment he cashes in. When he finally agreed to do a signature board for Greg Noll Surfboards, it was their biggest seller, not only when it first hit the market and sold eight thousand units in the sixties but again a quarter of a century later when it was rereleased. Even the ads for Da Cat boards were famous; they featured quixotic shots of a melancholy Dora, never surfing, always ruing his lost utopia. It was an odd marketing strategy, including an infamous shot of Dora crucified on a cross constructed from two surfboards. It's a quintessentially American theme, as old as the cowboys who decried the legend at the same time they were printing it, and as new as pierced and tattooed X Games athletes licensing their bad-boy images for the highest dollar. Dora may have been an innovator, but he saw "managing the brand" as yet another job and so never joined the entrepreneurial ranks of those who followed him.

However inefficiently he did it, Dora did sell out his beloved paradise, and the knowledge that he had done so deepened an unforgivable nastiness that ran through him. His stepfather was famed for his "redneck mean streak," racism, and anti-Semitism, and there were echoes of those hatreds in Dora's anger, or "viciousness," as he proudly referred to it. Dora bequeathed the sport a dark legacy of localism, the idea that the beach and its waves belonged to a select few and that newcomers entered the lineup at their peril. There's a triptych of photographs from the post-Gidget era, when the California coast exploded with new entrants to surfing, that shows (1) Dora knifing through the water; (2) aiming his board at another surfer; and (3) knocking the other guy off his board with surgical precision. For all that one can admire about Miki Dora's quest for the perfect wave and the deep joy he took in his own abilities, the brutality of these three photographs and the lingering effect of his "locals only" savagery have forever tainted the sport he loved.

Irrespective of, or perhaps because of, his viciousness, Dora became the first literary superstar of the surfing world. He crafted a snarling, witty persona in interviews and penned short essays for *Surfer* magazine about the end of his personal Eden. "Bad omens," he wrote, "are in the air." Whereas *The Day of the Locust* famously concludes with a fire ravaging the assorted cretins and hucksters of Nathanael West's LA, Dora's twist on the apocalyptic imagination presages our own fears of climate change, global warming, and rising waters. Dora was forever waiting for "that moment when the sea gods come and reclaim their domain."

But before those gods arose from their depths, Dora was determined to have the best and most interesting time he could. There's a contact sheet of headshots Dora did in 1962 in which he looks like nothing so much as a Magyar Marlon Brando, with two-day stubble and a cigarette dangling from his lips. The fact that Dora had met Brando and liked him was no doubt an influence, but what you get when you see pictures of Dora from this period is that he and his compatriots had perfected cool. Look at Dora leaning against a wall, wearing faded khakis, a T-shirt, and a crooked smile, and you see the American image of youth, power, and inchoate rebellion that every sports lifestyle brand the world over is still selling for billions.

Dora supported this intriguing life with an endless series of scams and subterfuges, bouncing checks and even forging plane tickets to chase waves. Like many charismatic individuals, he was famously difficult to get close to. No matter what level of intimacy someone thought they had with Dora, the likelihood was that he would turn on them, conning them or cutting them off or, most likely, both. Early on, he and two friends went down to Rio for Carnival, scammed the locals into thinking that Dora's father owned the hotel where they were staying, and then stiffed the organizers of a charity benefit for fifty grand. Dora hustled at golf, tennis, sports car racing, anything to keep moving forward.

Eventually, Da Cat just took off. In his last competition, the 1967 Malibu Invitational Surf Classic, he caught a great wave, turned his back on the judges, spectators, photographers, and assorted hangers-on, and dropped his trunks, mooning the whole lot of them—a postadolescent version of Garbo's wanting to be alone.

He spent the next four decades roaming the globe, surfing waves, charming some, stealing from others, and served time in the United States for fraud and grand larceny. His general misanthropy metastasized into full-on racism and conspiracy-mongering when he chose to live in the apartheid state of South Africa, where he bragged of having "coolies," saying that "everyone should own one," and ful- minated about a race war. He died of cancer in his Hungarian-born father's house in Santa Barbara in 2002, at the age of sixty-seven. To this day, you can still see the graffiti that the surfers he inspired to their own acts of rebellion and renunciation put up in honor of their mysterioso missing Magyar mentor: "Dora Lives!"

The word "Kakania" sounds like it could come from a luau in *Gidget Goes Hawaiian*. Miki Dora would have brought it back from the islands to Malibu's Pit, just because it sounded scatological. "Kakania" is in fact a coinage of Robert Musil's to describe the Austro- Hungarian Empire, "that misunderstood State that has since van- ished." Musil's pitiless masterpiece, *The Man Without Qualities*, offers a postmortem of the last days of the *österreichisch-ungarische Mon- archie*, which the author called Kakania because "it was *kaiserlich- königlich* (imperial-royal) and it was *kaiserlich und königlich* (imperial and royal); one of the two abbreviations applied to every thing and person, but esoteric lore was nevertheless required in order to be sure of distinguishing which institutions and persons were to be referred to as k.k. and which as k.&k." *The Man Without Qualities* is set just before World War I in a 1913 Vienna that cared deeply about such now utterly meaningless monarchical hairsplitting. Musil's is one of the great novels of the twentieth century precisely because it concerns the end of the world of the nineteenth century.

In spite of all its stifling k.k. and k.&k., or perhaps even because of it, Kakania gave birth to much genius. Freud, Kafka, Erdős, von Neumann, Wittgenstein, Klimt, Schrödinger, Schoenberg, Schum- peter, Loos, and others too numerous to mention were born into the empire. Whatever the field, from music to mathematics, physics to architecture, Kakanians were inventing modernisms across their realm. But on the battlefields of the First World War, Kakania expired, and more than a quarter century of misery, depression, pestilence, and war ensued.

So many of the best left, and some of the more talented ended up on the shores of the new Eden. Los Angeles in the thirties and forties has been called Weimar on the Pacific, but I like to think of it as Kakania on the Koast. There were enough of them to create a community, but it was a small enough group to ensure remarkable crossovers. If Bertolt Brecht could make the film *Hangmen Also Die* with Fritz Lang just before Thomas Mann, with Theodor Adorno's help, wrote *Dr. Faustus*, featuring a character based on Arnold Schoenberg, all of them living within a few miles of one another, then we can craft the following fiction about a late-summer evening in the middle of the twentieth century:

> The Kohner family drives east on Sunset from Brentwood to Little Hungary, where Miki Dora's father greets them at the door. Miki's not there. He's sleeping in the Pit at Malibu, waiting for dawn to break. The Kohners are seated next to a table where the Budapest-born actress Hedy Lamarr sits alone, puzzling over the torpedo-protection technology that earned her a patent and the grateful thanks of the War Department. As the Kohners leave, they pass an older man coming in the door. He is an architect who has walked up to Sunset Strip from his house on Kings Road. Did they all have goulash, or was there a special on schnitzel? Given that this is sheer invention, I choose goulash.

The latecomer to this fictional dinner was Rudolph M. Schindler, who—though close to forgotten at midcentury—is now acknowledged, along with fellow Austro-Hungarian expat Richard Neutra, to be one of the two finest modern architects to have worked in Los Angeles. The modest residence from which he walked to Little Hungary is now universally acclaimed as one of the great modernist private homes. The Schindler House is the next stop on our connectionist journey around Southern California, because it both prefigures and outlives the cultural and economic transformations to which Gidget and Da Cat contributed.

Schindler wasn't running away from persecution in 1911 when he left Vienna for America. Instead, he was seeking space, light, and opportunity, the classic California trio. Along the way, he stopped in Chicago for a few years to work for Frank Lloyd Wright, and it was Wright who convinced him to head even farther west. The plan was to have Schindler supervise the construction of Wright's Barnsdall house in Hollywood. After breaking away from Wright, Schindler and his wife, Pauline, decided he should stay in Los Angeles and establish a combination residence and studio, on the model of Wright's own Taliesin. The Schindlers forged a relationship with Clyde and Marian Chace. Pauline and Marian had been friends in college, and Clyde was a builder interested in new materials and construction. All were utopian modernists, interested in remaking the world through form and action. They decided to pool their resources and create a space for a new way of living in which each of the residents would function as an artist, a communal space in which cooking was transformed from womanly drudgery into shared pleasure, in which the boundaries between family and community, between the personal and the political, and between work, life, and play, would dissolve.

Erected in the then only partially developed unincorporated area of West Hollywood, Schindler's 1922 house was designed to be a house for radicals. But nothing about the way they lived was as radical as the space in which they were living. Two couples were intended to share the main house, arranged in a symmetrical pattern. There was an additional studio attached for the use of a single individual. The materials were simple: concrete, glass, unadorned wood. The construction was unconventional, with concrete walls poured on the ground and then raised up, slits for windows, and numerous sliding panels designed to facilitate movement across boundaries, from interior to exterior and among the couples' shared spaces. There were Japanese theatrical performances in the garden, the residents wore toga-like garments free of buttons and zippers, politics leaned left, rumors of polygamous couplings were bandied about, and all in all the neighbors were scandalized. The architectural critic Reyner Banham famously described Schindler's design as creating a structure that was built "as if there had never been houses before."

The key aspect that so radically breaks with earlier architecture is the melding of interior and exterior. The landscape flows into the home, and the home, via its outdoor patios, fireplaces, and sleeping porches, intermingles with the outdoors. While his erstwhile friend, colleague, and eventual Schindler House–mate Richard Neutra became more famous, Schindler was there first. The style that Schindler and Neutra developed on the fringes of architectural civilization became central, two decades later, to the program of *Arts & Architecture*. The magazine sponsored the Case Study House program from 1945 to 1966, and its pictures of the new style of architecture—often by photographer Julius Shulman—influenced the entire post-war building boom. The ranch home with pool, sliding glass doors, and stripped-down aesthetic, its seamless flow, whether kitsched up for the suburbs or not, owes its mass appeal to these case-study homes, but even more to the photographs of them.

Just as surfing is a sport that most people experience through photography—there are lots of readers of *Surfer* and Surfline.com in Indiana and Arkansas—so, too, is high-modern architecture something that most people experience only through images. It can even be said that surfing and modern architecture are designed for the perfect moment of photography: in surfing that instant in the tube before the wave closes in, in architecture that brief interval between the end of construction and the day the clients move in their possessions. There's an odd symmetry between the spiritual claims of soul surfing and the West Coast's high-modern architecture as well. Each claimed the desire for a personal connection to and communion with nature, achieved through the spare use of the most contemporary materials and techniques. Yet this communion, often discussed in the loftiest of terms, was also quite exclusive, and those who achieved its satori often fought to keep others away. We have already condemned Miki Dora's nasty localism after the Gidget wave rolled in, but what are we to make of Pauline Schindler's decade-long attempt to restrict Kings Road to zoning for single-family homes? No renters, or even condos, in her workers' paradise, I suppose.

It is in the mix of production, promotion, sale, and compromise that these Kakanian émigrés—the Kohners, the Doras, and the Schindlers—come together. Just as Schindler was breaking down the boundaries between inside and outside with his radical archi-tecture, and Dora was melding shore and break with his grace, Gidget and her father were erasing the distance between people who could actually surf and those who just wanted a piece of the surfing lifestyle. X-treme sports marketing, which sells T-shirts rather than skills and sunglasses instead of experiences, can trace its multibillion-dollar industry back fifty years to this odd group on the run from the ruins of the Austro-Hungarian Empire. It's gnarly on the Ringstrasse, dude!

3 THE FACTORY MODEL OF DESIRE

UNTITLED #5 (FREEWAYS) I 1994 I PLATINUM PRINT I 2 ¼ X 6 ¾ INCHES (5.7 X 17.1 CM)

Walt Disney, Hugh Hefner, and the Transformation of Sex, Death, and Boredom in America

Once upon a time, there were two young men from the Midwest who wanted to change the world. Both ended up in Los Angeles, where their dreams came true, but what merits our attention is the similarity of what they accomplished and how they did it, though one tapped into childlike wonder and the other stuck to adult, if not necessarily mature, content. What was shared by Walt Disney (small-town Marceline, Missouri's most famous son) and Hugh Hefner (proud product of the Windy City) was a profound understanding of the twentieth century's transformations of sex and death. These men's names are universally recognized because each took his intuitions about our primal urges and inevitable demise and expertly made them over into new lifestyles built around Entertainment Everlasting.

The sex of the millennium is pornography.
—Germaine Greer

If anything is more irresistible than Jesus, it's Mickey.
—Carl Hiaasen

Life had a choice to make early on. Immortality, or infinite mutability punctuated by death and rebirth? Though a few single-celled organisms are still burbling around, life in its wisdom abandoned self-replication and embraced sex, the intertwining of individuals to produce other individuals, who adapted to their environments, matured sexually, and repeated the process, albeit with ever-shifting results. In other words, life would rather fuck and evolve than endure the stasis of immortality, and we are all the better for it.

Sigmund Freud was hardly the first to link eros and thanatos, but conditions in Freud's Vienna were more akin to the hunter-gatherer's ancestral veldt than to today's developed world. In Freud's time, sex remained intimately yoked to death. Men and women dallied outside marriage, but as a recreational sport, sex was closer to running the bulls at Pamplona than playing doubles tennis. As for death, childbirth was still dangerous, infant mortality sky-high, and the sick and the dying not yet exiled to old-age homes. No wonder, then, that this was the heyday of the cemetery as leisure space. What better Sunday amusement than wandering amid its shady bowers, sketching its marbled memorials, and pondering one's own mortality over a picnic of cold poached chicken in aspic?

This was the world into which Walter Elias Disney was born, and the stories on which he was raised were not only appropriate to those conditions but dictated by them. The fairy tales of Hans Christian Andersen and the Brothers Grimm were for children whose lives were mired in death. The old perished at home, friends and relatives succumbed without treatment, children regularly lost siblings. Not even the richest families were immune. Arthur Guinness, founder of the brewery that thrives to this day, had twenty-one children in the second half of the eighteenth century, only ten of whom survived to adulthood (the heroic martyrdom of Arthur's wife, the former Olivia Whitmore, will have to go unmemorialized here).

Even the most pampered of Guinness children required stories to inoculate themselves emotionally. This is why Red Riding Hood gets eaten, the Little Match Girl perishes in the bitter cold, and the Little Mermaid willingly suffers, for her love of the prince, on legs that burn like fire. Fairy-tale worlds brim with violence, privation, and premature death, their narratives rife with ravenous wolves, jealous stepmothers, and unprotected adolescent female protagonists. Blame Jack's ever-growing beanstalk for bloodying poor, innocent Rose-Red. Fairy tales incarnate not only the chill of mortality but also the heat of unchecked hormones.

Walt's genius was to understand that as the context shifted, so, too, must the texts. His most famous character, Mickey Mouse, first caught the public's attention in *Steamboat Willie*, which was released in 1928, the same year the Scottish scientist Alexander Fleming discovered penicillin. The children who grew up with Walt's early animations, then, were protected by the explosion of antibiotics and immunizations that characterized the first half of the twentieth century. By the time those children's children were watching *Escape to Witch Mountain* on TV and buying personalized felt mouse ears at a kiosk next to Mr. Toad's Wild Ride, scarlet fever was no more terrifying than the common cold, polio was a thing of the past, mothers gave birth in hospitals and came home without fail. The floor plans of middle-class homes expanded so that the sounds and smells of sex were cordoned off from the rest of the household, and Grandpa and Grandma were packed off to Leisureworld before "passing" in a sterile hospital ward. The children born in the second half of the twentieth century were truly modern. "Things" didn't happen *to* them; they and the adults around them made "things" happen *for* them.

Walt made things happen in a big way. By the late 1930s, Mickey Mouse was as much of a cultural sensation as Charlie Chaplin. The European avant-garde embraced Mickey as a symbol of the anarchic liberation of the New World and its entertainments. The Soviet director Sergei Eisenstein wrote, "I'm sometimes frightened when I watch [Disney's] films. Frightened because of some absolute perfection in what he does… He creates somewhere in the realm of the very purest and most primal depths." During this same period, however, the critic Walter Benjamin expressed concern about the totalitarian implications of "the Disney method" that normalized power relationships—in other words, Donald Duck gets whacked because that's his fate in life: he's a whackable duck and no amount of social organizing will make him less whackable. Neither were the fascists happy: the Nazis took Walt to task for appropriating the tales of the German *Volk* and "Americanizing" them, stripping away their stern morality for the sake of entertainment.

We have a word for taking an ancient tale or a gritty neighborhood and bleeding the edge from it: that word is "Disneyfication." In the Brothers Grimm, stories end with terrible retribution: on their way to Cinderella's wedding, each of the wicked stepsisters has one eye pecked out, and then on the way home, the other. Walt's 1950 film, by contrast, doesn't even bother to mete out punishment to the stepsisters, instead concluding with a newlywed kiss between Cinderella and Prince Charming. Decades later, in a direct-to-video sequel, even that was too harsh, and one of the two stepsisters is rehabilitated, morphing into yet another Disneyfied good-girl-who-also-happens-to-be-beautiful.

By the time of the corporate resurgence of animation two decades after Walt's death, the Disney company entirely inverted Hans Christian Andersen's most famous fable. Instead of the Little Mermaid making the ultimate sacrifice, turning into the "seething foam" of the sea so that her prince might be happy and she might achieve God's grace, the mermaid (now named Ariel) marries the prince, defeats the sea witch, reconciles with her father, and lives happily ever after, ushering in a multidecade run of animated fairy tales—from *Beauty and the Beast* (1991) and *Aladdin* (1992) to *Frozen* (2013) and *Coco* (2017)—that have generated billions for the House of Mouse. Let it be said, however, that the road to Disneyfication is not always smooth. In 1995 an Arkansas woman filed suit against the Walt Disney Company, insisting that an oddly shaped structure on King Triton's underwater castle of gold resembled an enormous, erect penis. The suit was eventually dropped, but it should be noted that the allegedly phallic turret has been banished from subsequent releases of the film.

Like fellow midwesterner Walt Disney, Hugh Hefner had a warm, supportive mother and a distant, demanding father. Such is the classic family dynamic of the nascent entrepreneur, and indeed, though Hef and Walt were a generation apart, their similarities vastly overwhelm their differences. Both had backgrounds in commercial art; both served in wars but saw no action; both were serial entrepreneurs, though neither was particularly interested in the minutiae of business; both became world famous for success in a single medium, only to move on to create complex ecosystems of entertainments and environments. Most significant, Walt and Hef simultaneously perfected what I call the Factory Model of Desire, wherein the only fantasies that endure are those that can be fulfilled by a preexisting, branded, mass-marketed commodity.

Before all of that, though, Hef was a World War II vet who returned home to Chicago poised to make a contribution. After the requisite setbacks—in school, in marriage, in business—he borrowed eight hundred dollars from his mother, raised a few thousand more from friends, and founded a magazine he called *Stag Party*. However, before the first issue came out (featuring Marilyn Monroe "with nothing on but the radio") another men's magazine called *Stag* threatened to sue, so Hef changed his magazine's name to *Playboy*. With the mascot's metamorphosis from deer to rabbit, the epochal Playboy Bunny was born.

As with Walt, history rewards the prescient artist, and *Playboy* emerged at the same time as the first successful clinical trials of the oral contraceptive pill. Hef's magazine became the public face of technologized, midtwentieth-century hedonism; *Playboy* incarnated sex severed utterly from reproduction. In the first issue's now-famous introduction, the young editor and publisher wrote: "We like our apartment. We enjoy mixing up cocktails and an hors d'oeuvre or two, putting a little mood music on the phonograph and inviting in a female acquaintance for a quiet discussion on Picasso, Nietzsche, jazz, sex.... If we are able to give the American male a few extra laughs and a little diversion from the anxieties of the Atomic Age, we'll feel we've justified our existence." The telltale reference to nuclear holocaust reminds us that death, regardless of how it morphed in the twentieth century, remained tethered to sex, while sex itself was undergoing its own radical reenvisioning. Walt may have rewritten old stories for modern children, but Hef invented brave new tales for brave new adults in a brave new era.

Turn on Hef's earliest television show, *Playboy's Penthouse*, and watch Hef, pipe in hand, rather stiffly invite us in to join his swinging party. And what a party it was, with foulmouthed comedian Lenny Bruce ogling real-life Playmates and Nat King Cole tickling the ivories. This social leveling of hepcats and kittens—blacks, Jews, and women who later could be seen without their clothes on in the magazine—was too incendiary for some stations in the South, yet Hef and his people preferred losing markets to succumbing to fears of race mixing. This was the man who was proud of publishing some of the biggest literary stars of his time, who staked out liberal positions on civil rights and censorship disputes and found common cause with second-wave feminists over birth control and abortion.

Yet by the time he moved his personal operations to Los Angeles in the 1970s, Hef's emphasis on sex had devolved ever more surely into an emphasis on *Hef's* sex. The Mansion in Chicago may have been a swinging pad, but the Mansion West, located in Holmby Hills near TV producer Aaron Spelling's palatial spread and the Disney manse, was weird, and became weirder, the site of a Me Decade–long bacchanal documented play by play in Hef's house organ. The baby oil–slathered pornotopia was assuredly not all fun and games. One night, while performing cunnilingus, poor Hef accidentally inhaled a Ben Wa ball out of July 1977 Playmate of the Month Sondra Theodore. The canny centerfold deployed the Heimlich maneuver, the gleaming silver orb flew out of Hef's throat, and the lucky girl framed the unique souvenir above the motto "Lest We Forget." It was in this period that Hef admitted, "The most successful sex object I'd ever created was me."

Back in the middle of the twentieth century, psychologist Abraham Maslow distilled his years of research on human needs into a powerful graphic that has been taught in undergrad psych courses for decades. A marvel of information design, Maslow's pyramid cleverly shows how humans negotiate their needs. At the bottom are what Maslow called "deficit needs" because we feel them most acutely when they are unfulfilled: these are our needs for air, water, and food. In the middle are our needs within the social sphere, like finding others with whom to work and connect. At the apex of the pyramid we confront the most abstract "being needs," which, when met, literally make us into better people.

What Maslow's pyramid does *not* address is a phrase that now returns two million hits on Google: "entertainment needs." As insightful as Maslow was, Walt and Hef were more forward thinking. Both acutely understood that as casual sex flowered and death moved offstage, so, too, would the hierarchy of human needs evolve. Instinctually, Walt and Hef understood that the Enlightenment notion of enlightenment that Maslow located at the top of his pyramid would never be as popular, much less as profitable, as entertainment.

Entertainment becomes ubiquitous and audiences theoretically unlimited with the advent of what we now call "transmedia." No one before or since has gotten that as profoundly as Walt, who began his career with animated shorts about funny animals; won an honorary Academy Award for *Snow White and the Seven Dwarfs* (eight Oscars, actually, one regular sized and seven more miniatures—for the dwarfs, of course); moved into comics (we have him to thank for Carl Barks's sublime *Donald Duck*); then low-budget live-action movies (*Swiss Family Robinson, The Shaggy Dog*); television (*The Wonderful World of Disney, The Mickey Mouse Club*); licensed goods of every description (from watches to pajamas to anything you can slap a copyrighted character image onto); and finally into what he called "theme parks" (never, ever the more common "amusement parks").

Inspired by sources as disparate as Copenhagen's Tivoli Gardens and Glendale's Forest Lawn cemetery, Walt opened Disneyland in 1955 as a *Gesamtkunstraum*, a totally integrated aesthetic space, walled off from the world and formed as much by the cinematic imagination as by any kind of architectural impulse. Disneyland was a space for pure entertainment, conceived in large part around Walt's brilliant but little-known concept of "weenie-tecture." In the movies, dog trainers stood off camera and waved frankfurters to get their charges to move across the stage as bidden. Walt took the concept of the hot dog, or weenie, as focusing device and deployed it throughout the Magic Kingdom. The ultimate weenie, of course, is Sleeping Beauty's castle, which pulls people down Main Street toward Fantasyland. At every major juncture there are weenies deployed in alternate directions, ensuring predictable, manageable foot traffic. In Disney's theme parks, crowds find their way toward the secondary weenies, those visual magnets beckoning enraptured guests from ride to character greetings to shops to exit.

It's hard to resist creating double or even single entendres about weenies and *Playboy*, but just five years after Disneyland opened, Hef likewise determined that there would be a demand for a *Gesamt-kunstraum* for his particular kind of entertainment. He founded the first Playboy Club in Chicago and then went on to create a string of such clubs from Los Angeles to New York, London to Tokyo, Manila to Macao. Like Disney's lands and worlds, Playboy Clubs were extrusions of the cinematic. Hef, a lifelong movie buff, was obsessed with the erotics of the silver screen, and the Playboy Clubs instantiated his cinema-inspired architectural fantasias, fleshing out the bachelor pads and urban boîtes of his fevered imagination. These were set-designed and fully staffed spaces where the average Joe (after forking over the then-estimable sum of twenty-five dollars for a "key") could live life as though he were James Bond. So successful was this merging of fantasy and real space as entertainment that filmed entertainment returned the compliment. In *Diamonds Are Forever*, an execrable seventies installment of the venerable franchise, Sean Connery as 007 is shown with a London Playboy Club key—a weenie if ever there was one.

Walt and Hef both, then, offered their paying customers a chance to break through the fourth wall, to enter the dreamscape and interact with its cast (Mickey or Cinderella at Disneyland; fluffy-tailed bunnies in the Playboy Clubs). These cast members were subject to strict regulations about fraternization and to minutely orchestrated rituals of appearance and behavior. Walt, for example, insisted that they emerge from hidden elevators and that characters like Goofy never be seen without their heads on. Hef liked rules as well. The *Bunny Manual* prohibited the "girls" from sitting (though each was schooled in the Perch, which involved leaning against a chair back) and elaborated upon the crucial Bunny Dip, the key to smooth drink service: "a Bunny... does not awkwardly reach across the table" but "arches the back as much as possible, then bends the knees to whatever degree is necessary." This kind of live performance of cinematic spectacle, of course, became a sine qua non of later cultural entrepreneurs, from Ray Kroc and the McDonald's Playland to the ESPN Zone and every other horrible, themed entertainment eatery that's opened in a mall or downtown redevelopment district near you. But unsurprisingly, Walt and Hef got there first. In Southern California, when asked what they did for a living, Walt's people would say, "I work for the mouse," while Hef's responded, "I work for the bunny."

As mentioned, both had homes in Holmby Hills, nestled between those two more famous enclaves for the rich, Bel Air and Beverly Hills. But Walt and Hef were most truly neighbors in a wondrously named and entirely imaginary place called "the uncanny valley." In a 1970 paper, Japanese roboticist Masahiro Mori coined the term to explain why it was that as robots became more human, they engendered ever-greater unease in spectators and users. Mori claimed that we recognize machines as they begin to look and behave like us, but, ironically, the closer they actually get to us, the creepier it makes us feel. Mori charts his research with industrial robots (nonhumanoid machines) on one end of the scale and healthy humans on the other, demonstrating that as robots approach the human, they rise at first, only to fall into the valley as their *unheimlich* qualities, both eerie and familiar, recall prostheses, corpses, and zombies. The uncanny valley extends into 3-D films as well, and it's the reason that the toys in *Toy Story* are so much more involving than the few people we see; and why 2010's *Avatar* was so much more successful than 2001's *Final Fantasy: The Spirits Within*, a translation of a successful video game into one of the biggest money-losing animated feature films of all time. It's not just that animation advanced over the course of the decade; it's that *Avatar*'s sultry Neytiri, being not quite human, was that much less likely to tumble into the uncanny valley than *Final Fantasy*'s photo-realistic CGI "human," Dr. Aki Ross.

Obviously, Walt and his corporate descendants have been taking the standard route into the uncanny valley ever since the first animatronics in the Hall of Presidents. The Imagineers worked long and hard on defamiliarizing and refamiliarizing their animation of the nonliving to create simulations that delight rather than disturb. But juxtaposing Walt and Hef leads to one completely unexpected discovery: the uncanny valley has more than one route into it. If roboticists, animators, and Imagineers have entered from the south, think of Hef as a pioneer in a baby-oil-and-vibrator-filled covered wagon arriving from the north, uninterested in creating the lifelike from the inanimate and instead taking living humans and rendering them so seamless, inflated, and plastic that they approach the condition of unreality. In other words, if *animation* is the southern route into the valley, then *airbrushing* takes you in from the north. Each is drawing of a kind, but the animator takes the drawing and makes it "real," while the airbrusher takes photography and creates an ideal.

The Playboy Playmate might have begun as a girl next door, but she was always buffed and re-buffed by the magazine's expert photographers, burnished to a high-gloss sheen before being printed on heavy-gloss stock. The addition of ubiquitous plastic surgery, literally from head to toe, Brazilian waxes, Oompa-Loompa orange tans, and bleached hair yielded squads of pornofied California blondes (sometimes zygotic twins and triplets) who became pneumatic specimens of the posthuman *unheimlich*. *The Girls Next Door* of TV fame were filmed at the Mansion but lived in the uncanny valley along with other plastic-surgery addicts, including the Disney-obsessed Michael Jackson, catwoman-socialite Jocelyn Wildenstein, and even the rictus-jawed Hef and his third and final wife, Crystal Harris, who was in her early thirties when he passed at the age of ninety-one, and who herself has claimed to be a sufferer of "breast implant illness."

So what, then, do these two multimedia, midcentury, midwestern megalomaniacs have to teach us about life in the uncanny valley? Walt sees death receding and builds a Magic Kingdom out of princesses who don't die but don't get to fuck much either. Hef, like Walt an avid cartoonist in his youth, fills a mansion in the Hollywood Hills with the Girls Next Door, who grew up wanting to be princesses, but strips off their robes and pumps up their chests, creating a masturbatory simulation of sex without reproduction. In 1967 the underground magazine *Ramparts* commissioned *Mad Magazine* cartoonist Wally Wood to combine Disneyland's Main Street with the Playboy Mansion. A half century ago, Wood's orgiastic princesses and rutting cartoon creatures read like caricatures. Now, in an era of ubiquitous streaming pornography, furries, entertainment on demand, cosplay, personal digital assistants, deepfake technologies, and Instagram filters, they read as reportage.

4 RIOTS GOIN' ON

UNTITLED #7 (FREEWAYS) | 1994 | PLATINUM PRINT | 2 ¼ X 6 ¾ INCHES (5.7 X 17.1 CM)

Jazz on the Stem, Pop on the Strip, and What Happens When Cops Try to Crush Culture

Arthur Taylor Lee died sure that you'd have heard of him, but you probably haven't. In the summers of 1965 and 1966, had you been the kind of kid who hung out on Sunset Strip, you definitely would've known about the African American front man for the rock-and-roll band Love, a pop singer so protean he has been called the father of psychedelic style and, with the single "7 and 7 Is," the earliest godfather of punk. But Lee's momentum was lost during the upheaval in the fall of 1966 known as the Riot on Sunset Strip.

Let's ignore for the moment that Lee's life pre- and post-Love parses like a supercut of every MTV rise-and-fall music documentary— the teenager who sets the record for baskets in a single game at South Central's Dorsey High and wanders north to Hollywood to stare at

Everything I've seen needs rearranging
And for anyone who thinks it's strange
Then you should be the first to want to make this change

—Arthur Taylor Lee, "You Set the Scene" (1967)

They came in and flooded a community that wasn't prepared to meet them. . . . We didn't ask these people to come here.

—LAPD chief Bill Parker on race relations

the stacked platters of the Columbia Records building, knowing, just *knowing* that fame awaits. A chance meeting presents Lee with a collaborator who brings out the best in him. An audition for other players dredges up Bobby Beausoleil, future Manson Family killer (Bobby doesn't get the gig). Love, the band that emerges, generates so much heat on the Strip that it is neck and neck with the Byrds in the cool Olympics, and Lee serves as mentor to some UCLA dropouts who have read just enough William Blake and Aldous Huxley to name-check *The Doors of Perception*. But long before Jim Morrison became the Lizard King and his band shaved its name down to the Doors, Lee and Love were already renting a twenties-era mansion on Mulholland Drive known as the Castle, which for decadence and debauchery rivaled anywhere Hugh Hefner ever lived. The Castle and the Strip

were so all-enveloping, in fact, that Lee refused to tour, which deci-
mated record sales, which led to increasingly paranoid drug and
alcohol use, which broke up the band. Ensuing years brought the inevitable re-forming of Love in and around the deaths of its members
and Lee's five-year stint for grand larceny in the state pen. Regardless
of the drama, Love's first three albums remain classics.

But what if Lee and his band, Love, were victims of a more complex etiology, unknowing players in a long history of subterranean
conflict between the Dionysian mysteries of music and the martial
policies of law enforcement in Southern California? As it turns out,
Los Angeles is the only U.S. city that had not one but *two* popular,
profitable musical movements destroyed by police power in the quarter century after World War II. To see this clearly, we have to travel
both spatially and temporally, going back more than a decade and
moving south, and then forward two decades and due west. The
villains will change uniforms, the music will shift tempos, but the
story remains depressingly the same.

Starting from the Strip, head east on Sunset toward downtown.
Cutting through Chinatown, move next to Little Tokyo, and take Central south from First Street. This trip takes us from the locus of white
pop music in 1966 over to Central Avenue, the center of African American LA. But first we have to go back decades, to the city before the war.

> Los Angeles, a city
> Out in the Golden West
> Where flowers bloom in plenty
> And nature speaks of rest
>
> —Edith Brown-Young, "Los Angeles" (1909)

Twenty-first-century Southern California is incredibly diverse, with more residents of Korean descent than any city outside Korea, more Cambodians than anywhere outside Cambodia, more Samoans, and so forth, and that's not to mention enough Mexican Americans to make Los Angeles second only to Mexico City when it comes to framing cultural and political issues for Spanish-speaking North America. But between 1900 and the Second World War, any official civic diversity agenda was more limited—to Anglos and Saxons, in fact—with the city fathers pushing a Protestant paradise by the Pacific. In the first few decades of the twentieth century, LA's population exploded, but it didn't fundamentally *change*. That was because the bulk of the newcomers flowed west from the white-bread heartlands of the South and Midwest, so much so that "Iowa by the Sea" picnics, with seating arranged according to the expat Iowans' counties of origin, were some of the most popular entertainments in the region, with 100,000-plus attendees.

Southern California's rulers not only liked but encouraged this homogeneity. These oligarchs were unabashedly anti-Semitic, anti-Catholic, antiunion, anticommunist, and—need it be added?—racist to the core. The East Coast, and even San Francisco to the north, might have been overrun by cosmopolitans, union thugs, sausage eaters, heathens, Semites, and papists, but that would not be permitted in the Southland. Henry Huntington, General Harrison Gray Otis, Harry Chandler, and the Committee of Twenty-Five that followed them ruled downtown LA for most of the twentieth century. They were conservatives who knew what kind of city they wanted: one that understood that capital creates jobs and that working people should know their place. Above all, they wanted a city that was a reflection of their own ethnic and religious identity.

The songbook of the first decades of the twentieth century in Los Angeles reflected their profoundly conservative, boosterish spirit, from Edith Brown-Young's pastoral "Los Angeles" in 1909 through Bing Crosby's suburban anthem of 1944, "San Fernando Valley (I'm Packin' My Grip)."

The Second World War changed everything. Los Angeles is as far west as you can go before hitting the "Far East," and that made it the engine of the American war in the Pacific. Kaiser Steel fed the boat-yards where the massive battleships were built; high technologies powered the Douglas and Hughes factories that produced the air-planes, with Chrysler auto plants repurposed to build their engines; and the Willys-Overland plant cranked out jeeps, many of the lines running twenty-four hours a day. But to keep this production going, Southern California's factories needed new workers, and they weren't all going to be like their midwestern, Anglo-Saxon predecessors.

During the war years, Los Angeles grew faster than any other metropolitan region in the country, with the county's population increasing 50 percent between 1940 and 1950, to some four million people. Even more dramatic was the increase in the population of people of color, whose numbers more than doubled. As Southern California shifted to an all-encompassing war footing, industry de-manded an expanded labor force and recruited from hitherto un-tapped demographic groups, including women (think Rosie the Riveter) and people of color. Demanding and accepting, however, were not the same thing. There were stories about black workers herded into boxing rings at Douglas Aircraft factories to fight for their white foremen's amusement. The infamous Zoot Suit Riots of 1943 pitted Anglo sailors and marines against Mexican Americans in their wide-shouldered, peg-legged "drapes," with the LAPD not only ignoring but encouraging the rampaging servicemen. And, of course, there was the wholesale internment of the region's Japanese Americans, including the forced evacuation of Little Tokyo to Manzanar and other desert camps. LA's mayor during the war, Fletcher Bowron, spearheaded this xenophobia and brought catastrophe down upon his own Japanese American citizens. As Chester Himes, author of the magisterial noir novel *If He Hollers Let Him Go*, wrote in his autobiography, "The mental corrosion of race prejudice in Los Angeles" left one "bitter and saturated with hate."

As much as the demographics changed, so, too, did the entertainments. With jobs aplenty, production lines running day and night, and soldiers, sailors, and airmen on three-day leaves, there was money in people's pockets, and they wanted to spend it on more than movies and malteds. That's where Central Avenue came in. Central, also known as the Stem, had been the heart of black LA since the 1920s, and the Dunbar Hotel had been the beating muscle of that heart. African Americans were excluded from most hotels in Los Angeles, and from all of the better ones. A black entrepreneur, John Somerville, decided to build an establishment to surpass any other that catered to African Americans. When it opened in 1922, W. E. B. Du Bois came to celebrate, calling the hotel "a jewel done with loving hands... a beautiful inn with a soul."

For the next quarter century the hotel, later renamed after the African American poet Paul Dunbar, hosted brave travelers who consulted their invaluable Negro Motorist Green-Books, which listed lodgings, restaurants, and even beauty salons around the country that were either black-owned or amenable to black patrons. The Dunbar sheltered the great, like poet Langston Hughes and jurist Thurgood Marshall, as well as the entertainers who could perform in the clubs at whites-only hotels like the Ambassador but weren't permitted to sleep in the rooms. The latter included Billie Holiday and Duke Ellington, who would bring his whole orchestra, transforming the Dunbar into an all-night jam session. The Dunbar's energy attracted other celebrities and entrepreneurs, including the former world heavyweight champion boxer Jack Johnson, who opened the Showboat, an after-hours club of his own inside the hotel. Most famous, however, was the Club Alabam, which opened just next door and became the best-known jazz club on the West Coast.

The clubs up and down the Stem changed names and styles over the years, moving from the expatriate New Orleans Dixieland sounds of Jelly Roll Morton in the early 1920s to the vibraphonist Lionel Hampton's big bands of the thirties to the swinging scat of Slim Gaillard's nonsense lyrics in the forties—"A puddle o'veet! Concrete / First you get some gravel, Pour it in the vout"—to the postwar, hard-bop intricacies of bassist Charles Mingus. At its height, the Stem was a party that flowed from the Club Alabam to a raunchy juke joint like the Eagles Hall to late-night eats at Ivy's Chicken Shack. Huntingtons, Otises, and Chandlers be damned, it was a party to which everyone was invited—at least everyone who had the cash: touring musicians mingling with local players, neighborhood regulars mixing with white kids from all over the county, Mexican Americans from the Eastside, Cool School artists from Venice, and Hollywood swells swarming in from points west via hired car.

In *On the Road*, Jack Kerouac's characters crisscross midcentury North America, lavishing love and piling up scorn as they go. Of all the cities they bum through, none gets it worse than Los Angeles: "the loneliest and most brutal of American cities." But the Beats found one bright spot in the City of Angels: "The wild humming night of Central Avenue… howled and boomed along outside. They were singing in the halls, singing from their windows, just hell be damned and look out." Two of Central's best were Dexter Gordon and Wardell Gray, their symbiotic saxophone rivalry one of the Stem's highlights. Gordon was tall and played smooth, Gray was stocky and blew hard. When they staged sonic battles with each other, it was epic. Dean Moriarty, the novel's arbiter of hipness, bowed "before the big phonograph listening to a wild bop record, 'The Hunt,' with Dexter Gordon and Wardell Gray blowing their tops before a screaming audience that gave the record fantastic frenzied volume." Gordon and Gray were evenly matched, and their records exude furious energy and charming playfulness, but within just a few years neither they nor the clubs they electrified would remain on the Stem.

Did the Stem die of natural causes, or was it murder? The answer to this whodunit is that it was death by cop, and, serial killers that they were, the cops did it again a few decades later. The question of why is all the more interesting.

> This is the city:
> Los Angeles, California.
> I work here,
> I'm a cop.
>
> —Jack Webb's opening lines in *Dragnet* (1951–1959)

Start at the top with William "Bill" Parker, LA's chief of police from 1950 to 1966, a reformer who transformed a notoriously corrupt police department. In the years before World War II, the LAPD was beset by scandal, regularly in league with the very gangsters it was charged with fighting. Bill Parker joined the LAPD in 1927, during the reign of famously crooked Chief James "Two-Gun" Davis, but regardless of temptation, Parker stayed true to his origins as the righteous son of a single mother who moved her boy from Deadwood, South Dakota, to Southern California, the sun-kissed land of opportunity. Parker's religious faith instilled in him a rigorous internal compass; he rose in the force as a straight arrow among the bent. He joined the army, attained the rank of captain, and received a Purple Heart after being wounded in the Normandy invasion. Parker spent much of his time both during and after the conflict denazifying police forces in Italy and Germany. His European experiences taught him that it was possible to root out corruption in even the darkest situations. After the war, Parker returned to the LAPD, first to head up Internal Affairs, and then as chief, serving sixteen years until his death, longer than anyone before or since. There is no question that he was the most influential lawman in the history of Southern California, and, after the FBI's J. Edgar Hoover, the second-most-famous law enforcement officer in America.

Parker rooted out corruption, rationalized and technologized the department, and—inverting the inward focus of Internal Affairs—established a public relations department par excellence in the world capital of make-believe. Parker and his minions promoted the LAPD as the twentieth century's new centurions, an incorruptible, mobile, all-powerful organization that would live up to its motto "To Protect and to Serve." Parker made the LAPD America's police department in the same way the Dallas Cowboys were to become "America's team" in football. The LAPD used its access to the global media machine that is Hollywood to promote this image in magazines and newspapers, on radio, in cinemas, and on television. Most powerfully, there was actor/producer Jack Webb, who began *Dragnet*, his love letter to Parker's force, on radio and then had not one but two different runs on television. "Just the facts, ma'am" was the mantra of Webb's Sergeant Friday, who would never allow a free meal in a diner to besmirch the department's reputation.

Parker's professionalized cops policed with an efficiency that made taxpayers and governments ecstatic; the LAPD covered more square miles, deploying fewer officers per capita than any other major police force in the country. These economic and logistical competencies came at a steep social price, though. The mobile squad cars that made it possible to cover extensive territories meant that human contacts between officers and citizens were few, and often at the end of a baton. Parker's stress on intelligence, a result of his time cleaning out fascists from police departments in Europe, meant that the LAPD developed a cult of control that rivaled Hoover's FBI. Under Parker the LAPD created intelligence-gathering networks and covert counterintelligence units to support his high-tech mobilized paramilitary police force.

For all the shine Parker buffed on the apple of his department, there was a worm hidden within—more of a serpent, really. The LAPD was racist when Parker joined up as a rookie cop. It remained racist throughout his tenure as chief. In neighborhoods where people of color predominated, the LAPD was an occupying army. By the 1950s, there were, in fact, targeted racist policing policies in Los Angeles designed to deal with the city's post–World War II diversification. Parker was a genuine reformer, creating the modern American police force as we know it today, but he never cared enough to excise its cardinal sin, and that very racism birthed the LAPD's two colossal failures. The first came in Watts in 1965, when Parker, still chief but battling the illness that would kill him the following year, watched his force misconstrue the events on the ground to apocalyptic results. In other words, the LAPD's racism blinded them to the rebellion's causes and prevented both rank and file and the command staff from understanding that the department's humiliations, both minor and egregious, of African Americans in Los Angeles had primed segregated Watts to explode, no matter how much violence the cops meted out to the rioters to restore order.

A generation later, after the Rodney King police brutality trial in 1992, Chief Daryl Gates, Parker's onetime driver and personal choice to head the LAPD after him, bungled the police response even more shockingly. African Americans, horrified by the special weapons and tactics (SWAT) units sent into their neighborhoods, incensed by the battering ram–equipped police vehicles busting down their doors, and just generally exhausted at being seen as an enemy population rather than citizens, blew up again. Los Angeles burned twice, and both times its self-styled centurions neither protected nor served its citizens.

The legacy of Parker's "arrogant racism," as a 2009 *Los Angeles Times* editorial put it, resonated for decades. The African American community took the brunt of it, especially when it came to Parker's personal concerns about miscegenation. Parker referred to Los Angeles as "the last white spot," and he meant to keep it that way, no matter what was happening on the Stem, or anywhere else on his rapidly diversifying beat, in the years before the Watts riots. Of course, Central Avenue was no postracial utopia, but it was a place where the parts of Los Angeles that didn't normally mix came together, if only for a sweaty Friday night. This alone was cause for the LAPD's growing hysteria.

As bassist David Bryant described it in the groundbreaking oral history *Central Avenue Sounds: Jazz in Los Angeles (1921–1956)*, "All the stars and all the [white] people would come over to Central Avenue and listen to the music, man." The LAPD "didn't like the mixing, so they rousted people around and stuff, and that's how they closed it up." Trumpeter Art Farmer maintained that the authorities saw anything that brought the races together as a felony waiting to happen: "[T]he only thing they saw anytime they saw any interracial thing going on was crime.... It was a crime leading to prostitution and narcotics." Of course, the vice that was most threatening was the attraction of white females to black males, especially black musicians. In Parker's LAPD, the idea that jazz might be art, or that a minority-majority community like the Stem had a right to go about its business unmolested, was trumped by race panic. The flowers of white femininity howling in ecstasy to ferocious rhythms performed by African American musicians brought out the LAPD's head knockers.

Thus, when the most famous of all bebop innovators, Charlie "Bird" Parker, came to play Central Avenue in the late forties, it wasn't just his heroin habit or the six-month stay at a mental hospital just outside LA, immortalized in his 1947 release "Relaxin' at Camarillo," that foretold doom for the Stem. Whether the community knew it or not, Bird, his band, their producers, and their fans were a vanguard, not just in aesthetics but also in politics. Bird's audiences might have preferred the intricacies of his melodies to the silly rhythms of Jack McVea's novelty hit of 1946, "Open the Door, Richard" (an updating of an old comedy routine), but even the most die-hard bebop fan understood the double signification of McVea's call to expand opportunity to all, regardless of color: "Open the door, Richard / Richard, why don't you open the door?" But there were people on the other side of the door who were holding it closed, some of them with badges and guns.

The interweaving of race, class, and power in Los Angeles is ever changing. By the late fifties, Bird was dead at thirty-six, so ravaged by his habit that the coroner thought he was in his sixties; Wardell Gray likewise succumbed to addiction; Dexter Gordon fled first to New York and then to Copenhagen; and jazz itself diminished into the niche music it is today rather than the soundtrack of hipster youth it once was. Bill Parker's policing machine went on to become the most famous in the world, judging by the dubbed versions of *Dragnet* and *Adam-12* (also produced by Jack Webb) that played everywhere from Spain (*Área 12*) to the Soviet Union (*Адам-12*). But within a few years the Watts riots would reveal the fateful limits of police power, and from the ashes of the Stem's death were born glittering new phoenixes.

Rock and roll in LA got off to a promising start in the midfifties, with roots in the R&B scene that had emerged from the wreckage of Central Avenue. There were hits from African Americans, like the Penguins' doo-wop classic "Earth Angel" in 1956; from the Mexican American icon Ritchie Valens of "La Bamba" fame (1958); and even from squeaky-clean Ricky Nelson, the TV star son of *The Adventures of Ozzie and Harriet*, who became a would-be Elvis with a string of singles that started with his number one album *Ricky* in 1957. But by the early 1960s, both the LA record industry and local audiences had lost interest in rock and roll.

It took the arrival of the Beatles in the United States in 1964, with their appearance on *The Ed Sullivan Show*, followed six months later by a sold-out concert at the Hollywood Bowl, to refire the rock-and-roll dreams of LA teens. Beatlemania was not merely about fandom; it ignited a culture in which it was not only possible to go out and form a band, it became a duty. In Southern California in the midsixties, the best of those bands (including the Byrds, whose "So You Want to Be a Rock'n'Roll Star" was simultaneously an instruction manual and a hazard warning) answered the call on Sunset Strip: "... when your hair's combed right and your pants fit tight / It's gonna be all right." It is there that we now travel back to, fourteen miles north and west of Central Avenue, but by the midsixties, light-years distant musically and economically from the Stem.

Never officially demarcated with a start or a finish—though most agree that it includes the mile and a half from Crescent Heights in West Hollywood to Doheny Drive just east of Beverly Hills—the Strip is as much a state of mind as a physical environment. A center of entertainment for decades, with the Mocambo and the Trocadero hosting Hollywood celebrities, Southern California's café society, and tourists ready to pay stiff tabs to bend elbows with the stars, it had by 1964 undergone a "youthquake," as they put it in those generation gap–obsessed days. The "kids" of the Strip began to grow their hair long and adopt ever-more-flamboyant costumes. The fashions matched the bright, syncopated sounds we now refer to as "LA Pop," which embraced the psychedelia of Love, the magnetism of the Doors, the craft of the Mamas and the Papas, the charm of the Turtles, and even the showbiz schmaltz of Sonny & Cher.

With this concentration of talent came an explosion of audience, and that audience in turn generated a scene that didn't necessarily depend on having a ticket to get into a show or the money to buy an album. It was enough to be present on Sunset Strip, milling about, checking out the other kids, grooving on the vibe. What made the scene so compelling, in fact, was that it delineated a place that, while not "local" to many, if not most, of its participants, nonetheless felt *shared*—this in a city that, as urbanist Mike Davis observes, habitually trades public space for private view, ignoring parks in favor of the vistas from hillside mansions. But the sense of shared space did not last. LA Pop's demise can be dated precisely to November 12, 1966, the first night of the Riot on Sunset Strip. A historical obscurity now, this riot anticipated the larger conflicts of the late sixties and reflected back like a fun-house mirror the simmering strife on Central Avenue a decade earlier.

"For What It's Worth" ("Stop, children, what's that sound...") is almost universally remembered as a Vietnam protest anthem, with references to a "thousand people in the street," "battle lines being drawn" and "a man with a gun." But in fact Stephen Stills, a member of Buffalo Springfield, the house band at the Strip's iconic Whisky a Go Go, wrote it from his ringside seat, reportedly in fifteen minutes, on the historic night when mounted sheriff's deputies and helmeted LAPD riot cops clashed with kids in caftans and hip-huggers on Sunset Strip. A different venue, a different enemy, but the law in LA was at it again, destroying a musical movement.

The Stem still has the Dunbar, now transformed into low-income housing, but the same can't be said of the riot's flash point, bulldozed into oblivion. Today at the intersection of Sunset Boulevard and Crescent Heights there's a traffic triangle anonymous even by the standards of Southern California streetscapes. But rewind to the sixties, and that little triangle was the location of the aptly named Pandora's Box, a fifties jazz club that had morphed into an all-ages café. Its manager, Al Mitchell, not only was interested in Sunset Strip's burgeoning youth culture but, as a key figure at the *LA Free Press* (a pioneering underground paper better known as the *Freep*, sold for a quarter with the pitch "Don't be a creep, buy a *Freep!*"), was invested in struggles for racial justice and solidarity around Southern California. Closing down Pandora's Box was an attack on the entirety of the burgeoning youth culture, and not just its manifestations on the Strip.

The trouble began when LAPD officers and sheriff's deputies began enforcing a 10:00 p.m. curfew to bring "order" to the crowds of mostly underage kids roaming up from coffeehouses to cafés to clubs. A group called Community Action for Facts and Freedom (CAFF) got the word out that the police were set to close the lid on Pandora's Box. A thousand kids turned out to protest, peacefully at first, then less so, with some in the crowd throwing rocks and even tipping over a city bus. The Sheriff's Department and LAPD responded to these provocations in full force. Not only were the deputies and cops just "doing their jobs," but they were also using the Riot on Sunset Strip as a do-over of their embarrassing performance during the Watts riots the year before, only this time with a younger and less combative crowd. The LAPD's fearsome Metro Division formed a flying wedge. Massing against the unarmed teenyboppers and budding hippies, the cops were on a mission to clear the streets and restore order, even if that meant cracking skulls. To swaths of sixteen-year-olds from the Valley were added a smattering of celebrities, including the actors Jack Nicholson (he left early) and Peter Fonda (he was arrested). At a later protest, Sonny & Cher showed up. Did I mention that in addition to their CAFF armbands, the duo wore coordinating white faux-fur toppers and hoods?

The protests, and the repression of these protests, ground on through the summer of 1967, but the result was the deadening of the Strip's street life and a disruption of the vital connection between artist, audience, and cityscape that defined the LA music scene. Jim Morrison called out a law-and-order ideology specific to the LAPD as shaped by Chief Bill Parker: "LA cops are idealists, almost fanatical in believing in the righteousness of their cause.... They have a whole philosophy behind their tyranny." Historian Dave McBride pushes past Morrison, claiming that the Riot on Sunset Strip was "essentially about the counterculture's right to the city," a right they lost as a result.

If race panic was the defining reason for the assault on the Central Avenue jazz scene, what propelled the cops and deputies into crowds of middle-class white kids? Why did a culture that didn't (and still doesn't) provide much in the way of organized spaces or activities for teenagers fear them so much when they congregated to listen to music, hang out in coffeehouses, and promenade back and forth in front of one another in increasingly distinctive generational garb? Why did middle-class parents allow the police and sheriffs to criminalize their own children? In a democracy, how do politics and profit combine to direct policing?

On the Strip, the ultimate answer is a poisonous combination of money, real estate, and taste. The Riot on Sunset Strip was a conflict ignited by shifting demographics and economics, pitting the new scenesters against the Strip's established clientele. Journalist Kirk Silsbee reminisced about the moment of transition in the midsixties: "The Old School Hollywood supper clubs—Ciro's, the Mocambo, the Trocadero, the Moulin Rouge—had a steep profit margin that they had to maintain. They relied on the patronage of moneyed Hollywood that could pay for dinner and a show every night. Kids couldn't do that. They could go to Ben Frank's or Canter's or The Fifth Estate and nurse a cup of coffee all night long or hang out in the parking lot."

After the riot, musician Terry Randall released a single, titled "S.O.S.," about the Strip, which today sounds like nothing so much as white garage proto-rap. Over a three-chord thrum, Randall talk-sings, "We've got as much right to be here as anyone," and questions why the forces of order are harassing them. He concludes with the plaintive "We're not hurtin' nothin', but what do we hear?" and then pantomimes the voices of the cops and the deputies as they fling the kids up against the wall and demand they cut their long hair.

Sunset Boulevard's commercial landlords, the management of the established clubs and restaurants, and even the organized crime figures who ran the topless bars were aligned against the "kids" and their ways. The sheriffs and the police were called in to make the Strip safe for surf-and-turf dinners, exotic dancers, and other "adult entertainment." In other words, Sunset Strip was better left to professional strippers teasing businessmen than to kids who might actually have sex with one another—a triumph of the simulation over the real as profound as any Southern California had ever manifested.

In the summer of 1967, LA artists traveled north to a music festival co-organized by the Mamas and the Papas' John Phillips. The Monterey International Pop Music Festival shifted what remained of the LA Pop scene's energy to San Francisco's emerging psychedelic swirl. Even the hippies had roots in Los Angeles, though, with health food pioneer Gypsy Boots and eden ahbez, a songwriter and robe-and-sandals-clad Jesus look-alike. As early as the forties, they lived bucolic, bohemian lives as self-styled "Nature Boys," to

the point of sleeping alfresco under the Hollywood sign and camp-
ing out in Topanga Canyon and inside caves in the Coachella Valley.
But by 1967, the hippie scene as well became associated with the
Bay Area, another sign that the epicenter of the youthquake had
moved north. May through September of '67 was branded the Bay
Area's "Summer of Love," even as kids were still occasionally battling it out with the cops and deputies on the Strip down south.

A year later, schlockmeister Sam Katzman produced an exploi-
tation flick called *Riot on Sunset Strip* that featured documentary
footage, a rockin' soundtrack of the title track by the Standells, and
a ludicrous plot about a girl force-fed acid who is saved by her cop
dad. The Strip, however, had survived worse movies, and as the decades passed, it escaped no one's notice that there was still money
to be made and talent desperate for venues. There were other high
moments, to be sure—singer-songwriters later in the sixties, hard
and glam rockers in the seventies, punks in the eighties. But the lows,
especially the innumerable spandex-clad hair bands of the late eighties and nineties, sealed the Strip's fate, a pleasant, enduring senes-
cence of expensive restaurants and venues where bands had to pay
to play.

The same cannot be said about the Stem. The music and crowds
return once a year for the antiquarian Central Avenue Jazz Festival,
patrolled by the LAPD officers who moved into the "new" Newton
precinct house that takes up the entire block between Thirty-Fourth
and Thirty-Fifth on Central. The few people who stop to read historical plaques are unlikely to note that the LAPD's substation on
the Stem—"Shootin' Newton," as it used to be called in the bad old
days—sits on the site of the former Elks Club at 3416 Central. The
ironies abound in this now majority Latinx neighborhood, with the

very police force that destroyed the vitality of its former African American cultural identity installed in the space of one of its most influential halls.

Both the Stem and the Strip were cultural infrastructures, places where people created and consumed music and culture. When police power was applied—whether for rocker Arthur Lee or sax man Dexter Gordon, or even the cuddliest of the Strip's sixties bands, the Turtles—the end results were the same: the cultural ecology that sustained them was undone and their energies scattered. For Lee it was into the decades-long downward spiral that left him imprisoned, for Gordon a life of exile in Europe, for the Turtles an endless roundelay of oldies festivals. In this accounting, it looks like the score is Cops 2, Culture 0.

In 1988, when the Stem was a musical ghost town and the Strip was poised between the Scylla of sappy monster ballads by hair-metal bands and the Charybdis of rich suburban kids arranging to buy their way onstage, I moved to LA and tried to use radio to understand my new home. I would listen to "Loveline" on FM's KROQ, a late-night call-in show that astonished me as to the sheer polymorphous perversity of my new city, but on AM radio I learned about its emerging power politics. At the end of the dial, I found KDAY 1520, the first commercial station to play rap and hip-hop exclusively. Over a few months, I noticed that one group was getting more and more play, eventually ending up with 50 percent of the airtime on the afternoon *Mack Attack* show. Many readers will already know that I'm talking about N.W.A. and, given the year, that I was listening to their path-blazing first album, *Straight Outta Compton*, the origin point of West Coast gangsta rap. After a while, I bought the tape, mostly because the radio versions of my favorite tracks were so heavily bleeped. The second track—though hardly the most censored—caused the most furor. Written, at least in legend, after some cops hassled Ice Cube, "Fuck Tha Police" is a four-minute public opera that flips the script of the narratives of power that have animated the stories I have been telling up to now.

In rap and hip-hop, when MCs "flip the script," they are calling for changes in power relationships. The term implies surprise, a judo move that upends opponents and social situations. "Fuck Tha Police" flipped the script by having young artists of color from Compton spinning a tale of revenge and justice, taunting the police for their implicit claims of having "the authority to kill a minority." When N.W.A. declared, "Fuck that shit, cause I ain't the one / for a punk motherfucker with a badge and a gun," the implications of their verses hardly went unnoticed. The FBI wrote N.W.A. a letter accusing them of encouraging "violence against and disrespect" for law enforcement; at a concert in Michigan the off-duty Detroit officers providing security told N.W.A. that if they played the song, the cops would arrest them. The group played it anyway, the Detroit cops arrested them, and the legend of N.W.A. just got bigger.

But "Fuck Tha Police" was less a threat than a warning, like the Trojan princess Cassandra's unheeded prophecies in Aeschylus's *Agamemnon*. The global impact of the song, the group, and gangsta rap in general cannot be denied. But its local significance was even greater. Because for any Southern Californian who was actually *listening* to what Ice Cube, Eazy-E, DJ Yella, MC Ren, and Dr. Dre had to say, the events of 1992 came as no surprise. Whether you call it "the riots" or "the rebellion," it began with a video recording the aftermath of a car chase. In the spring of 1991, a group of LAPD officers engaged in a hundred-miles-per-hour chase. They dragged the driver, Rodney King, from his car and fell upon him with batons. A civilian named George Holliday watched this unfold from his balcony in the San Fernando Valley community of Lakeview Terrace. He had a Handycam on him and recorded what he saw as obvious abuse. Holliday tried to interest the LAPD in his footage as evidence to discipline the officers, but when the department ignored him, he sent his tape to local television station KTLA. They aired it, and the tape was picked up and shown over and over again, not just in Los Angeles but globally. Holliday's twelve-minute tape can be considered an early example of viral video, prefiguring the importance of personal recording technologies now remaking the relationship between police and the policed throughout the United States. In the era before the cell-phone camera, much less the Movement for Black Lives, what people were seeing was revelatory, even revolutionary, footage of police brutality.

The officers involved were eventually put on trial for their assault on Rodney King, but because of the video's notoriety, the trial venue was changed to the far-flung suburb of Simi Valley, a conservative bastion that houses the Reagan Library and was well known for being an LAPD bedroom community. When the 75 percent white jury acquitted the 100 percent white officers, the chief of police was out of town, and there was little thought of how the city would deal with the aftermath. First South Los Angeles and then other parts of the city erupted in protest and violence that lasted for days, brought out the National Guard, led to a billion dollars of economic losses, injured thousands, and brought death to more than fifty Los Angeles citizens. The story is too complex to be adequately covered here, but there is no question that the LAPD, under Parker protégé Chief Daryl Gates, once again failed to protect and failed to serve.

In the middle of the twentieth century, Central Avenue jazz and Sunset Strip pop demonstrated that policing aesthetics directly and with violence affects not only the vitality, viability, and direction of artists, venues, and audiences but the totality of an art form. But a generation later, the police no longer had this power. Some of this had to do with shifting demographics, not only in Southern California but also across the country. It also had to do with the importance of rebellion as a commodity in popular culture—rap and hip-hop may have started out as outliers in the global entertainment world, but by the time *Straight Outta Compton* was released, publicly traded commercial behemoths like Viacom, Time Warner, and NBC Universal depended on youth culture's ever-mutating ability to generate shock and excitement to fuel their corporate profits. So the LAPD could seethe when N.W.A. released an album, the FBI could write letters, and the Detroit PD could even arrest them when they sang "Fuck Tha Police," but N.W.A. didn't just survive; it thrived, becoming a linchpin of the most successful global musical movement of the last quarter century. White sixteen-year-olds in Oshkosh, Wisconsin, and Bloomington, Indiana, couldn't buy N.W.A.'s music fast enough; they were desperate for access to the gangsta rappers' "street knowledge." The late twentieth century's commodification of cool was complete by that point, and corporate media's capacity to capture and monetize rebellion made it economically disadvantageous and politically impossible to police N.W.A.'s aesthetics and messages. Rather than face death, exile, or obscurity, the group's DJ, Dr. Dre (Andre Young), sold Apple his Beats-branded headphone and music company for $3 billion, and the biopic about the group is the highest-grossing film ever in its genre.

The further we get from "Fuck Tha Police," the more it seems like a paranoiac precognition out of a Philip K. Dick novel. Here it's the musicians who are scorching the earth, and not just getting away with it but becoming billionaires. It's not that the battles between Dionysus and Mars are over in the City of Angels, just that the script's been flipped, at least for now.

5 SPACE PORT ALPHA

UNTITLED #8 (FREEWAYS) I 1994 I PLATINUM PRINT I 2 ¼ X 6 ¾ INCHES (5.7 X 17.1 CM)

Libertarians, Libertines, and the Ineffable Lightness of Southern California's High Tech

O n top of Temescal Canyon in the Santa Monica Mountains, at the end of a long, private driveway, are the scattered remnants of an experiment. There's little left of the Sandstone Foundation for Community Systems Research, Inc., which was founded back in 1968 by a former Lockheed aerospace engineer, John Williamson. Sandstone, an old Malibu estate, must have appealed to Williamson because from its vantage point you can look out over the Pacific Ocean into the black night sky and see, twinkling there, the stars, our destination. Or so it seemed to many in Southern California for the decades when building planes and rockets was a great way to make a living, and to guarantee the United States' dominance over the globe. Williamson was looking at the Pacific at the far western edge of Manifest Destiny. From that

Extremism in the defense of liberty is no vice.

—Barry Goldwater, accepting the 1964 Republican
    nomination for president

I can honestly say I saw more naked stars than any other woman
in Hollywood.

—Barbara Williamson, the Sandstone Foundation

golden locus, the frontier might, at first glance, have appeared to be fully conquered. The oceans mapped, the continent colonized, the world wars won, power projected, Americans poised to plant the Stars and Stripes on the moon itself. What frontiers were left, what "community systems research" still needed to be done?

Starting with the view from Sandstone, we will trace the impact of aerospace technologies on the cultural imaginary of Southern California, with stops at secret weapons laboratories, Goldwater for President lawn signs, spy plane cockpits, systems theories, leather pants, and 0° 40′ 26.69″ N, 23° 28′ 22.69″ E (0.67408°, 23.47297°), better known as the moon's Mare Tranquillitatis. Difficult as it was to reach that part of the lunar landscape in 1971, the inner space of the psyche may be even more elusive. That's the realm where psychonauts and astronauts meld magic and martial science, sex and rockets.

At the end of our travels, we will have an answer as to why, when John Williamson looked down from the skies above Temescal Canyon and back over his shoulder at Sandstone, the pool was filled with so many naked bodies.

One body that John Williamson would not have seen, either behind him in the pool or in front of him in the air, was that of a former coworker at Lockheed, Anthony "Tony" LeVier. It's doubtful that Williamson ever met LeVier, and he probably never saw him working either. Williamson was one of many, a skilled technician in a region overflowing with them. But Tony LeVier was unique. He was a test pilot. No, he was, as the National Aviation Hall of Fame puts it, "the world's foremost experimental test pilot." In addition to having incredible skill, remarkable luck, and depthless determination, LeVier was also one of the few men in the world who could wear a shearling-lined flight jacket and not look silly. LeVier tested the fastest, deadliest toys in the world at Lockheed's Skunk Works, one of the most clandestine facilities in the United States.

What generals asked for, Congress approved, executives planned, engineers designed, and production workers welded together were, until actually flight-tested, only concepts for airborne war machines. Like Chuck Yeager, who was made famous in Tom Wolfe's *The Right Stuff*, LeVier was an inheritor of the cowboy mythos, test pilots combining daredevilry with a warrior's ethos. Some of the planes that Tony LeVier took up literally dissolved around him. He described the first-ever landing of the U-2, a superlight plane designed for high-level surveillance whose wingspan was enormous for its weight:

I got into [a turbulent stall] and had no idea where the goddam ground was. I just had to keep the goddam plane under control. I kept it straight and level and I hit the ground hard. Wham! I heard thump, thump, thump. I blew both tires and the damned brakes burst into flame right below the fuel lines.

Tony LeVier had a lifetime total of more than 24,000 flights in over 250 different airplane designs, including the first flights on eleven of the Skunk Works planes. He had 101 air accidents and incidents, including eight crashes, fifty-eight near crashes, five tailspins to "low" altitudes, twenty-six forced landings, five canopy losses, twenty pilot errors, one midair collision, and nine near midair collisions. He was the exception to the rule he cites in his autobiography—"there are bold pilots and there are old pilots, but there are no old bold pilots"—and that may be why there's an air-safety award named after him.

Tony LeVier was in Burbank because that was where the action was. At the height of the Cold War, fifteen of the twenty-five largest aerospace and defense contractors were based in Southern California. Behind the facade of sunshine and movie stars, beach boys and beatniks was the reality that Southern California was the true "arsenal of democracy" for the war in the Pacific. The hardscape of airplane production lines and rocket test sites and the lived histories of hundreds of thousands of aerospace workers have been crowded out by the celluloid screenscapes of the region's dream factory. As noted, for a hundred years Hollywood has so dominated LA's consciousness, not to mention its image, that the region's "real" economies have been almost forgotten. The roughly five decades from the 1940s through the 1990s belonged, in alchemical terms, to the air; in empirical terms, to the aerospace and defense industries, which were the dominant force shaping the region's built environments and mental topographies.

The roots of all these wings go back more than a century, to 1910. Local boosters, including the *Times* and the *Examiner* papers, hosted the Los Angeles Air Meet, the first such show in the United States. Famed French aviator Louis Paulhan was the main attraction, and he did not disappoint, setting a new world record by ascending to 4,600 feet. That same year, Glenn Curtiss established the first training center for military pilots in the San Diego area. By the 1920s, the California Institute of Technology (better known as Caltech), under then-President Robert Millikan, had founded a state-of-the-art aeronautical research division to train a new generation of engineers. A decade later a group of students, faculty, and associated enthusiasts, including Theodore von Kármán, Frank Malina, and Jack Parsons, started what would eventually become the Jet Propulsion Laboratory (JPL), famed for designing everything from rocket engines to the Mars lander.

The region's wide-open spaces and perfect weather attracted pilots and aircraft manufacturers, and the airfields in Westchester (first called Mines Field, then LAX) and Burbank (known for more than a quarter of a century as the Lockheed Air Terminal, then named after comedian Bob Hope, now branded as Hollywood Burbank Airport) became central to the industry. Amelia Earhart, the most famous female pilot in history, took her first flying lesson out of Long Beach in 1917 and began her last voyage out of Burbank two decades later, a doomed attempt to circumnavigate the globe. Burbank was also the airport where she'd taught flying for the better part of a decade. Entrepreneurs including James McDonnell and Donald Douglas, brilliant pilot and future lunatic Howard Hughes, and Allan and Malcolm Loughead (who later phoneticized the spelling of their Scottish surname to Lockheed) all set up shop in Southern California. In World War II, more than $40 billion flowed into the state (half a trillion in today's dollars), and Southern California's aeronautics facilities geared up for a global conflict.

The rush to dominate the battle space in the air spawned its own culture in Southern California. The industry needed workers, and so many of them came from the South and the southern Midwest that they came to be called, with a mixture of affection and derision, "Aviation Okies." As the wartime journalist Ernie Pyle put it, this new population was "better off than were the dust bowl Okies," those climate and economic refugees who fled their drought-stricken homes during the Great Depression, only to be turned back from California's borders by an illegal blockade of police and sheriff's battalions. After the hot war was over in 1945, the Aviation Okies stayed, and others joined them in the new suburbs and towns developed around the region to house them, from Lakewood outside Long Beach to broad swaths of Orange County. These workers were now combatants in the Cold War against global communism and, for that reason, the beneficiaries of investment by the federal government, a transfer of wealth unprecedented in U.S. history. By the midfifties, the industry added rockets and rebranded itself "aerospace." In Huntington Beach, North American Aviation constructed the command module for the Apollo spacecraft, and in Torrance, Hughes Aircraft designed and built Syncom, the first-ever geosynchronous communications satellite.

Fighting the totalitarian threat, either fascist or communist, required these workers to keep what they were doing secret—secret from their spouses, secret from their children, secret from their siblings, their parents, their friends, their neighbors, secret from the other members of their bowling leagues. But secrecy—even in the defense of liberty—brings its own problems. Chief among these is how the covert comes to define the interactions of a society. As with the chicken and the egg, the question becomes which precedes and engenders which. Are people with secrets drawn to secrecy as a way of life, or does secrecy as a regime encourage people to generate other secrets, beyond the ones they are paid to keep?

Moving from the post–World War II era to the sixties, another question arises. How did a generation that both deeply believed in security and profited handsomely from the military-industrial complex give birth to a generation that revolted so fully *against* that mission, that is, those teenyboppers rioting on Sunset Strip and the hippies who followed? One answer may be that homes, communities, and whole regions that require secrecy simultaneously demand hypocrisy. La Rochefoucauld, the urbane French memoirist, coined the maxim "Hypocrisy is the homage vice pays to virtue." When archconservative Barry Goldwater ran for president in 1964, one of his slogans held that extremism in the defense of liberty was not a vice but a virtue. In Southern California, that extremism supported a comfortable lifestyle, complete with a split-level in the suburbs, a pool in the backyard, and a new station wagon in the driveway.

During the Cold War, security clearances were clandestine status markers, and the entire world of aerospace was, if not dark, definitely gray. But what of a society in which many heads of households can't discuss their work when they return home? Historian Mihir Pandya maintains that the very secrecy central to military aerospace has deformed the way we think about Southern California history. The silence imposed on every level of employee, from management to line worker, meant that there was no oral tradition about the industry passed on within families, which in turn diminished aerospace's impact on the region's collective memory of itself.

In all of the secret world, nothing was more secret than the Advanced Development Projects space, known as the Skunk Works, that Lockheed set up in the San Fernando Valley to develop its most experimental planes and rockets. Even as trustworthy a Skunk Worker as Tony LeVier was constantly tested and resworn to secrecy with every new advance. When he signed on to the U-2 project, he was told in no uncertain terms: "What you just saw you must never mention to another living soul. Not your wife, your mother, nobody. You understand?" Like everyone else at the Skunk Works, LeVier appreciated the deadly seriousness of their mission.

How did such a serious place end up with such a funny name? The story goes that the offices were next to a particularly foul-smelling chemical company, and that engineer Irv Culver came to call it the "Skonk Works," after an odiferous "skonk oil" factory at the edge of Dogpatch in Al Capp's comic strip satire of southern life, *Li'l Abner*. The name resonated, but in deference to Capp's litigious nature, the spelling was changed to Skunk Works.

The whole place was run by a brilliant aeronautical engineer, Clarence Leonard "Kelly" Johnson. Johnson's strategy was to build the best planes in the world—to innovate, fail, iterate, fail again, iterate again, succeed; and to do so from within the inherently conservative environment of the military-industrial complex. Inside a system in which four-star generals field reports from majors, who liaise with senior management, who maintain lines of communication to finance, design, and the factory floor, a truly radical new plane could take over a decade to be brought into production. Johnson had no patience for red tape, so at the Skunk Works he flattened the hierarchies within Lockheed and encouraged risk taking rather than ass covering as the default mode for everyone, from welders to project managers to CFOs. The planes designed and prototyped under his watch included the U-2 spy plane developed for the Central Intelligence Agency; the SR-71 Blackbird, which flew three times the speed of sound (Mach 3) and set records that still stand; and the F-117 Nighthawk, which pioneered radar-invisible stealth technologies.

By the time the Nighthawk was revealed to the public in the late 1980s, the romance of the Skunk Works concept had seduced corporate America, and not just in entities involved with ultrasecret "black projects" for the Defense Department. Johnson became famous not only for producing his planes in record time and often under budget, but also for his management strategy of KISS—Keep It Simple, Stupid—to avoid encumbering every aspect of a project with layers of unneeded communication and command. With KISS, Johnson and the Skunk Works created the model of the "California" R&D-driven company to come. By the twenty-first century, countless tech companies had embraced KISS, cultivating risk and streamlining corporate organization charts. Whether they actually called them Skunk Works, as Apple did, or camouflaged them as "X labs," like Google, Johnson's influence spread far beyond aerospace.

What those Northern California tech firms were trying to tap in to was not just Johnson's management style but the particular sense of boundlessness that aviation and rocketry had lent to Southern California a half century earlier. Flying brings liberation from the constraints of gravity, mobility unmatched even by the automobile, and supersonic speed. Add rockets to the mix, and the sense of liberation redoubles, the notion that leaving the "big Blue Marble" is the inevitable next stage of evolution. Aerospace contributed to the Southern California mythos of anything imaginable in fact being possible. The freedom to reinvent yourself in a new place. The freedom to use your talents to make your own destiny. As M. G. Lord writes in her memoir of growing up in an aerospace family, the engineers felt liberated from older hierarchies, creating a meritocracy where it didn't "matter what your father could do. It matters what you can do."

But freedom is never emotionally neutral. It can give birth to fears about change and anarchy as easily as it generates utopian notions of remaking society. One response to this freedom was the radical individualism of libertarianism. Libertarianism comes in as many flavors as there are people calling themselves libertarians, but a few commonalities emerge. It is a philosophy that sees itself less as the heir of liberalism than as liberty itself enacted as principle. Libertarians prize the individual above the community (or the "collective," as they often deride it) and see government restrictions on individual thought or action as oppression, government regulation of business as intrusive, and taxation of almost any kind as theft. An early classic of Southern California libertarian thought is "Freedom Is a Two-Edged Sword," written in 1946 by JPL cofounder Jack Parsons. Offering hyperrational approaches to political and economic problem solving, libertarianism was a natural fit for the engineering mind-set.

Libertarianism's political economies emphasized personal self-sufficiency, free-market ideology, and a commitment to small government. These concerns dovetailed with the emergent postwar conservative movement, especially as manifested in the 1964 presidential campaign of Arizona Republican senator Barry Goldwater.

What emerged in Southern California was a combination of libertarian economics and a traditionalist set of concerns about morality, the family, and patriotism (especially as manifested in anticommunism). This "fusionism" defined aerospace's political influence in Southern California. Historian Lisa McGirr refers to the emergence of "suburban warriors" in Orange County, not far from the stereotype of the crew-cut, pocket-protected engineer with a wife in an A-line skirt and a Goldwater sign on the front lawn.

The coexistence of libertarian antistatism and massive federal funding may seem oxymoronic, but it was incredibly seductive to a generation of men and women certain that their place in this new society was a direct and unique reflection of their own talents and perseverance rather than any structural advantages. Getting the Aviation Okies and aerospace engineers to ask any of the following might prove difficult for reasons that transcended mere ideology: Why was there a permanent war footing during the Cold War? How could anyone support the insanity of mutually assured destruction (MAD) in an atomic conflict with the Soviet Union? Did President Eisenhower's domino theory, wherein the fall of French Indochina would lead to a series of communist victories cascading through Southeast Asia, make any sense? Even if it did, what were the ethics of a democracy pursuing proxy wars in places like Vietnam and El Salvador? The production workers and rocket scientists weren't asking these questions, though, because in the end, support for these policies supported their own, very comfortable way of life. As the novelist, radical socialist, and onetime candidate for governor of California Upton Sinclair noted, "It is difficult to get a man to understand something, when his salary depends on his not understanding it."

Fusionism came back from the disaster of Goldwater's 1964

campaign with a stunning victory sixteen years later when Ronald Reagan won the presidency. Reagan reshaped the Republican Party as one of the West and South, establishing the neoliberal economic agenda with libertarian overtones that grinds on to this day, while supporting, or at least giving lip service to, evangelical social conservatives and other revanchist culture warriors. But the concepts of freedom and liberty do not belong solely to the right, nor does libertarianism.

Southern California was a "new" place, at least new to the millions who flowed into it during the twentieth century. The stolid midwesterners may have been Methodists when they left, but they arrived in a place where the ecstasies of Pentecostalism had been invented, where the ties of tradition loosened, and where entirely new kinds of answers were being offered. The Simi Valley–based Divine Order of the Royal Arms of the Great Eleven was headed up by a mother-daughter pair of prophets known as the Blackburns. They wore purple robes while sacrificing mules (their scriptures referred to them as the "Jaws of Death"), promising at least one rich believer that, with enough financial support, God's own archangels Gabriel and Michael would dictate the "Great Sixth Seal," revealing hitherto unknown oil and mineral deposits. The two scammers were convicted at trial but won on appeal, the ruling stating that "it is not actionable to the court if the defendant made certain representations as to being divine." Mankind United, on the other hand, was less theistic, promising to connect believers to an underground race of metal-clad superbeings while offering anyone willing to follow its precepts, in the words of chronicler Carey McWilliams, "a $25,000 home, equipped with radio, television, unlimited motion pictures, and an 'automatic vocal-type correspondence machine.'"

These cultists were preposterous, but they responded to the same yearnings as health-foodists eating exotic treats like yogurt and tofu, and the occasional naturist group taking advantage of the region's abundance of sunshine. Throughout the middle of the twentieth century, Los Angeles was a place that maintained a sense of *public* decorum. Enforced by the ruling businessmen's Committee of Twenty-Five, who took lunch together at Perino's on Wilshire; a squadron of dour preachers in the pulpits and on the radio; and a police force that, while corrupt, still managed to keep vice under wraps, the city seemed placid enough on the surface. But underneath, in *private*, more and more of its citizens were discovering the pleasures of reinventing every aspect of themselves in this new Eden at the edge of the Pacific, unencumbered by family and religious obligations. Here was the other edge of freedom's sword, not the economic libertarianism that fused so well with traditional conservatism but a spiritual liberation wherein individuals were the arbiters of their own morality. This was where the libertarian shaded into the libertine. Hugh Hefner outlined his vision of libertine liberation in his epic "Playboy Philosophy," a twenty-five-part, 150,000-word manifesto published between 1962 and 1965. For the libertine libertarian, freeing the body from the exterior constraints of religion or social mores can be as important as the enlightenment of the mind or the unshackling of the economy.

John Williamson was an Aviation Okie who transformed himself by dint of effort and intelligence into a white-collar engineer and then an entrepreneur. He grew up in the backwoods of Alabama and had uncles in the bootlegging trade. His mother's mother was a "buxom showgirl" who ended up leaving his grandfather and marrying a much older sugar daddy in New Orleans. Young John visited the Big Easy and got a taste for an entirely different way of life. Bright and skilled with his hands, John claimed he could have gotten an appointment to the Naval Academy in Annapolis but instead chose to enter the service directly at seventeen. The navy recognized him as an intuitive mechanic and also trained him as an electronics technician. He was based for a number of years in the Pacific and, while there, met and married an anthropologist from Germany. Together they moved to Cape Canaveral, Florida, after she became pregnant, and John became that which he detested—a working stiff with a steady job, a family man with conventional restrictions, someone who watched while other people were living, really living.

In that period, Williamson had two especially dark days, one secret, another horribly public. He came home despondent one day in May 1960 but couldn't say a word to his wife about why. His depression coincided with the very moment when key Lockheed employees were informed about the capture of the Skunk Works–designed U-2 spy plane, which had been shot down by surface-to-air missiles over Soviet territory. The conjecture is that John had worked on this plane and that he took its downing as a personal blow. A year later, John was tinkering with a loud engine at his canal-side home and didn't hear his three-year-old son, Rolf, fall into the water. When John looked up some time later, he found his son dead. Within a year, John was living in California and his wife had filed for divorce, returning to Germany with the couple's surviving daughter.

In Los Angeles, John opened his own electronics firm supplying the aerospace industry, partaking in the region's entrepreneurial spirit and making a lot more money in the process. He read widely, searching for meaning after Rolf's death and purpose beyond material success. Among the most significant works he encountered were the radical Austrian psychotherapist Wilhelm Reich's *The Sexual Revolution* (1945), Robert Heinlein's science fiction blockbuster *Stranger in a Strange Land* (1961), and that dismal classic of libertarian thought, *Atlas Shrugged*, by Ayn Rand (1957). Think about what an engineering mind-set could do with the raw materials these three books provide: Reich's concept of the "orgone" combines "orgasm" and "organism" and promises liberation from psychic oppression via intercourse; Heinlein's protagonist, Valentine Michael Smith, is the lone human survivor of an ill-fated mission to the Red Planet. Smith was raised by Martians, only to be returned to Earth as a prophet promising that a mix of sex, all-encompassing empathic understanding, or "grokking," and a will to change would engender a new race of *Homo superior* (as we will see later, this was also a very important book for Charles Manson). And finally, there is John Galt, the hero of Rand's pulpy opus, a libertarian *Übermensch* who, together with other titans of industry and assorted geniuses, retreats from a society that refuses to respect his superior contributions, only to reemerge to remake the world in his image. That Galt manages this with a lithe and sexually liberated fellow industrialist named Dagny Taggart at his side is just icing on the cake.

So in 1966 we find Williamson in Los Angeles, single, a self-made man, cut off from his roots, uninterested in religion, but missing something. It was at this point that he concocted Project Synergy. Cobbling together voguish notions about freedom, sexuality, human communication, and systems theory, Williamson envisioned "a telocratic, synergistic, large-scale community" within the bounds of which the basic structures of human relationships would be reworked (note that he is using the royal, or at least conjugal "we" here): "We believe that with the improved feedback and integration of tribal organization, this body of knowledge could and would be used to directly aid, rather than exploit or endanger, continued evolution." The Sandstone Foundation for Community Systems Research, as it came to be called, would experiment with small numbers of people, yielding benefits to many more later, a classic extrapolation. Williamson would reengineer fucking and thereby transform the world.

But first he needed humans to have sex with. Fate, or perhaps the market, provided him a perfect partner. One day in 1966, New York Life Insurance Company agent Barbara Cramer walked into his office, and both their worlds transformed. As Barbara remembers it, John said she was "the perfect mate for Project Synergy. Professionally successful, independent, self-assured, sexually liberated." And, yes, of course, she reminded him "of Dagny Taggart, the heroine in *Atlas Shrugged*." Like John, Barbara was self-made and a refugee from rural life, hers on the outskirts of small-town Missouri. She'd risen by sheer force of will to be one of the few female agents for New York Life, earning a salary that allowed her to drive a new red Mustang convertible to meet clients. But like John, Barbara Cramer was also at an impasse. Years later she reminisced: "I was on a sales appointment and met that mystical person, that sense of completion, in a man named John Williamson. I call him a man... he was more like an idea, a movement, a category of one. I came to sell him an insurance policy and he sold me a great destiny. We found that we wanted the same things in life. So, with John's engineering and problem solving background, we agreed to design and create an alternate lifestyle."

That lifestyle depended on what they saw as "radical honesty,"

loosening the bonds of coupledom to include multiple sexual partners, breaking through hypocrisy and secrecy to embrace pleasure
rather than shame. Their first attempt at swinging included two of
John's colleagues from Lockheed: the man, an engineer like John;
the woman, an office worker and former stewardess (to keep the
aerospace imaginary going). The richest account of John and Barbara Williamson and Project Synergy is found in *Thy Neighbor's
Wife* by Gay Talese, one of the era's preeminent New Journalists.
Talese spent a large part of 1970 living at Sandstone, which he declared was "undoubtedly the most liberated fifteen acres of land in
America's not-always-democratic republic: It was the only place . . .
where there was no double standard, no place for mercenary sex, no
need for security guards or the police, no reason for fantasies as
substitute stimulants." In other words, Talese was a believer that the
shift of "John Williamson's career ambitions . . . from mechanical
engineering to sensual engineering, from the wonders of electronics
to the dynamics of cupidity," had borne ripe fruit.

From the distance of a half century, the mix of Esalen Institute–
style encounter group, Ayn Rand–ian objectivism, nudist magazine-
inspired frolicking, and hard-core fucking seems sui generis to the
place and the moment. The long-term residents, usually heterosex-
ually coupled, formed the Sandstone "family" (a quintessentially
sixties concept that withered after the horrors of the Manson murders). Along with the Williamsons, they were the ones who made
sure that the pool was kept at ninety-three degrees, the hillside was
landscaped, the kitchen supplied with food, the two-person tub
clean, and the enormous "Ballroom" attractively lit and stocked
with plenty of pillows. This last was vital for the weekends, when
the guests would arrive.

The only way to visit Sandstone was to sign up for membership, shelling out a considerable monthly sum to obtain the right to attend the weekend revels and encounter groups. Male guests had to bring one or more women with them, as a way to cut down on the problem of lonely and abusive horndogs, as well as one-way voyeurism. The point was participation and, in a Reichian sense, to open oneself up emotionally through sex, both with people one was close to and with strangers. Hence the Ballroom's centrality, as a place to "ball," in the parlance of the times.

Barbara long claimed she saw more naked stars and starlets than any other woman in Hollywood, and the Sandstone membership rolls and occasional visitors make for eye-popping reading. Just a few of the boldfaced names included crooner/dancer/actor Sammy Davis Jr., who arrived one night together with his wife, Altovise, and Marilyn Chambers, the star of the pornographic movie *Behind the Green Door*; fellow Rat Packer and Kennedy family confidant Peter Lawford; the English sexologist Dr. Alex Comfort, who wrote about Sandstone in his bestseller *The Joy of Sex*; former teen idol Bobby Darin; George Plimpton, the editor of the *Paris Review*; and acid guru Timothy Leary.

One regular was an ex-marine turned game theory scholar turned intelligence analyst named Daniel Ellsberg. If that name sounds familiar, it's because at the same time he was at Sandstone and other "swinging" establishments, Ellsberg was collecting secret documents revealing that the military and Presidents Johnson and Nixon were concealing the disaster of the Vietnam War, lying not only to the public but also to Congress. In 1971 Ellsberg leaked the Pentagon Papers to the *New York Times*, helping to end the war, even at the cost of being charged with espionage.

Ellsberg had access to the papers because he was working at the RAND Corporation in Santa Monica, an independent think tank that had grown out of a Douglas Aircraft group doing research and development (RAND, as it was acronymed during the war) for the U.S. armed forces. After World War II, RAND was a powerful force supporting Southern California's Cold War aerospace juggernaut, merging public and private sources, military needs and academic research, a meeting place for accountable politicians and unaccountable spooks. Beyond the odd coincidence of RAND analysts (including Ellsberg colleague and co-conspirator in the Pentagon Papers leak Anthony Russo) frolicking in the Sandstone pool before retiring to the Ballroom for cocktails, there is the commonality of systems thinking to both Sandstone and RAND. As RAND historian David Jardini notes, in the early years "systems analysis served as the methodological basis for social policy planning and analysis across such disparate areas as urban decay, poverty, health care, education, and the efficient operation of municipal services such as police protection and fire fighting."

It was John Williamson who brought systems analysis to bear on human sexuality. Why systems? Because World War II was won through what strategists called C^3I—command, control, communications, and intelligence—and part of the postwar world was devoted to maintaining this dominance. Linked to the dissemination of cybernetics and computing in the fifties and sixties, C^3I mutated into various attempts to build systems theories for everything, and the aerospace culture of Southern California was a testing ground for systems theory, as a way not only of engineering but also of organizing the social.

It should have come as no surprise that this kind of thinking would eventually be applied to the most intimate of social relation-ships, and Sandstone's libertine libertarianism was precisely the kind of turn that social conservatives, even those with fusionist leanings, would attack. In "Libertarianism or Libertinism?" a 1969 essay in the conservative *National Review*, Frank Meyer catego-rized libertines—in whose company he surely would have placed the Williamsons—"like those other products of the modern world, ritualistic liberals, socialists, communists, fascists," as "ideologues first and last" who would "replace God's creation of this multifari-ous, complex world in which we live, and substitute for it their own creation, simple, neat and inhuman—as inhuman as the blueprints of the bulldozing engineer." That bulldozing engineer reached an apotheosis in Sandstone's Project Synergy.

The Williamsons' erotic utopia was open for only three years, long enough to be written up in magazine articles and a few books; there's even *Sandstone*, a 1975 feature-length documentary. Eventu-ally, in the way of so many communes in Southern California, it slipped away—just like Llano del Rio, a socialist community founded in the Antelope Valley in the 1910s; the same fate as the thirties col-lectives of the Mankind United cult; and similar to the Source Fam-ily run by Jim Baker/Father Yod, who clustered together in a Los Feliz mansion they called the Mother House in the seventies. When the Williamsons came to realize that their systems approach to hu-man emotions was no more sustainable than any of those other communities, they sold the Temescal property to one of the mem-bers, only to see it shuttered soon thereafter, the pool no doubt drained (wouldn't you?) and the Ballroom's bathroom given new wallpaper to replace the pornographic flocking that had surrounded the extra-large tub. John and Barbara eventually moved to Nevada and opened a sanctuary for tigers and other "big cats" outside Las Vegas. John received a respectful, if perplexed, obituary in the *New York Times*, and Barbara admitted to the reporter that after Sandstone closed, she and John had grudgingly "merged back into the culture that we disliked so much."

The norms that the Williamsons worked so passionately to dismantle were precisely those that Tony LeVier dedicated his skills and bravado to defending and sustaining. As an employee during the Cold War for the most secret of Lockheed's divisions, LeVier saw himself as the tip of the spear of democracy. He maintained that if it "hadn't been for aircraft like the F-104, which was strategically targeted at key Russian facilities, and the U-2, which let us know everything the communists were doing, there may well have been a World War III."

In 1963 Tony posed for a PR picture with his teenage daughter Toniann. They were wearing flight suits and exiting Tony's beloved supersonic F-104, a two-seater plane nicknamed the Starfighter, complete with a decal that read FREE WORLD DEFENSE on the fuselage. Tony's in front, sporting a pair of aviator shades, while Toniann, in the back, all of eighteen at the time, is wearing her flight helmet and beaming. They were taking off from Andrews Air Force Base in California, heading to Washington, DC, and along the way making a few promotional stops. During one of them, Toniann switched seats with her dad and cranked it up to Mach 2 over the Mojave Desert. That got Toniann labeled the fastest teen on planet Earth. She knew that when she got home from John F. Kennedy's Camelot, the thrills wouldn't stop. She'd be arriving all set to inherit the absolutely bitchin'est existence that humankind had ever managed to create.

But, but, but. It was her very cohort, set to inherit this bounty, that caused so much consternation over the next decade. Not all kids were like Toniann, along for the ride. Millions of young people in the 1960s rebelled against the previous generation. The rebellion confounded and even enraged their parents, many of whom had fought in and lived through the wars against fascism in Europe, Japanese imperialism across Asia, communism in the Korean hot war, and the proliferating proxy skirmishes during the long grind of the Cold War. Not only had these sacrifices on the battlefield created the bubble of the Pax Americana, but it allowed, as we've seen, the residents of Southern California to profit from their patriotism. Aerospace's good jobs supplied plenty of cash to buy real estate and pursue leisure. The industry provided a lot of the money spent at Disneyland, modifying cars to race the drag strips of the Inland Empire, and ensuring that young kooks and groms from Newport in the South Bay to County Line, just north of Malibu, could buy their first boards at the coastline's many surf shops, all flourishing under the Southern California sun.

With the good life all around them, fueled by the proceeds from jet fuel, how could children so blessed by abundance and security abandon the conservative fusionism that sustained their parents to embrace the libertarian libertinism of sex, drugs, and rock and roll? How could a culture that maintained such an arsenal of democracy give birth to sybarites writhing to pagan rhythms? Who were the seducers of these innocents, and how could such a different tribe of people infiltrate Southern California so successfully?

Take, for example, the lords and (a very few) ladies of Laurel Canyon, who emerged in the aftermath of Beatlemania and reignited LA's dormant rock scene in the midsixties. By that time, the children of Aviation Okies and rocket scientists alike were flocking to Sunset Strip clubs like the Whisky a Go Go and the Rainbow to catch sets by bands like the Byrds, Buffalo Springfield, the Mamas and the Papas, the Mothers of Invention, and the Doors, all of whom lived just above Sunset in the verdant hillsides of Laurel Canyon. The rock stars' moral compasses were skewed and their commitment to hedonism legendary. But was the distance between them and their fans as vast as it looked from the stage? In fact, those LA rockers had themselves suckled at the breast of the military-industrial complex to a degree that, in retrospect, boggles the mind.

Lead freak in the Canyon and musical innovator par excellence Frank Zappa may have been surrounded by the Mothers of Invention, but his own father, Francis Zappa, was a chemist working in the defense industry, moving from Maryland's Edgewood Arsenal chemical warfare facility to Edwards Air Force Base in Southern California. To get a sense for what Father Zappa was working on, it may be worth considering that the Zappa family grew up with gas masks at the ready. David Crosby (first of the Byrds, then Crosby, Stills & Nash) may have been famed for sheer excess in everything from drugs to booze to sex, but one reason he was able to connect with the aerospace kids in Southern California may have been that he understood the stresses of living in a household filled with state secrets. David's father, Floyd Delafield Crosby, attended Annapolis and during World War II developed visual reconnaissance technologies for the Army Air Corps. John Phillips, leader of the Mamas and the Papas, did Crosby one better, not only by having a father who was a retired Marine Corps officer but also by attending Annapolis himself (though, not that surprisingly, he didn't make it through his plebe year).

Gram Parsons of the Byrds and the Flying Burrito Brothers may not be as well remembered as Zappa, Crosby, and Phillips, but he was justly admired by his peers for bringing country and western together with rock and roll to create what he called cosmic American music. Parsons commissioned Nudie Cohn, LA-based tailor to the C&W stars, to make him a "Nudie" suit emblazoned with rhinestone pill bottles, marijuana leaves, poppy blossoms, a naked woman, and a bright-red cross exploding off the back. This was the greatest libertine outfit of the era. Parsons's father, Major Ingram Cecil "Coon Dog" Connor II, a World War II bomber pilot who flew more than fifty combat missions, never did see his son wearing his Nudie suit on the album cover for *The Gilded Palace of Sin*, as Major Coon Dog shot himself in the head six years before Gram—born Ingram Cecil Connor III—dropped out of Harvard and moved to Laurel Canyon to find his fortune and escape the family's demons.

There were even more rockers with highly placed military fathers, including Stephen Stills, all three members of the band America, and even the later-to-emerge singer-songwriter Jackson Browne, but only one had a father who rose high enough to command a full fleet of navy ships, submarines, and air wings. That would be Rear Admiral George Stephen Morrison's son, who never went by "James Douglas," preferring the informality of "Jim." Rather than follow his father into the military, Jim ended up studying poetry and film at UCLA. There he dropped acid, poured himself into tight leather pants, and cofounded the Doors. Rear Admiral Morrison, on the other hand, commanded the fleet during the Gulf of Tonkin incident that enmeshed the United States in the Vietnam War. The emergence of the Lizard King, as the younger Morrison styled himself, from a rear admiral's house was both the macro and the micro of what was happening in the rest of Southern California's aerospace families.

The disaffected young came to see the industry as part of a war machine without end, where secrecy bred hypocrisy and the whole edifice—executive suites to factory floors to the workers' homes—stank. That stink spread through a mammoth network of suburbs that ate up wilderness and souls at an equal clip. However they felt, aerospace remained a mainstay of the Southern California economy until the end of the Cold War. The fall of the Berlin Wall in 1989 and the dissolution of the Soviet Union in 1991 meant that those things Southern California made better than anyone else in the world—fighter jets, long-range bombers, suborbital platforms, guided missiles—were not needed to the same extent. The engineering mind-set that the aerospace industry baked into its workers was also challenged. The kind of system that designs rockets that can take humans to the moon and get them back safely can conversely produce 300 percent cost overruns and weapons systems that are obsolete before they make it to the battlefield. There had long been a call to take aerospace's engineering acumen and turn it toward consumer markets. It wasn't as though the industry was unaware of advances in computation and telecommunications. The branches of Southern California aerospace that worked on engineering and launching communication satellites were at the forefront of cellular communication and the kind of packet switching that later defined the internet. As early as the U-2, Kelly Johnson was grumbling that the information technologies in the spy plane were attracting more attention from the brass than the design of the plane itself.

One milestone was the 1969 transmission of the first message of the modern internet, which was sent from Leonard Kleinrock's lab at UCLA to the Stanford Research Institute. The message was supposed to read "log," but the system crashed and only the two letters *lo* made it northward. Fifty years later, Kleinrock maintained that this glitch could be seen as prescient, standing in for "lo and behold"—which I see as a digital-era updating of fellow engineer William Mulholland's "There it is. Take it." But the mantra of the high-tech marketplace that the internet enabled—release early, release often, clean up later—never meshed with Southern California's aerospace ethos. Unfortunately for LA, over the course of two decades, the center of the state's engineering culture moved in the same direction as that first internet message: from Southern California, where people worked on government contracts to build planes and rockets, to Northern California, where entrepreneurs built personal computers and social media.

Exactly one hundred years after the Los Angeles Air Meet inaugurated Southern California's first century of aerospace, Northrop Grumman moved its corporate headquarters from Century City in Los Angeles to Falls Church, Virginia, in the Washington metroplex. Northrop Grumman was just following the lead of other companies like Science Applications International Corporation and Lockheed Martin Corporation, which had pulled up stakes a decade earlier. But Northrop Grumman was the last. When it relocated, there was no longer a single aerospace giant headquartered in Southern California. Those moving vans literally and symbolically marked the decline of the influence—economic and cultural—of an industry that had done so much to define the region and, through it, the nation.

The end of the first century of aerospace is not the end of aerospace in Southern California. There's been an explosion in what's called the alt-space business, with private companies like entrepreneur Elon Musk's SpaceX, based in unglamorous Hawthorne. What the cultural impact of the alt-space movement will be is too early to tell, but if it can channel the limitless guts of Tony LeVier and the galactic weirdness of John Williamson, perhaps space will once again be open to human exploration.

Libertarianism is the civic religion of the engineers' new home, Silicon Valley, with the founders of everything from Uber to PayPal espousing braided strains of libertarianism. For they also see themselves as self-made men free from constraints and unwilling to acknowledge the trillions of dollars of public investment in the platforms over which they hold sway. The voters in Southern California have become solidly blue, even in the formerly blood-red Orange County, and are far less enchanted with libertarianism than in the heady days of the Goldwater campaign. Libertinage has gone electronic to emerge on Grindr and Tinder, and in retrospect it can be seen as one of the forces that helped to open cultural spaces for gay liberation, feminism as a way of life, and trans rights as human rights. But right now, the alt-space movement continues, and at least some of us still dream of the moon, of Mars, of the stars.

6 EINSTEIN'S BATHTUB

UNTITLED #20 (FREEWAYS) | 1994 | PLATINUM PRINT | 2 ¼ X 6 ¾ INCHES (5.7 X 17.1 CM)

Science, Art, Magic, and Mayhem from Pasadena to the Moon

Sigmund Freud said that anatomy is destiny, but he was wrong—geography is. How else are we to explain the fact that the world's most famous scientist; a rocket engineer turned magus; the woman with whom that magus performed "sex magick," alongside the founder of one of the century's oddly enduring religious technologies; the inventor of science fiction fandom; the Nazi aristocrat who became the father of the American space program; a grade-school dropout who founded a death cult; and Yoda, the diminutive Jedi sage from the *Star Wars* franchise, should all be connected by a mapping that follows the Arroyo Parkway from Pasadena to downtown LA? The slippage between these people, these places, science, science fiction, pseudoscience, and sheer lunacy

One man's "magic" is another man's engineering.

—Robert Heinlein

Freedom is a two-edged sword of which one edge is liberty
and the other, responsibility. Both edges are exceedingly
sharp and the weapon is not suited to casual, cowardly or
treacherous hands.

—Jack Parsons

marks, with uncanny precision, the way Southern California ideologies and idols were packaged and exported to a world audience.

From the beginning of the Yankee era, Southern California aspired to live the future. Modernism has long been the de facto
idiom, resulting in cascading iterations of the techno-sublime, from
the lacquered surfaces and acrylic depths of the Light and Space
movement, to the melding of ergonomics and aesthetics in the design work of Charles and Ray Eames, to the gleaming metallic to-
pologies of Frank Gehry's architecture. The techno-sublime slides
too easily into machined kitsch, of course; the Space Age leaves its
mark on everything from Googie diners to rocket-shaped tail fins.
In any case, it wasn't all bright skies. The darker side of technology

manifested itself not only within the garrison state that was California during World War II and the Cold War, but also within its imaginary, from entertainment to religion to the realms of madness.

This wild and woolly story begins in the break between world wars, when the twentieth century's greatest scientist spent time in the rich and sleepy suburb of Pasadena. This was, of course, Albert Einstein, he of the bushy hair, luxuriant mustache, and soft-spoken demeanor. Einstein's ideas had an impact not only on his colleagues in physics but on the general public's very conception of the universe, his theory of relativity shocking everyone who expected time and space to be stable and matter and energy to be fundamentally different. Whether the masses partially grasped or completely misconstrued it, Einstein's relativity was as fundamental to their sense of modernity as were the movies or air flight.

Einstein is arguably the most celebrated intellect ever, a celebrity whose reach crossed borders and ages. By the early 1930s, he understood that the rise of fascism across Europe would make it impossible for him and his wife, Elsa, to stay on the Continent, much less in Germany. So Einstein became what in sports would later be termed a free agent—in his case, the greatest player in the game. He visited Oxford, but found it stuffy, and lectured at MIT and Princeton, but the strongest pull was a relatively new institution on the West Coast, the California Institute of Technology, in Pasadena, northeast of downtown Los Angeles.

Under the leadership of Nobel Prize–winning physicist Robert Millikan, Caltech was intent on becoming a powerhouse on the world stage. In a region already derided for vapidity, Millikan and the board of trustees set their sights on transforming an obscure technical college founded in the nineteenth century into an impregnable temple of knowledge and a storehouse of scientific and engineering mastery designed to power the whole of Southern California. Along with the adjoining Huntington Library and gardens and the observatory atop nearby Mount Wilson, the mandarins at Caltech were intent on creating an Athens among the oranges, a genteel grove at the far western edge of the West. And Millikan saw landing Einstein as key.

So it was that Albert and Elsa Einstein spent three winters in Pasadena from 1931 to 1933. At first they lived in a small house on Walnut Street. Einstein's genius attracted people, especially children, who would march straight up to his door and ask for help with their homework. This wasn't a problem for Einstein, but one day the walk to his office nearly killed him (his reputation for ambulatory distraction all too true), and Elsa insisted they shorten the commute. So they moved into the newly opened Athenaeum on the southeast end of Caltech's carefully designed and meticulously manicured campus.

The Einsteins got the best suite in the place, complete with a bespoke interior of white wainscoting, where for two winters they soaked up the sun and made decisions about their future. "Here in Pasadena it is like Paradise. Always sunshine and clear air, gardens with palms and pepper trees and friendly people who smile at one and ask for autographs." Einstein himself was famously uninterested in Hollywood, though. When asked by Millikan if he wanted to meet any of the entertainment elite, Albert admitted he didn't go to many movies. Elsa leaned over and reminded him that he had enjoyed some of Charlie Chaplin's films, and so the theoretical physicist was set up for an evening with the grade-school dropout. What the German refugee did not expect was that the English expatriate would invite him to ride together to the world premiere of Chaplin's masterful film *City Lights*. Einstein was staggered by the klieg lights and the frenzy of the crowd, which was calling out the name not only of the movie star but also of his guest. The story goes that Chaplin turned to Einstein and said, "They are cheering me because they understand me; they are cheering you because they do not understand you."

Physicist and historian of science Abraham Pais said of his one-time collaborator, "Einstein, creator of some of the best science of all time, is himself a creation of the media insofar as he is and remains a public figure." Indeed, the Rumpled Professor, with his wild hair and unruly mustache, became an iconic figure in much the same way as Chaplin's Tramp, with his baggy pants, bowler, over-sized shoes, and tidy, twitchable mustache. The respective "looks" of both scientist and comic were sketches, rudimentary outlines teasing out essences. In physics, light is simultaneously a wave and a particle. So, too, is celebrity, and only the rare few, like Chaplin and Einstein, manage to harness the particulate bursts of notoriety and the long waves of fame, achieving levels of renown seemingly outside both space and time. The same cannot be said of the next figure in our tale.

> I hight Don Quixote, I live on peyote,
> marijuana, morphine and cocaine,
> I never know sadness, but only a madness
> that burns at the heart and the brain.
>
> —Jack Parsons

If only minimal strokes are needed to render icons like Einstein and Chaplin, how to paint the portrait of a character named Marvel

Whiteside Parsons, known to friends and colleagues as "Jack" but remembered today mostly by the aficionados of fringe culture? We can start with one point of commonality: while certainly not everyone in Pasadena was aware that Albert Einstein was a neighbor, there was at least one teenage local—already a virtuoso at blowing shit up—who was keenly aware of the presence of genius just east at Caltech.

Jack Parsons was raised by indulgent grandparents who educated him as they would have a nineteenth-century aristocrat, complete with individualized tutors, a personal laboratory, and access to a private library. The latter's volumes on Arthurian legends forever endowed Parsons with a keen sense of antiquarianism and a love of ritual. More than anything else, though, what captivated him was a single, specific longing, one inspired by reading the earliest forms of speculative fiction late into the night. Boy Jack dreamed of space. Jules Verne's striking and technologically detailed 1865 volume *From the Earth to the Moon* was important to Parsons, but when he turned twelve, a new magazine came on the market called *Amazing Stories*, edited by the father of modern science fiction, Hugo Gernsback. *Amazing Stories* was filled with tales not only of the moon but of traversing the stars themselves, and there was only one way Parsons could envision interplanetary travel happening, and that was rocketry.

Rockets had been around since antiquity but in modern times were considered too unstable for most military applications and essentially unworkable for guided, much less manned, flight. They were, in other words, technologies best left to showmen and pyromaniacs. Anyone thinking about rockets differently was a hobbyist at best, a fantasist at worst. Jack Parsons, it turned out, was a brilliant hobbyist and a dedicated fantasist, and the combination of those qualities pushed him to the forefront of the nascent field.

The way forward, however, was neither clear nor easy. Parsons's family fortunes suffered greatly during the Depression, so much so that the boy who was chauffeured by limousine to his classes (causing no little amount of fighting with less privileged peers at John Muir High School) was forced to drop out of Stanford because of financial difficulties. But Parsons's thirst for space travel was unquenchable, and his proximity to Caltech yielded an opportunity that his education did not.

He and a high school co-conspirator, a gifted mechanic named Ed Forman, made the acquaintance of a graduate Caltech aeronautics student named Frank Malina. Malina, in turn, managed to convince the great physicist and aeronautical engineer Theodore von Kármán to allow the three of them to set up a lab. The Rocket Research Group at Caltech's Guggenheim Aeronautical Laboratory was nominally under von Kármán's leadership, but it was better known around campus as the Suicide Squad, given the incessant blasts that scared passersby and the occasional explosions that literally blew up parts of the building. These blasts prompted a move off Caltech's campus to the unpopulated Arroyo Seco at the northern edge of Pasadena, where Parsons and Forman had tested their rudimentary rockets back in high school. There, in a dry creek bed, on Halloween in 1936, the most famous photograph of the group was taken. Forman, Malina, and two other grad students, Apollo Smith and Rudolph Schott, all sprawl around an engine-testing mechanism looking rather exhausted. Parsons, reclining in his usual formal attire (the legacy of his posh youth), smiles in self-satisfaction.

That day's test was successful, and the legacy of the Rocket Research Group was the formation of the Jet Propulsion Laboratory (so named because even at that time, the term "rocket" struck the Caltech community as outré) and a commercial spin-off that became the successful Aerojet Company. During World War II, both JPL and Aerojet grew hugely important, and they stayed so for decades afterward. By any measure, both Parsons and Malina should have been lauded as the fathers of American rocketry, their visages immortalized on stamps. But, as will be seen, neither has gotten his due, though for very different reasons.

Let's work backward from Parsons's tragic, if not entirely surprising, demise. In 1952 an explosion ripped through the carriage house of Parsons's house on Orange Grove Avenue, aka Millionaire's Row. When the upstairs tenants ran down, they found Parsons near death, one hand and part of his head blown off. There were barrels of chemicals, sinister-looking powders, and other dangerous equipment lying around, as well as papers blowing everywhere. Curiously, after a tragedy of such magnitude—only amplified by the suicide of Jack's mother immediately after hearing the news— one of the first things the tenants did was to bolt upstairs and paint over a wall-sized mural. Understand that the mural was of an enormous devil's head. The tenants also collected and disposed of a variety of other magical talismans.

That an experimentalist with a penchant for mixing volatile chemicals should die in an explosion is not as surprising as the fact that the accident happened in his kitchen, but it's that satanic mural that really confuses things. What becomes clear in unfolding the layers of Parsons's life is that, curious as he was about the natural world, even as it extended into space, the supernatural was equally

compelling. As his scientific career slowed, his interest in magic—
or "magick," as he spelled it—escalated to where Parsons became
the most influential occultist in the United States and eventually
the chief American emissary of the infamous British warlock Aleister
Crowley. Crowley, who embraced the nickname the Great Beast,
was the charismatic founder of the Thelemic Church—a hedonistic, syncretic utopia devoted to experimenting with sex, drugs, and
excesses of all kinds—whose motto, "Do as thou will shall be the
whole of the law," was an incongruous fit with postwar Pasadena,
home of the Rose Bowl and Rose Parade, among other wholesome
and definitively nonsatanic pursuits. On the other hand, midcentury Southern California was filled with people who were open-
minded about a huge range of beliefs, from those they'd brought
with them to others they created in their new homes on the edge of
the West.

One of these people was the World War II naval veteran who
moved into Parsons's house on Millionaire's Row and had an affair
with Parsons's wife, while Parsons himself was sleeping with her
younger sister. After Parsons and the vet, who had turned to writing
science fiction stories to make a living, engaged in a series of sex
magick rituals together, Parsons was convinced to invest a considerable sum in purchasing a boat on the East Coast that the vet
would then sail through the Panama Canal and resell in California
at a profit. As it turned out, however, the vet and Parsons's soon-to-
be-ex-wife ran off with Parsons's money, bought the boat for themselves in Miami, and would have gotten away with it had Parsons
not flown to Florida just as they were leaving and invoked a spell
that brought on a tropical storm that forced them back to port.

Did I mention that the sci-fi-writing, wife-stealing, sex magick–partnering naval veteran was L. Ron Hubbard, who within a few years would found Scientology and claim, evidence notwithstanding, that the entire time he spent with Parsons he was on a "secret" mission for naval intelligence investigating paranormal threats to American security?

As the preceding suggests, the history of American rocketry is nothing if not explosive. But interestingly, when it comes to bestowing the greatest honors, the story gets even more bizarre. That's because this country's epochal space program doesn't have an American father; instead, it has a German *Vater*. Herewith, the true and truly improbable story of Wernher von Braun—Nazi, rocket scientist, American immigrant, Hollywood biopic subject, NASA stalwart, and Disney television star.

To fact-check von Braun's story, let's revisit young Jack in Pasadena, in the twenties, those halcyon days before Parsons's family lost their fortune. Back then, Jack was allowed to do the almost unthinkable: make personal phone calls overseas. When Jack called far-off Germany, who picked up the phone? Another young man, only two years older, likewise raised in luxury and obsessed with rocketry and speculative literature. The young man's full Prussian name was Wernher Magnus Maximilian Freiherr von Braun. Holding the title "Freiherr" is equivalent to being a baron, and on his mother's side he was a blood relation to royal families across Europe. Young Wernher had a spotty record in school but found his place in the world by relentlessly fantasizing about how to get off it. What sustained him through the twenties and thirties was a dream of using rockets to propel man into space, a dream that was fed by readings in science fiction and a burgeoning awareness that there was a fledgling community spread around the world already trying to generate financial backing and public support for what seemed to most to be either quixotic or idiotic. It's no surprise that like-minded dreamer young Jack would be aware of young Werner and envious of his growing success in Germany. However, the line between dream and nightmare is not always clearly delimited. That is to say, von Braun's futurist orientation appealed not only to Parsons and other fellow travelers but to the vanities, delusions, and strategic thinking of Germany's supreme leader, Adolf Hitler himself.

In short order, von Braun not only joined the Nazi Party, he became an officer in the SS. With direction straight from the Führer, he and his team set up shop in Peenemünde, an island in the Baltic Sea (some claim at the suggestion of von Braun's mother, who felt it was "just the place for you and your friends"). At Peenemünde they developed the first of what can be considered contemporary rockets: sleekly aerodynamic, with pointed nose cones and stabilizing fins. Originally known as A-4s, by the time they were deployed by the German military they had been rebranded as V-2s, the *V* abbreviating the German word for "vengeance." These were the rockets that leveled Antwerp and Rotterdam and rained terror on the residents of London.

Von Braun consulted personally with Hitler and SS chief (and chief architect of the Holocaust) Heinrich Himmler and later admitted to touring the Mittelbau-Dora concentration camp looking for workers for the factory at Peenemünde. After the war, von Braun claimed that he had been appalled at the conditions in the camps but was powerless to change them, and that everything he did—from donning jackboots to employing slave laborers to building war machines that expedited the deaths of any and all enemies of the Third Reich—was simply the action of a scientist striving to advance knowledge in his field.

So how is it that an SS officer from Prussia ended up as the paterfamilias of America's space program? The answer has to do with politics, and even the fallibility of memory, as much as it does science. In September of 1945, von Braun and his team rushed to surrender to American rather than Soviet troops, knowing that their talents were bound to be of use to the winners, and far preferring to take their chances stateside. They became the centerpiece of Operation Paperclip, an American military intelligence program that combed through the defeated German forces for scientists and technicians who might benefit American military and industrial needs. The administrators of the program were supposed to weed out "bad Germans"—committed Nazis and war criminals—in order to identify "good Germans," but as it turned out, the looming security needs of the Cold War carried more weight than did justice for the war's victims.

By the time von Braun and his team passed from London to Los Angeles, the U.S. military had waived a magic denazification wand over them, and their pasts were not so much forgotten as obliterated. Even new mistakes were sent down the memory hole, including one of the first American military rockets based on the V-2 launched from Arizona; it went off course and exploded in Mexico, another example of von Braun and those around him caring more about the launch than the landing. Not everyone was so forgetful or forgiving, though, as evidenced in Tom Lehrer's 1965 song "Wernher von Braun," in which the satirist rhymes "hypocritical" with "apolitical" and includes the lines "'Once the rockets are up, who cares where they come down?' / 'That's not my department,' says Wernher von Braun."

Von Braun ended up resettled in Alabama but flew to LA regularly to consult on the Redstone and Jupiter rocket programs. During these trips, he became close to multimedia impresario Walt Disney, who had a special interest in technology and how it would define the future. Von Braun had published a series of intricately illustrated articles about space flight in *Collier's* magazine, and Disney adapted them for a series of television episodes titled "Man in Space," "Man and the Moon," and "Mars and Beyond." In the midfifties, who else was Uncle Walt going to turn to? Jack Parsons was dead, his scientific work tainted by black magick. His JPL cofounder Frank Malina was the victim of McCarthy-era red-baiting and had decamped with his family to live and work in France for the rest of his life. This left von Braun—blond, tall, handsome, with an aristocrat's bearing— at the head of the table. And, let us not forget, as a former Nazi, von Braun was unassailably not a communist.

Thus, when former actor and General Electric pitchman Ronald Reagan opened the Disneyland Park with a flourish in 1955, you could see—all the way from Main Street to the Matterhorn—a version of the V-2, Germany's own *Wunderwaffe*, or "wonder weapon," stationed at the center of Tomorrowland. Remember that this consecration of von Braun's legacy took place a mere fourteen years after the United States entered the Second World War. It was as though, in 2015, the former director of Al Qaeda's 9/11 cyberpropaganda unit was designing America's latest social-media platform.

I have devoted my life to amassing over a quarter million
pieces of sf and fantasy as a present to posterity and I
hope to be remembered as an altruist who would have
been an accepted citizen of Utopia.

—Forrest J. Ackerman

It's hard to shake the image of young Jack calling the slightly older
but still-young Wernher to trade stories about payloads and trajectories, but these calls undoubtedly also covered the pair's mutual
interest in early pulps like *Amazing Stories* and *Weird Tales*. So
great was von Braun's love for science fiction that even when World
War II closed off most of Europe to American publications a decade
and a half later, he used his exalted position to obtain smuggled
copies of his beloved pulps.

By a twist of fate, many of the writers featured in these magazines were gathering regularly in Los Angeles with some of their
most dedicated readers, including Jack Parsons, who even got some
of the authors involved in his Crowley-inspired magickal gather-
ings. As compelling as the Thelemites must have been in their
robes, chanting and fooling around with broadswords, the growing
number of science fiction readers in Southern California still didn't
have much of a sense of their own peculiar destiny. That's where the
next figure in our tale comes in, the obsessive's obsessive, the person
who conjured up fandom as a way of life, the redoubtable and remarkable Forrest J. Ackerman.

Ackerman, known as everything from "4F" to "Forry" to "the
Ackermonster," claimed to have seen his first "imagi-movie" in 1922,
after which he moved on to pulps like *Amazing Stories*, eventually
creating one of the first fan clubs, the Boys' Scientifiction Club, in

1930 in downtown LA, at the other end of the Arroyo from Pasadena. It was there that Ackerman toiled as an agent (eventually for
both L. Ron Hubbard and Ray Bradbury); wrote fiction of his own
(some of it lesbian themed under the delirious pen name "Laura-
jean Ermayne"); and generally immersed himself in what he dubbed
the world of "sci-fi." He was one of the first members of the most
influential group on the West Coast, the Los Angeles Science Fantasy Society (LASFS), where readers like Parsons and writers like
Hubbard, Bradbury, and Robert Heinlein met to hash out the future, debate the ins and outs of rocketry and atomic energy, and
strike violent blows against the quotidian. Bradbury and Heinlein
are universally recognized as titans of the genre, while Hubbard,
who claimed to "hate the hell out of gadgets," started writing sci-fi
only because it sold well, though his friend Heinlein once generously asserted that the former's *Final Blackout*, serialized in *Astounding Science Fiction* in 1940, was "as perfect a piece of science
fiction as has ever been written."

Regardless of its literary quality, the genre was generating a notable passion among its readers, and eventually they decided to get
together to share it. When Forry attended the First World Science
Fiction Convention in 1939, he appeared in a green satin cape over
jodhpurs and boots inspired by the costumes in William Cameron
Menzies's 1936 film *Things to Come*. His outfit was put together by
one of the most important women in early fandom, fellow LASFS
member Myrtle R. Jones (better known as Morojo, her nickname
in Esperanto), who also sported a twenty-fifth-century ensemble.
Forry called what they were wearing "futuristicostumes," thereby
co-inventing what has since become known as cosplay. Adherents,

amateurs, acolytes, enthusiasts, and buffs worldwide may not realize that as they dress for the street in Tokyo's Harajuku or for the
convention hall at San Diego's Comic-Con they are enacting rites
that Forrest Ackerman and the LASFS pioneered decades ago. The
rituals of fandom have by now moved out of the comic-book store
and into the multiplex, the narratives of lonely adolescents having
become the central and most profitable stories of our age. Fandom's
triumph has been lauded by geeks and nongeeks alike, but there is
no denying that a certain poignancy has been lost.

There was a tangible sense of "difference" in early fandom, which
created open spaces for any number of what would eventually be
called subcultures. Before gay liberation, science fiction clubs were
congenial places for people with same-sex attraction to gather without the omnipresent fear of being raided by the vice squad. The
presentiment of other worlds and hopeful alternative realities led
people like the young Harry Hay to the LASFS years before he founded
the Mattachine Society, one of the first major homosexual rights
organizations in the United States. Drawing on his past experience
with radical politics, Hay structured the new advocacy group along
the lines of Communist Party cells, designed to protect the identities of their members. The inspiration behind its name was the So-
ciété Mattachine, a masked cohort that, according to legend, traveled
from town to town highlighting injustice in medieval France. The
fantasy element of the LASFS may well have encouraged Hay to
build off this medieval reference, but late in life, when he founded
the Radical Faeries, a gay spiritual movement, Hay made his indebtedness explicit. In addition to the passion he brought to organizing, Hay was also an accomplished musician, one of whose

gigs was playing the organ at Jack Parsons's Thelemic masses in Pasadena.

What the LASFS presaged was a particular variety of the Southern Californian imagination, one that was willing to enlist the sciences in dreams that were often spiritual, and that would let slide any disjunctions between the limits of rationality and the flights of fiction. The trip from the Einstein Suite at the Athenaeum to Parsons's Thelemic Lodge on Millionaire's Row to Ackerman's Science Fantasy Society downtown to Hubbard's Church of Scientology Celebrity Centre International in Hollywood encapsulates how readily fandom can descend into thralldom.

In creating a new "science of mind," as he termed it in *Dianetics: The Modern Science of Mental Health,* Hubbard bowdlerized psychology, psychotherapy, cybernetics, educational theory, and New Age metaphysics, wrapping his "technologies" in a shiny, atomic-age, jet-powered fuselage. The first publication of *Dianetics* was in *Astounding Science Fiction,* the same pulp so central to Parsons, von Braun, and Ackerman. Even Forry, or perhaps especially Forry, was not immune to Hubbard's claims, nor were others in the LASFS: "Everyone was going to be a 'clear,' were going to take off all their glasses, there would be no more colds, one fella even had a finger missing from a hand and he felt like a chameleon that he was going to be able to grow a new finger." As Forry said, "In Los Angeles we felt we were going to have a brave new world."

Why shouldn't Scientologists believe in the E-Meters and other "tech" that a former science fiction author not only created but bequeathed to his believers as physical objects? From a science fiction author who creates a technology that he eventually incorporates as

a church (in large measure to avoid government scrutiny of thera-
peutic claims), it isn't too big a stretch to find people who might
adopt a work of pure science fiction into a quasifaith. That's exactly
what happened to the work of Hubbard's other friend from the
LASFS, Robert Heinlein. Like Hubbard, Heinlein was a navy veteran, but Heinlein stayed the course with his science fiction and
became one of the genre's grand masters. Heinlein's work from the
thirties through the late fifties can be charitably described as scientized juvenilia, but his 1959 *Starship Troopers* broke through into
more adult themes, including the blend of libertarian politics and
libertine sexuality that characterized the outer fringes of Southern
California's subcultures. Heinlein was a nudist, had what would be
termed an "open marriage" with his second wife, and throughout
this period was interested in polyamory. But his greatest impact in
the realms of science-fictionalized spiritual tech came with the
writing of 1961's *Stranger in a Strange Land*, which we last encountered in chapter 5 as John Williamson's bedside reading at Sandstone.

A trippy book published at the start of a trippy decade, *Stranger
in a Strange Land* rambles through metaphysics, sexuality, martyrdom, and Mars, focusing upon the travails of the only survivor of a
human encampment on the Red Planet. Valentine Michael Smith
was raised by the Old Ones, the spirits of the Martian inhabitants,
who see little distinction between the living and the dead. Eventually he is repatriated (replaneted, perhaps) to Earth, where he has
to meld his Martian metaphysics with the mores of his ancestral
planet. He becomes a Jesus figure, surrounded by sycophants and
enemies. He and his followers practice a Martian kind of communi-

cation called "grokking," which involves a full "knowing" of the other, accomplished largely during "water ceremonies," which strike most around Smith as indistinguishable from pagan orgies and are the basis of his Church of All Worlds, which is subsumed under the very 1960s slogan "Thou art God." Eventually Smith is "disincorporated" by his enemies, but he is able to contact his followers and takes over the spiritual hierarchy of the dead. *Stranger in a Strange Land* was and remains a book best read while high.

One of the stranger *Stranger* fans was a young drifter incarcerated in the early sixties, bouncing back and forth between the prisons on McNeil Island in Washington State and Terminal Island in San Pedro. A three-time loser, the drifter was interested in learning how to control others, at first because he wanted to be a pimp, and later to understand how he might establish more comprehensive powers. From experienced felons he came to understand that for expediency's sake he should target girls who were "cracked but not broken," and that the secret to keeping them that way was doling out affection and abuse in alternating increments. He was interested in the Bible and Dale Carnegie's *How to Win Friends and Influence People,* but there were two texts that were game changers for him. Not that the drifter had actually read either of them. Being functionally illiterate, he needed to have others pore over these books and then spell out the salient points for him.

In *Stranger in a Strange Land* the drifter located his consummate role model in Valentine Michael Smith, a figure of otherworldly charisma and sexual power. And in L. Ron Hubbard's *Dianetics* he found an organizational strategy for a science of mind—one that needed little actual science, a plus for a grade-school dropout. The combination of *Stranger*'s grokking and *Dianetics*' clearing was unbeatable, and by the time he got out of Terminal Island in 1967 and drifted around California from Haight-Ashbury to the Spahn Ranch in the desert outside Los Angeles, he'd gathered a flock of the damaged and the lost, which he called a family. The Family was equal parts cult, gang, and halfway house. And their leader—our drifter—was none other than Charles Manson, whose notable achievements include masterminding the Tate-LaBianca killings of 1969 and the murder of that entire decade's peace-and-love mien.

Former rocker Ed Sanders made the strongest claims for a connection with *Stranger in a Strange Land* in his book *The Family*, pointing out that Manson named his son with Mary Brunner "Valentine Michael Manson" and claiming that when Charlie was finally captured, his backpack contained a copy of Heinlein's classic, along with sixty-four movie magazines. We do know with more certainty that Manson used Heinlein's language, including "sharing water" to indicate closeness and "grokking" for understanding, modeling his "fly-trapping" orgies on ceremonies from *Stranger in a Strange Land*.

In 1970 several strands of this story came together under the unforgiving skies of Death Valley. Toward the end of their murderous spree, Manson and the Family decamped to the desert and found themselves confronted by a grizzled prospector named Paul Crockett, a Scientology veteran who either recruited or deprogrammed (depending on your point of view) three of Manson's disciples. Never one to take poaching lightly, Charlie sent other members of the Family to "creepy-crawl" (as they referred to their deadly nocturnal forays) into Crockett's encampment. This alarmed the otherwise unflappable desert rat, and rather than engage with Charlie's ultraviolent shock troops, Crockett and his newly minted Scientologists chose the better part of valor, slipping away into the night. The heat-shimmering otherworldliness of Death Valley was the perfect site for this conflict between the devotees of two different science fiction writers. Like the origin stories of superheroes, the battle between the grokking water ceremonialists of Manson's Family and the E-Metering, Thetan-banishing auditors decamping with Crockett is encrusted in legend. Another origin story that figures here is that of Manifest Destiny, insofar as so many midtwentieth-century California cults—from Scientology to est to Synanon, even Anton Szandor LaVey's Church of Satan—depended on a sci-fi vision of the technology-enhanced new self, the made, remade, and ever-iteratively fashioned self of America at its westernmost limit.

Charlie and his drug-addled and splintered Family became infamous for just this kind of self-fashioning at the limits of sanity. Bobby Beausoleil tried (and failed) to become the bassist for the LA Pop band Love, but his desire for a music career continued through his involvement with Manson, who might not have gone quite as berserk had he been good enough to impress the Beach Boys with his talent, as opposed to his pimping abilities with bent flower children. Years later, even a band as powerful as Guns N' Roses was unable to do anything to mitigate the woefully repetitive banality of Manson's best-known song, "Look at Your Game, Girl": "Can you ever live without the game / The sad sad game / Mad game."

From prison, Beausoleil wrote the score for the mystical masterpiece of avant-garde cinema *Lucifer Rising*, originally shot in 1970 but reworked through the decade, finally released with his score in 1980. Beausoleil was actually supposed to star in it before his incarceration, but he had had a falling-out with its notorious, and notoriously difficult, director, Kenneth Anger, whose film trilogy—*Inauguration of the Pleasure Dome* (1954), *Invocation of My Demon Brother* (1969), and *Lucifer Rising*—was hugely influenced by Aleister Crowley, Jack Parsons's old mentor. For Anger, the melding of Crowley's Thelemite practices with the technology of cinema created a new "magick lantern," a mix of physics and metaphysics to usher in an Aquarian age. Like so many others in the 1960s, Anger concocted his worldview out of a grab bag of pseudosciences and half-digested spiritual traditions. If Anger were looking for a model for all of this, he couldn't have done better than with the artist known as Cameron, whom he cast in *Inauguration of the Pleasure Dome* as the Whore of Babylon, and who also happened to be Jack Parsons's widow.

Marjorie Elizabeth Cameron Parsons Kimmel—or Cameron, the name she preferred—was an artist, poet, witch, and beacon of the counterculture; she knew everyone and materialized everywhere, even as her own name has all but vanished. Cameron showed with famed sculptor Ed Kienholz at curator/gallerist Walter Hopps's Syndell Studio. She had a small part in Curtis Harrington's *Night Tide*, the first film to star the young Dennis Hopper. Later, Hopper said that Cameron scared him out of his mind. Hopper had been primed by stories he had heard floating around Cameron and Parsons that during one of their black masses "some guy had fallen down the stairs and broken his neck which had given him an erection and four women had fucked him before the emergency squads arrived. . . . Whether these were true stories or not, they were the kind of thing you heard and thought 'who is this woman?'" Far more verifiable is the fact that one of her erotic drawings provoked the LAPD to arrest Wallace Berman (who'd championed her in his legendary journal Semina) at his 1957 Ferus Gallery show—the scandal that put the LA art world on the map.

For Cameron art was life and life was art, so her biography is essential to understanding the visual work and poetry she produced over the second half of the twentieth century, a period in which she didn't just encounter alternative lifestyles but pioneered them. Cameron's life was turned upside down by World War II, but she never fit the profile of the women workers who settled back into family life after V-J Day. She was more like Rosie the Riveter's jazz-obsessed gal pal, who didn't retreat back into the kitchen after the armed forces got her the hell out of Belle Plaine, Iowa. As the nation geared up for the war effort, Cameron joined the navy as a mapmaker and was stationed in Washington, DC, before being disciplined for going AWOL. After the war, Cameron followed her family to Pasadena. One night she wandered into a wild party at a mansion on Millionaire's Row thrown by her future husband, the rocket scientist who just happened to be a warlock. Parsons had earlier written a poem cycle called "Songs for the Witch Woman" with the hope of conjuring a suitably mystical mate, and when the red-haired Cameron walked into the room, he was smitten. For the next six years they remained in each other's thrall, casting astrological charts (which are beautiful works of art in their own right), orchestrating sex-magick rituals for themselves and their acolytes, and experimenting with physical and metaphysical science.

Cameron and Parsons were bona fide members of the so-called Greatest Generation, but like Heinlein, Hubbard, and Ackerman, they belonged to a subset I choose to call the "weirdest generation." They persevered through World War II and then revolted against the imposition of peacetime conformity, living as free-loving protohippies—occult and esoteric. The sci-fi worlds they imagined fueled the libertarian and libertine culture of the sixties. College kids in revolt embraced Spider-Man precisely because of his relationship problems; hippies dug *The Lord of the Rings*' hobbits, who became heroes in spite of themselves; and an entire generation of nerds recognized themselves in an emotionless Vulcan named Spock on *Star Trek*. By the seventies, these phantasmatic universes were not merely one element of popular culture but were well on their way to their present status as popular culture in toto. Interestingly, sci-fi used to outrun our capacity to visualize it, but now blockbuster films, games, and immersive virtual-reality simulations are capable of rendering that which formerly could only be imagined. Indeed, these days you'd have to be something of a nostalgist to want to conjure the future out of prose as opposed to special effects, CGI, and deepfakes.

Always pass on what you have learned.

—Yoda

No audiovisual sci-fi has had the same impact as George Lucas's *Star Wars*, a multibillion-dollar franchise so successful it turned into a world of its own, with the largest fandom of any twentieth-century media product, an imperium of the imagination built from the kit of parts that Forrest Ackerman first identified. The cultural DNA of *Star Wars* was hybrid, drawing as much from Parsons's beloved sword and sorcery as from more scientific, or at least scientized, science fiction. This hybridity offered multiple points of entry into the narrative universe of *Star Wars* and an intensely personal connection not only with the stories but with their characters. The original films' sheer mass of narrative is surrounded and supported by associated animations, novelizations, games, and endless crowd-sourced and shared fan fiction. These new narrative modes were, of course, all enabled by internet technologies and connections not even dreamed of when the first films were released during Jimmy Carter's presidency.

The second film produced in the series, *The Empire Strikes Back* (1980), introduced Yoda, an elfin, nine-hundred-year-old warrior/ sage. With his inverted syntax and long green ears, Yoda has inspired a diverse set of devotees who see in his control of Lucas's mysti-cal "Force" an echo of their own dreams of mastery of that ever-so-Californian idea of a spiritual technology. Because the films' producer was a practicing Mormon, and because aspects of the Force also seem resonant with Mormon theology—Yoda's claim that "luminous be-ings are we, not this crude matter" was something of an echo of the Latter-day Saints' core belief that "as man is, God once was; as God is, man may become"—wishful thinking prompted a Mormon myth that the almost-thousand-year-old, wrinkly Jedi knight was based on the Mormons' own almost-hundred-year-old patriarch, Spencer W. Kimball, who led the church from 1973 to 1985.

The truth is—and here is the eureka moment—Yoda has a secu-lar inspiration. According to the *Star Wars* special effects and makeup designer, the wispy tendrils of hair around the head and the kindly face of the venerated resident of the planet Dagobah paid explicit homage to none other than Albert Einstein, that short-term win-terer in Pasadena. And so, as Disney opened new lands to celebrate (and further monetize) its corporate takeover of the *Star Wars* franchise, fans will be able to interact with Yoda, or at least buy a Yoda backpack.

For those few intrigued about the intersections between relativity and the Force, here is an insider's tip about where to stay: Albert and Elsa's former quarters at Caltech's Athenaeum, known as the Einstein Suite (www.athenaeumcaltech.com). There's a nice little terrace with a view down onto the campus's famed Olive Walk, and you can order breakfast sent up from the club's elegant dining room. The suite retains its vintage charm, with the exception of the bathroom, which has been thoroughly updated with Italian tile, marble, chrome, and a walk-in shower, meeting the global standard of the high-end hospitality industry. But whoever approved this renovation either forgot or was unaware that Archimedes experienced the original eureka moment when he was in the tub, so there goes your chance to bathe as a genius.

Physicists at Caltech are still generating empirical evidence for Einstein's theories—such as the proof of gravitational waves, which took more than a century to measure—but the field's momentum has moved beyond quantum mechanics into the all-but-untestable suppositions of string theory and hypotheses of multiple, simultaneous universes. This brings us back into a moment when science and the science fictional do not seem so far apart, and the time ripens for a new, weirder generation. In Southern California you need imagination these days to think about the stars because of all the light pollution. So if you try to pick out specific features of the lunar landscape, you're better off driving to some forlorn place, like the Spahn Ranch, for example. But if you drive all the way out there, even if you bring a good-enough telescope, there's still no chance you'll be able to see the crater located at 37.3° N 171.2° W. That's because it's on the dark side of the moon, forever invisible to us, but no less climactic to our tale. In 1972 that roughly circular impact crater was named in honor of John Marvel Whiteside "Jack" Parsons. Though no one asked Wernher von Braun or L. Ron Hubbard if they thought this geography reflected destiny, we do know that Cameron was pleased.

7 WHAT MAKES MEN HAPPY

UNTITLED #27 (FREEWAYS) | 1994 | PLATINUM PRINT | 2 ¼ X 6 ¾ INCHES (5.7 X 17.1 CM)

Student-Professor Liaisons, Modern Seating, the Story of Civilization, and How Every House Is Haunted

Those who combine success in work with success in love are said to be the happiest of all, especially if they manage long, healthy lives. But what of that even rarer group who combine work and love without ever leaving the house? How do they negotiate the myriad registers of partnership: emotional, vocational, and architectural? In an era when telecommuting challenges the classic concept of the workplace and the parameters of marriage have been expanded, looking back on two of the highest-profile coworking couples Los Angeles ever produced may be particularly instructive. And because biography is at base voyeurism, let's look inside their houses, and perhaps a few others.

Many of LA's most famous coworking couples have been actors acting at being couples. Mary Pickford and Douglas Fairbanks (who

We just did whatever was necessary.

—Ray Eames

Who did the housework while I pored over the heroes and heroines who were to give life to Volume VII? I did.

—Ariel Durant

were married) built one of the city's great showcase estates, Pickfair. Spencer Tracy and Katharine Hepburn (who weren't, at least to each other) hid their affair for decades at Tracy's villa in Palm Springs, just far enough from the Hollywood press to garner some privacy. Cary Grant and Randolph Scott (rumored to be playing at *not* being a couple) shuttled between a Los Feliz mansion and a Santa Monica beach cottage "jokingly" known as Bachelor Hall. Brad Pitt and Angelina Jolie (not married; married briefly; divorced) purchased so much real estate over the years that they could have opened a brokerage.

But Hollywood stars aren't the ideal subjects for this property-centric roman à clef. Neither, frankly, are Jack Parsons and Cameron, who, as we saw in the last chapter, managed to blow up their decrepit manse on Pasadena's Millionaire's Row. Instead, consider the following two coworking couples, both avatars of the city at mid-century.

Will and Ariel Durant were the Pulitzer Prize–winning authors of the multimillion-copy bestselling book series *The Story of Civilization*, which fused a European Enlightenment sensibility with a commercial appeal. The Durants lived and worked in a book-strewn *casa romántica* high in the Hollywood Hills, with stained-glass windows, hand-carved woodwork, an observation tower, and city-to-ocean views. But more on the Durants later. I promise cradle robbing and Malcolm X.

Charles and Ray Eames were the West Coast's most important designers. They produced an ever-replenishing supply of furnishings, exhibitions, and films, fusing European modernism with American mass marketing. The Eameses lived and worked in the Pacific Palisades, in a glass-and-steel home they designed for themselves with a detached home studio, filled with unique objects they collected in their world travels. But more on the Eameses later. I promise *horror vacui* and Marilyn Monroe.

First the story of working at home. It may have been commonplace in the rural America of the eighteenth and nineteenth centuries, but industrialization changed everything. By the end of the twentieth, only one in ten families worked out of their homes full time. The explosion of networking technologies in the twenty-first shifted that equation, and today four in ten Southern Californians report that they have the option to work remotely, at least in part, and both the amount of time and the number of days are on the rise. LA's creatives, who have long been outliers, did not need the internet to reach these kinds of numbers. From the nineteenth century's gentlefolk tending their citrus groves in Riverside to the screenwriters toiling in their home offices in Hollywood's Golden Age, the Southland's labor force has regularly blended vocational and domestic spaces. The private home was central to Southern California's transformations of earth into land and then into real estate, but when emotions enter the frame, things can get wildly complicated.

In Billy Wilder's *Sunset Boulevard* (1950), down-on-his-luck scribe Joe Gillis (William Holden) pounds away at a typewriter in a Spanish-colonial-revival bachelor pad. He has to quit his domicile/office to avoid his creditors (a polite way of saying he's on the run from the repo man) and ends up blowing a tire and skidding into the forbidding mansion owned by the faded silent-movie star Norma Desmond (Gloria Swanson). Gillis gets an upgrade to bigger digs, a nicer office, and a new "family" situation—isolated with Desmond and her chauffeur/ex-husband/former director Max von Mayerling (Erich von Stroheim). That all was not bliss in this polyamorous, if unconsummated, relationship (the less said about the funeral of Desmond's emotional-support chimp the better) is something that any viewer should be able to figure out even before the final reveal that the film is in fact a ghost story, the voice-over by a posthumous Gillis, floating facedown in the pool. On the other hand, Desmond's gondola-esque bed, a naked angel perched on its prow, looks like an awesome place to connect with your inner muse.

In the twentieth century, the private home was the ultimate expression of LA's architectural soul: faux châteaus à la Norma Desmond; midcentury-modern post-and-beams; Venice Beach shacks; Silver

Lake bungalows; half-timbered Tudors; stuccoed Spanish; arched Moorish; stylized neo-Tuscans; and a staggering number of one-offs, including architect John Lautner's Chemosphere, an octagonal house roosting atop a thirty-foot pole; set director Harry Oliver's Beverly Hills storybook home, known to generations of trick-or-treaters as the Witch's House; and Lloyd Wright's brooding Mayan pile, the Sowden House in Los Feliz, where the Black Dahlia may or may not have been brutally dismembered. It is by now a truism that LA is defined less by public spaces or civic works than by the places, however humble, grand, or mysterious, where its people live.

Houses, however, are more than the sum of their spaces and appointments. They are, like Wilder's *Sunset Boulevard*, ghost stories, haunted by their architects and clients and all those who follow in their wake. Take the Beverly Hills manor designed in 1930 for silent film star and "Man of a Thousand Faces," Lon Chaney (whose *Phantom of the Opera* featured the same ornate bed that would turn up in Norma Desmond's boudoir a quarter of a century later). A tour of Chaney's Italian-revival structure would reveal that its architect, Paul Revere Williams, was, like his client, a master illusionist, veiling modern construction techniques in used brick and mature landscaping to create a sense of instant gravitas. Williams, whose iconic design of the Beverly Hills Hotel signage and its clubby Polo Lounge remains virtually unchanged since the forties, had a knack for connecting with the newly rich and famous, balancing the desire to demonstrate wealth and entitlement against the need to seek refuge from the pressures of living life on display. Strategies about how to simultaneously attract and deflect attention came out of

Williams's own experiences—as an orphan as well as a pioneering African American architect, the first to graduate from USC, the first to be inducted into the American Institute of Architects.

Williams triumphed in a racist America, but as he went about the business of design, he was wary of having "the doors of Opportunity closed roughly in his face," to quote W. E. B. Du Bois, writing on the "double consciousness" of the African American. When designing homes in Flintridge, Williams would carefully time his visits because that rich suburb just north of Pasadena was a "sundown town," where African Americans could be arrested or roughed up if they stayed after dark. Even after clients decided to engage his services, Williams often had to pull from a special bag of tricks. One of these involved training himself to sketch all of those sweeping staircases and charming lanais upside down so he could sit across from, rather than directly next to, his clients when he was conjuring up their new spaces. He'd come to understand that having a table between himself and the clients reduced the racial anxiety that close proximity engendered. In the end, what mattered most to him was making sure the doors of opportunity stayed open, even if it meant sublimating his own ego.

Some houses are haunted by reticent ghosts, others by spirits so vainglorious that not even death can squelch them. High above Beverly Hills is a house that offers stunning vistas: by day, a panorama of the lupine-covered hills; by night, the classic "diamonds on black velvet" expanse of the twinkling lights of the city. But even in LA, even in the hills, a house is more than its views. Reincarnated many times, 1129 Miradero Road flickers with the spirits of Greater and Lesser Gatsbys.

The most outsize of these is the house's designer. A poor kid from Texas born Jon Nelson Burke, he moved to the Golden State to start a new life. His good looks convinced him to take a stab at being an actor, but it turned out his métier was construction. He started a business named Craig Ellwood (after a local liquor store) and soon enough changed his name to match. At that point he had experience as a cost estimator and had taken a couple of courses in engineering, but he couldn't sign off on a drawing, much less a whole building. But just as Jonnie Burke understood he could become Craig Ellwood, so, too, did he realize that he could live the life of an architect without bothering to actually become one. In LA this is the hoped-for conclusion of "fake it 'til you make it." In any case, licensed practitioners could handle the pesky paperwork. Ellwood was busy willing his vision of modernism into existence.

Of everything he ever designed, Ellwood's most perfectly realized creation was himself. He understood that selling the client meant more than any credential, and he ensured those sales by cloaking himself in the signifiers of the modern: a Lamborghini with a license plate reading vroom; a closet containing thirty-two of the best Italian suits; a pipe in the Hugh Hefnerian mode. Ellwood deployed an actor's charm, using it to seduce (figuratively) both clients and their wives. Ellwood certainly had experience with wives, as he had four of them himself, his longest marriage to an actress, appropriate for a designer who played at being an architect, all while serving as the consummate salesman of the SoCal lifestyle at midcentury.

So well regarded was Ellwood that he was the only designer to create three homes for *Arts & Architecture* magazine's landmark Case Study House project, which supported the construction by progressive Southern California architects of new types of housing for the post–World War II era. Known as Case Study House #18, 1129 Miradero Road is the most accomplished of the three, with intersecting spaces constructed from prefab glass-and-steel-beam units organized in a flexible open plan. The house was meant to fashion a modern dwelling at an affordable price. The operative verb is "was," because at some point afterward it underwent its own reinvention, sloughing off its modern restraint and adopting structural and decorative elements borrowed from the French provincial, Hollywood regency, and Spanish colonial idioms. As of this writing, yet another reincarnation is in the offing, with the house up for sale as a "development opportunity," which in Realtor-speak means "tear-down." To that end, the sales prospectus conspicuously avoids mentioning the house's illustrious past, promising instead that the lot will be delivered with fully permitted plans for an eleven-thousand-square-foot McMansion.

In the unlikely event that the sellers of 1129 hold an open house, you can bet it will be swamped by those hoping to connect to one of the signature talismans of modernity before it joins too many other ghosts in LA's architectural *bardo*. Realtors tend not to appreciate such "looky-loos"—a term the *Oxford English Dictionary* claims originated in Los Angeles in 1978. But in Southern California, the Sunday open house (along with its cousin, the Tuesday broker's open) is not only for potential clients and real estate professionals. It is for architectural aficionados, nosy neighbors, the lonely, the curious seeking to understand the city's platzgeist. The looky-loo, driving from open house to open house, is to Los Angeles as the flaneur, strolling the *grands boulevards*, is to Paris.

It has been decades since the last open house was held at 5608

Briarcliff Road in Los Feliz, also known as the Casa della Vista, as per the curlicued script woven into the wrought-iron gate that keeps looky-loos enamored of history at bay. Through the gate, beyond the lacy trees and sculpted hedges, stands a perfect specimen of California Romantica. These houses, often built during the boom years of the 1920s, remixed Italian, Spanish, and Moorish vernaculars, resulting in built structures that quoted with verve while being tied to their own place and its particular dream—the good life as lived on the edge of the Pacific.

For forty years, Casa della Vista belonged to the writers Will and Ariel Durant, who produced within its walls a series of staggeringly successful nonfiction books. How Will and Ariel came to be America's best-known historians in a city not known for history is a tale in and of itself, but equally compelling is the story of how they found each other in the first place. Will was a seeker, born on a Massachusetts farm in the late nineteenth century into a devoutly Catholic family. Bookish from childhood, he fled the seminary for academia and then the wider world, eventually landing a job as the one and only teacher at Manhattan's radical Ferrer Modern School. It was a heady time for young Will, and it became headier still when he met the woman who would become his wife. Ariel was her fourth first name. She was born Chaya Kaufman to a Jewish family in Ukraine. After immigrating to the United States, her name was anglicized to "Ida." Will gave her two nicknames: first "Puck," after Shakespeare's sprite; and second "Ariel," which she took as her legal name when she became Mrs. Durant.

It's not entirely accurate to talk about twenty-seven-year-old Will meeting the "woman" he would marry in 1912, because she was a girl of fourteen at that point, and one of his students. A year later, she roller-skated to City Hall for the wedding, hanging her skates over her shoulders during the taking of vows, which may have been one of the reasons the judge accused her new husband of being a "cradle robber." The Durants' *Dual Autobiography*, published from the vantage point of a sixty-year relationship, is a curious document not merely because it demonstrates how fully they subsumed their individuality to the primacy of the couple—in love, in work, and for posterity—but also because several sections seem like nothing so much as fodder for future forensic psychoanalysts. For example: "We spent our wedding night in my mother's apartment, having as yet no rooms of our own. Everything went well until Will took me into his bed and asked for his marital rights. I was not quite prepared for this, and raised objections, until my mother, hearing my protests, came to us and reassured me, 'It's all right my child; don't be afraid.'" The Freudian kicker: "I could never resist my mother."

Marital rights ensured, Will pursued a doctorate in philosophy at Columbia while teenage Ariel tended bar at the Gypsy Tavern in Greenwich Village. To contribute to the family finances, Will turned to public lecturing and writing for the pioneering Little Blue Books series. These were wide-ranging pamphlets, on sale for as little as a nickel, aimed at working- and middle-class audiences. Two young New York publishers, Richard Simon and Max Schuster, asked Will to pull together his most successful pamphlets, which they published in 1926 under the rather immodest title *The Story of Philosophy*. Within three decades it had sold more than two million copies, and to this day it has never gone out of print. The book presaged the Durant house style: biographical, stuffed with anecdotes, humanistic rather than ideological.

With *The Story of Philosophy* to support them, the Durants went on the first of many world tours, gathering material for what would become their life's work: eleven volumes of narrative history ranging from ancient India through the rise of Napoleon. They wound up settling in LA, combing through bank-held properties until they found a dilapidated mansion that had been built on spec in the Roaring Twenties and had never found a buyer. By 1944, the weeds in the garden were four feet high, but this neglected manse cast a spell on Ariel. She and Will spent the next decade transforming it into a combination retreat and atelier, vowing they'd "abide there till the Reaper finds our door"—which the Grim One did in 1981, Will dying precisely two weeks after Ariel. Their longtime New York–based editor, Michael Korda, reminisced about the couple's adjustment to Los Angeles: "They fitted in there . . . they were vegetarian. When you went to their house, you got peculiar herbal teas and nut burgers and . . . odd food like that. . . . They wore health faddist space shoes that are molded to the foot out of some curious substance that isn't leather but also isn't plastic."

Will and Ariel wrote eight of the volumes of *The Story of Civilization* in the Casa della Vista, working fourteen hours a day, seven days a week. Will would sit in a rocking chair with their notes strung out in front of him while Ariel paced as they debated each point before generating their four pages for the day. The work was the life was the relationship. Though they raised a child inside its walls, there was something of the factory about the Casa della Vista, or better yet, a medieval scriptorium straight out of the imaginings of a gothic romance novelist. As Ariel once told a *Life* magazine reporter, "He's a monk and I'm a nun, we just happened to get married."

As the medieval church was built on a hierarchy in which only male priests could perform sacraments, so, too, were our culture's sacred rituals of authorship reserved for Will for much of the period of their collaboration. Will and Ariel always spoke with one voice about their work, but the sexual politics of the era, as well as the fact that Will held a doctorate, while Ariel's formal education ended after high school, militated against her being given public validation for her efforts. The shift to coauthorship would have righted a sense of injustice on her part. She was, after all, the spouse with the temper, which she often directed at their publishers, whom she saw as unfairly benefiting from the couple's work. One night, invited to Simon's Fifth Avenue mansion, she saw a Chagall hanging on the wall and exploded in rage. In the Durants' instantiation of the war between writer and publisher—the literary world's version of labor versus capital—Korda often served as intermediary, claiming it was only through his intervention that Simon & Schuster agreed to credit joint authorship with the seventh volume, *The Age of Reason Begins*, which was published in 1961. Despite their trepidation about messing with a successful formula, the addition of Ariel's name on the spines did not negatively impact sales, especially after the Book of the Month Club began offering the series as a bonus to entice customers to join. With over two million copies in print, the rainbow-colored volumes became a staple of the middle-class American home, two feet of decor as much as a storehouse of wisdom.

Books as decor have had a long history in Southern California. In the nineteenth century it was expensive to import European art and antiques all the way to California, but books, being compact and durable, were a different story. One of the ways those who'd struck it rich proved it was by accumulating serious libraries, as did early-twentieth-century railroad magnate Henry Huntington and copper baron turned U.S. senator William Andrews Clark. With plutocrats leading the way, the market for books took hold, and the stretch of Sixth Street from Main to Alameda became known as Bookseller's Row. Two of the most memorable bookmen of the era were Texas expats Jake Zeitlin and Stanley Rose. "Club" Zeitlin on Sixth was a conduit for modern art and design, with a small gallery attached in which the genteel Zeitlin hosted photographer Edward Weston's first-ever show. Rose was a whole different kettle of fish. The artist Fletcher Martin reminisced that Rose was "the least bookish person I've ever seen and I often wondered whether he ever read a book." His Hollywood shop was "a combination cultural center, speakeasy, and bookie joint.... [He] would get whiskey and/or girls for visiting authors." Located near the legendary Musso & Frank restaurant, Rose's store attracted an entertainment-oriented clientele, including Charlie Chaplin, Marlene Dietrich, and Raymond Chandler. Chandler, who knew that his affable drinking buddy used to help pay the bills by engaging in the shady trade of high-class porn, used Rose as the model for the fiendishly corrupt smut peddler Arthur Geiger in his hardboiled classic *The Big Sleep* (1939), the perfect foil for Humphrey Bogart's knight-errant private eye in the 1946 film version.

The Durants themselves were no strangers to the intermingling of the literati and the Hollywood set. In 1945 Will drafted "The Declaration of Interdependence," a humanist's call for peace and harmony concluding with the high-minded sentiment that "all men are brothers and that mutual tolerance is the price of liberty." Will and Ariel introduced the Declaration at a gala in Hollywood hosted by the intriguing if incongruous duo of Nobel Prize–winning novelist Thomas Mann and Academy Award–winning actress Bette Davis. They followed that up with a public event on July 4 at the Hollywood Bowl that was equal parts glitzy and homespun, featuring Jewish, Catholic, Anglo Protestant, and African American Protestant choirs singing "America the Beautiful," followed by a group recitation of the Declaration before a justice of the Supreme Court, imported from Washington especially for the event.

The Declaration reflects the Durants' optimism, which was driven by the personal—the Casa della Vista was an interfaith household; the setting—LA was a booster's paradise; and the professional—the couple's positive vision of human potential was key to their marketability. That last bit, naturally, enraged academic historians, who excoriated the Durants for their penchant for pontification and oversimplification. But the disdain went both ways, with the Durants seeing academics as specializing in perfectly researched atrocity exhibitions. Will spoke of civilization as "a stream . . . sometimes filled with blood from people killing, stealing, shouting and doing the things historians usually record, while on the banks, unnoticed, people build homes, make love, raise children, sing songs, write poetry and even whittle statues." All of which—except for the love-making part—sounds like a near-exact description of the three hundred animatronic children lined up on the banks singing "It's a Small World" in Walt Disney's riverboat attraction of the same name. The ride debuted at the New York World's Fair in 1964, just as Will and Ariel were putting the finishing touches on Volume IX,

The Age of Voltaire. That acerbic Frenchman might have found the Durants' approach too close for comfort to that of *Candide*'s Professor Pangloss, expert in "*métaphysico-théologo-cosmolonigologie,*" who famously intoned that "all is for the best" in this "best of all possible worlds."

For all the midcentury hopefulness that Disney and the Durants shared, it is worth noting that although "It's a Small World" has been installed in every Disney theme park around the world, it's invariably located in Fantasyland. Cynicism aside, the question the Durants posed late in life, "Who will dare to write a history of human goodness?," remains important. Their genial pantheism meant they wrote about a range of spiritual traditions with respect, and many Americans' first positive encounters with Islam, Hinduism, or Buddhism came directly from *The Story of Civilization*. The American scholar of Hinduism Pravrajika Vrajaprana notes that the Durants were among those most responsible for bringing the tenets of Vedanta "into the American public domain." In his autobiography, Malcolm X writes of being an incarcerated high school dropout who found the Durants in prison, and how they and others opened his mind "about Egypt's Pharaohs; about the great Coptic Christian Empires; about Ethiopia, the earth's oldest continuous black civilization," offering him an escape from the ways in which history had been, in his parlance, "whitened." Malcolm X was an autodidact and his story an intimation that the Durants' legacy will not be found in the university seminar room but rather in the eighteen-minute public oratories known as TED Talks and anywhere else the desire for understanding through narrative and anecdote continues to thrive.

Across town, another couple was likewise invested in opening up the American imagination to global consciousness, though they were doing so in the antithesis of the Durants' house. To get from the Churrigueresque embellishment of the Casa della Vista to the stark geometry of Charles and Ray Eames's modern live-work space entails leaving the Hollywood Hills and heading west to Pacific Palisades, a now staggeringly expensive suburban enclave perched cliffside above the ocean. In the 1940s, however, before the 10 freeway connected the coast road to downtown, Pacific Palisades was the hinterlands of the city before it fell away into the sea. Land that far out was cheap, and this, at least in part, explains why halfway down a canyon road that snakes to the beach, off an anonymous shared private drive, Charles and Ray were able to design and build one of the most radical experiments in the history of American domestic architecture.

Like Ellwood's 1129 Miradero Road, the Eames House at 203 Chautauqua Boulevard was sponsored by *Arts & Architecture*, and thus goes by Case Study House #8. Conceived as a modern dwelling for two partners in love and work, it is a single-story, seventeen-foot-high steel-and-glass rectangular box split into two, with one side for living and the other a studio for working. The massing of the two parts—the living area bigger by half than the studio, with a small patio court to the west of the living room and another court separating them—is harmonious and logical. The large rectangular surfaces of the house are themselves composed of smaller rectangles, with black and multicolored panels interspersed with glass, crisscrossed by supporting struts that create diagonals. The facade looks like a Mondrian painting interpreted by a toymaker with

grand ambitions. The interior, especially the living room, is simultaneously spacious and intimate. Like Rudolph Schindler's house
on Kings Road in West Hollywood, the Eameses meld the interior
and the exterior, but the architecture is even more directly linked to
its environment.

The site features a small meadow and a rise that offers a staggering view of the ocean. Somewhat perversely, given that the gold
standard of coastal living is seeing the waves crash from your living
room window, Charles and Ray decided the house should turn its
back on the Pacific and front onto the meadow. Though you have to
traipse through the grass and perch at the edge of the cliff to get a
glimpse of the water, the siting lends the home a magical sense of
remove and repose. It was from this house without a view that the
Eameses came to dominate design in the middle of the American
Century.

In 1958 Julius Shulman, the great documenter of Southern California's modern architecture, took a color photo of the couple relax-
ing in their living room, enacting their version of creative coupledom
in California. "It was all theatre," noted a coworker. "Every visit was
totally staged. Ray storyboarded it all in her head." Ray's maximalist
aesthetic provided much of the drama, counterposing the house's
modern architecture with the couple's eclectic collectibles, ranging
from a wood-carved stool from Africa shaped and painted to re-
semble a leopard to Indonesian masks to striped Mexican fabrics
tossed insouciantly over the sofas. There's a glimpse of a George Nelson bubble lamp hanging from the ceiling, and in the foreground another equally iconic signifier of midcentury modernism, the Eameses'
own leather lounger and ottoman, designed so sitters would feel
as if they were cradled in a broken-in catcher's mitt. At the dead

center of the image are Charles and Ray, attired with their signature studied informality—she in flats and jumper, he in chinos and open-necked shirt—seated on low stools, eyes only for each other, encircled by the fruits of their imagination, hard work, and world travels. Twenty-first-century social media influencers have nothing on this pair, who understood how image and product come together to create aspirational "lifestyle" half a century before the launch of Instagram.

Charles grew up in Missouri, trained as an architect, married, had a daughter, and started a firm, all before he was thirty. He might have ended up a well-respected regional practitioner had he not encountered Eliel Saarinen, director of the prestigious Cranbrook Academy of Art in rural Michigan. Saarinen offered him a fellowship to continue his studies, and the young man so impressed his mentor that within two years Charles was in charge of the entire Department of Industrial Design.

It is at this point that we switch our attention to California, and the young Ray-Bernice Kaiser. Always interested in art and design, she left her home in Sacramento to attend college in New York, where she studied dance with Martha Graham and painting with Abstract Expressionist Hans Hofmann. Ray had some success—the Whitney Museum acquired one of her paintings for its permanent collection—but in 1940 she returned to California to care for her ailing mother. After her death, Ray decided to diversify into graphic design and moved again, this time to attend Cranbrook, known for both its interdisciplinarity and its insularity.

When she entered Charles's classroom, Ray was only five years younger than her professor, but he was already on faculty, with an architectural practice behind him and a wife and daughter installed on campus. Ray, just starting grad school and unsure as to where she wanted her career to go, had never had a serious relationship and carried the burden of recently having lost both her parents. But within a year, Charles was divorced and writing her the following:

Dear Miss Kaiser,

I am 34 (almost) years old, single (again) and broke. I love you very much and would like to marry you very very soon. I cannot promise to support us very well—but if given the chance I'll sure in hell try.

They married just before decamping to Los Angeles in 1941, arriving as Southern California was gearing up for the war effort. The navy commissioned the pair to design emergency-transport splints for wounded sailors. After experimenting with materials, Charles and Ray decided to manufacture them out of pressed plywood. Their splints were sinuous objects, functional enough to serve the war effort, but to this day have a collectors' market, a view of one hanging on the wall signifying the owner's midcentury-modern bona fides. After the war, Charles and Ray took their experience with molded plywood and reworked the occasional chair, stripping away its overstuffed Victorian affectations to create the LCW of 1945–46. The LCW is composed of three forms—back rest, seat, and base—which come together as a modern seating solution, beautiful, comfortable, and affordable. Architecture critic Esther McCoy wrote that the chair was "the darling of young architects, the obligatory foreground object in photographs of the new modern house of the late

'40s." Since the day it rolled off the assembly line, the LCW has never been out of production.

Like the Durants' *Story of Philosophy*, the LCW allowed the Eameses to make money in their sleep. They took this freedom and ran with it, establishing an office in Venice, where they went deep into furniture design as well as crafting toys, making films, and designing exhibitions. If the Durants' house could be likened to a medieval monastery, where Will and Ariel worked single-mindedly on one project for years at a time, the Eames House was more of an R&D laboratory, with any number of experiments going at any one time. Charles was obsessed with math and science, which he saw as "essentially an artistic or philosophical enterprise carried on for its own sake... more akin to play than to work... a system of interlocking puzzles." And Charles and Ray were always excited by puzzles.

Take the one Billy Wilder posed them. Yes, the same Billy Wilder whose *Sunset Boulevard* trenchantly critiqued the folly of living in the past was a fiend for all things modern—Charles and Ray among them. Billy and his wife, Audrey, were in fact so close to Charles and Ray that they invited them to tag along when they eloped to Vegas. As for the Eameses' house, Billy so admired it he commissioned one of his own, until Audrey nixed the plan because she didn't want responsibility for keeping so many windows clean. If Billy couldn't get an Eames House, he did end up commissioning an idiosyncratic piece of furniture. On set, he'd become accustomed to taking catnaps on makeshift platforms of plywood beams propped on sawhorses. He wanted something similar, albeit more comfortable, but couldn't "afford to have something that looks like a casting couch," because it was "too obvious a symbol of lechery." So the Eameses designed an upholstered leather sling chaise, just wide enough for Billy to lie on (alone) with his arms crossed, ensuring that he'd wake the moment they dropped to either side.

Herman Miller, the company that manufactures Eames furniture, duly acknowledges Billy Wilder in all promotional materials. Why wouldn't they? It's great marketing. But Charles was not always so generous with credit. There were complaints over the years from designers in the Venice studio, and regardless of Charles's protestation that "anything I can do, she can do better," Ray's contributions always seemed to be mentioned second. Whenever there was media coverage, it tended to focus on the deeper-voiced, more conventionally attractive and media-savvy Charles. Later in life, there were also credible allegations concerning serial infidelities. Regardless, Charles and Ray weathered this and more from inside that most influential of the Case Study Houses until the day Charles died, August 21, 1978. Ray lived on alone in their house until her own death, ten years later to the day.

While Will and Ariel got an LA public library branch named after them (a modernist box, ironically, given their architectural tastes), the Eames House is the city's memorial to Charles and Ray. Their Venice studio has been repurposed as high-tech office space in Silicon Beach, and their vast archives transferred to the Library of Congress. A Vitra Design Museum model of the Eames Lounger that fits on a bookshelf costs more than twice as much in contemporary dollars as the original did as full-sized seating. High-end furniture stores all over the richest neighborhoods of LA are filled with originals and copies of their designs, demonstrating the extent to which their work remains a defining taste marker well into the twenty-first century.

The Eameses created a mood—call it modern meets folkloric—that is now de rigueur in open houses that strive for the bourgeois bohemian buyer in the turbocharged real estate markets of Venice, Silver Lake, Echo Park, and the gentrifying areas of the downtown-adjacent Eastside. Home stagers pair an Eames knockoff with two Moroccan poufs and a couple of Mexican vases, surrounded by a few artsy photos and an "edgy" painting or two. Such stagecraft seems as natural to the house as hardwood floors or arched door-ways, but the way in which it is aspirational speaks to the complicated legacy that the Eameses established with their work. What read as respectful appreciation in the 1950s can feel today like contextless appropriation, just as the Durants' middlebrow humanism and totalized, synthetic narratives do not parse well in an era that rightfully demands a diversity of voices telling their own stories.

What *does* feel contemporary is how the work of both couples anticipated its future—our present—of a multiplicity of narratives available across media platforms. Like their Enlightenment heroes, Will and Ariel were encyclopedists who created a precursor of Wikipedia via the Book of the Month Club. Over decades they were the smallest possible crowd—just two—sourcing and producing an enormous resource to be "mined," as opposed to a series of books to be "read." Will and Ariel's typewriter is a material link in a historical chain that connects the *philosophes'* quills to the Wikipedia editors' keyboards.

While Will and Ariel restricted themselves to text, Charles and Ray were actually inventing the ways in which our information-besotted culture now overloads itself with ever-multiplying screens, each one a combination portal and mirror. In 1959 the Eameses contributed to the first joint exhibition by the United States and the USSR since the Russian Revolution, staged in Moscow. Rising to the occasion, Charles and Ray created their own declaration of interdependence, a multimedia extravaganza called "Glimpses of the U.S.A." Shown on a grid of seven twenty-by-thirty-foot screens and installed in a geodesic dome designed by their friend and colleague R. Buckminster Fuller, "Glimpses" featured more than two thousand still and moving images to show, in their words, "the complexity and diversity of American life." One sequence in particular charmed the audiences at Sokolniki Park. A blindingly blond actress smiles and winks; the crowd loves it, and her. They don't recognize the actress, however, because in the Soviet Union, none of Marilyn Monroe's films have screened, but her charisma (and the skills of Billy Wilder) were apparent to all.

That moment of mediated seduction was a particularly Californian approach to bridging the Cold War gap between the superpowers. If Will and Ariel played to the desire for ever more information packaged distinctly "for us," Charles and Ray were starting to explore the design languages and visual logics that would embed "us all" in immersive experiences. Even the image of the couple at home begins to shift from that of two people next to each other talking, reading, watching, or listening together to those same two, still physically adjacent but now haunting the all-encompassing social environments created by our interconnected electronic devices.

Will and Ariel and Charles and Ray may have anticipated their future, our present, but each couple's work resonates differently now. Today not one volume of *The Story of Civilization* is in print, their house belongs to a movie producer, and Will and Ariel are all but forgotten. The Eameses, by contrast, are more famous than ever.

The Design Within Reach catalog alone sells over one hundred Eames items, including one sofa for over thirteen thousand dollars. Their house, universally acclaimed as a modern masterpiece, is listed in the National Register of Historic Places. That both couples met in school, with the future husband the teacher and the future wife the student, rubs wrong in our era, as do the previous questions of attribution, with both Ariel and Ray often wittingly or unwittingly being written out of the partnerships. Yet the idea of living and working with the same person over decades, building both a home and a practice, remains undeniably attractive, a dream for a dream house. In 1950 Will wrote a short piece titled "What Makes Men Happy?" The question itself reiterates the problem but is no less meaningful for its lack of inclusivity. Let us ask instead, what makes *us* happy? As per Charles and Ray, you can buy the good life for the price of a well-made chair. As per Will and Ariel, the answer is hope—hope that exposure to philosophy and history will make you a better person.

For a time early in the twenty-first century, Los Angeles's most famous couple were the actors Brad Pitt and Angelina Jolie. They were jointly obsessed with buying properties, and Pitt was particularly interested in modern design. They met, as such couples so often do, on a movie set, but perhaps the first emblematic portrait of them emerged in a *W* magazine pictorial. It was a fashion spread titled "Domestic Bliss: Angelina Jolie and Brad Pitt at Home," and many of the photos mimicked iconic photographs by Julius Shulman. Promoting a 2005 film called *Mr. & Mrs. Smith*, Pitt and Jolie utilized a midcentury palette to illustrate the very domesticity they would enact for real just a few months later, at least for a time. The re-creation of Shulman's most famous image, a photograph of Pierre Koenig's Case Study House #6, is particularly mimetic, with Pitt standing by a counter mixing a drink for Jolie, who sits on a low-slung modern sofa admiring her manicure.

Just a few years and children of their own later, these famous architectural enthusiasts made an unsolicited, multimillion-dollar bid on a beautifully restored *casa romántica* in the Hollywood Hills. It was, of course, Will and Ariel Durant's old place. The owners turned down the offer, but the tabloids reported it anyway. As Will wrote, "Happiness lies in the old-fashioned and natural relationships of the home."

8 CALIFORNIA ROLLS

UNTITLED #30 (FREEWAYS) I 1994 I PLATINUM PRINT I 2 ¼ X 6 ¾ INCHES (5.7 X 17.1 CM)

Cars, the Women Who Drive Them, the Men Who Design Them, Avocados, and a Stop in Manzanar

Two women.

The first confronts you with her pitiless gaze. An accomplished figure at the height of her career, she leans against her vehicle, cigarette in hand, arms crossed, wearing a clingy maxi-dress that could never be called cringeworthy, like so much of seventies fashion. The photograph is black-and-white and cool, cool, cool. It defines its moment perfectly yet is timeless.

The other woman, her eyes obscured behind New Wave sunglasses, is draped over her vehicle, thrusting out a chest of superhuman dimensions, hair bigger and blonder than Barbie's wildest fantasies. This woman is too much for one photograph. Her image is one of many, blown up building size and deployed across Los Angeles, their strident neon colors and fussy cursive text locking them

I live my life a quarter mile at a time. Nothing else matters. . . .
For those ten seconds or less, I'm free.

—Dom Toretto, *The Fast and the Furious*

"I'm glad you have a TV. . . . Some sushi bars are too Zen
to have one."
"I like sports," said the sushimaker.

—Karen Tei Yamashita, *Tropic of Orange*

always and forever into an eighties vibe that's a little tacky, a little
cheesecake-y, a little porno-y, a little postmodern-y.

So what links the famously slight Joan Didion—one of Southern
California's best-known writers, her work spanning decades and
encompassing fiction, reportage, memoir, and screenwriting—to the
pneumatic Angelyne, a woman semifamous for being semifamous,
the proto–reality TV, preselfie self-promoter of pure self?

The answer is simple. Both women pose with the same car: a
Corvette Stingray, the greatest of all American sports cars, an emblematic alchemical machine, a fire-breather, igniting the oil sucked
up from the earth to burn rubber, vaporizing tires into smoke that
drifts off into the air as it roars off into the hot summer night. Didion slouches against hers, the car's opulent curves balancing her

sleek angularity. Angelyne pours her body over hers, the signature Coke-bottle contours and pink too-much-ness as much a part of her personal brand as the bouffant or bee-stung lips. That two such divergent figures should converge on the same muscle car is providential, giving us an excuse to range across Southern California's freeways, traveling from the shade-giving palms of Beverly Hills to the bleakness of the Owens Valley, 250 miles north, to uncover some uncomfortable truths about how icons are created. There will also be sushi.

But first, consider the slowly dissolving actress Maria Wyeth, Didion's most famous character, the protagonist of her 1970 novel *Play It as It Lays*. Maria has only one unalloyed pleasure: driving. Her drives are not so much aimless as existential. Maria navigates the freeways "as a riverman runs a river, every day more attuned to its currents, its deceptions, and just as the riverman feels the pull of the rapids in the lull between sleeping and waking, so Maria lay at night in the still of Beverly Hills and saw the great signs soar overhead at seventy miles an hour." Maria drives to forget, Maria drives to fill the time that would otherwise devour her, Maria drives to feel.

Like Gidget, Maria is another character in LA's literary history who is inextricably linked to a real person. Not only do Didion's descriptions of the character reflect with near exactitude the image the author saw in the mirror, Maria drives Didion's car. In the little-seen 1972 film version of *Play It as It Lays*, the real-life actress Tuesday Weld portrays the fictional actress Maria Wyeth, the alter ego of the author, Joan Didion. The movie is a family affair if ever there was one. Didion cowrote the script with husband John Gregory Dunne, who in turn coproduced it with his brother, Dominick Dunne. The strongest connection among actress, character, and author is the Stingray, which Didion described years later as "a yellow so bright, you could never mistake it for anything other than Daytona yellow." It is Didion's car described on the page, pictured in the author photo, and, moreover, featured in motion in the film. As Didion once said, "There's a point when you go with what you've got. Or you don't go."

In the eighties and nineties, Angelyne likewise went with what she'd got. And what she had was an actual spandex-encased body that existed in large part as a placeholder for its virtuality. Before we had globe-spanning social media, we had the quaint concept of "local" celebrities: Bozo the Clown in Chicago, prior to WGN taking him national, or New York's manic electronics pitchman "Crazy Eddie" Antar. So Angelyne emerged, from somewhere deep inside LA's id, via the splashy medium of billboards spread across Hollywood and the Westside. No one knew why the billboards existed: Angelyne wasn't promoting an album, though she did release some music early on ("Kiss Me L.A." in 1982); nor was she hustling a new film, though she had bit parts in movies like *Earth Girls Are Easy* (1988). Her billboards were simply advertisements for the self, crystallized into two components: A Girl and Her Car. And then there was the girl *in* her car. By the early nineties, I regularly spotted Angelyne in traffic, every few years in a new model, but always pink, always with the classic yellow-on-black license plate reading ANGY-LYN, because, well, vanity.

Angelyne as phenomenon marks a high point in a particularly Southern Californian trajectory that has since become ubiquitous: the capacity, through sheer will, to create specialness. This is the story of celebrity, of course. "What do you think a celebrity is?" Angelyne once queried. "It's someone sent to us as a gift, to bring us joy." Celebrities are different from the rest of us. They inhabit the aether and contribute to the quintessence. They literally radiate light. Light attracts attention. Ergo, celebrities inevitably get "discovered." Everyone knows the legend of Lana Turner being discovered in 1937 at the counter at Schwab's on Sunset Boulevard by director Mervyn LeRoy. Never mind that it was *not* Schwab's (where Gloria Swanson really did buy her makeup and F. Scott Fitzgerald his teetotaler's candy bars), but a mile and a half farther east, at the Top Hat Café, where then-Judy went after ditching typing class at Hollywood High just across the street; and that the person who spotted then-Judy-later-Lana was *not* LeRoy but Billy Wilkerson, publisher of the *Hollywood Reporter*, who referred her to agent Zeppo Marx, brother of Groucho et al.

Before she ascended to the mythic, Lana Turner was a working actress. Conversely, we have the contemporaneous Gabor sisters, who emerged from Hungary after World War II and became known less for their acting, singing, and dancing (negligible) than for their intricate personal lives (substantial). Eva was married five times; Magda six; and Zsa Zsa, the winner or loser, depending on how you define such things, nine times. One of Zsa Zsa's husbands had also been married to Magda. Another was Conrad Hilton of the hotel family, great-grandfather (via another marriage) of Paris Hilton, an early reality television star and employer of a young closet organizer named Kim Kardashian, who eventually became even more famous for being famous than her erstwhile benefactress.

The missing link between the sisters Gabor and Kardashian is the singular Angelyne, who once claimed, "I can feel myself getting more and more famous every day." Like the artists Andy Warhol before her and Jeff Koons after, Angelyne evinced a relentless devotion to her chosen métier of self-creation. Given that, we shouldn't be surprised that Angelyne turns out to have been every bit as much a fictional character as Maria Wyeth. A young redheaded girl from the San Fernando Valley (by way of Holocaust-surviving Polish parents), Renee Goldberg wanted to be famous but never got closer than opening for the Screamers at the Whisky a Go Go as part of her then-boyfriend's punk band, Baby Blue. So she decided to play her cards as they lay. Reinventing herself as Angelyne, she joined the uni-*nomenklatura* of Madonna and Beyoncé, becoming a human hashtag well in advance of the technologies: "Although I act, model, dance, paint, write and create magic, I'm most known for my persona, the essence of who I am." As if she weren't busy enough, Angelyne (the person, not the persona) ran for governor in the chaotic election of 2003, which saw another absurdly proportioned celebrity—bodybuilder turned action star Arnold Schwarzenegger—elevated to the highest office in the state. Angelyne came in a somewhat embarrassing 28th in the overcrowded field of 135, but nobody could argue with her campaign slogan: "We've had Gray [Gray Davis, the governor being recalled], we've had Brown [Jerry Brown, who had been governor before and would be governor again], now it's time for some Blonde and Pink."

Pink was hardly Didion's color. Her Corvette was yellow. And what's more, it wasn't simply another perfectly matched element in an overdetermined, over-the-top ensemble. It was the wild card in the deck. For Didion, the Corvette was a marker of difference. That a writer—of books, not even screenplays, though Didion did that as well—should have a car like that was more than surprising. It signified power. In the iconic photograph by Julian Wasser, commissioned by *Time* magazine for a feature about her nonfiction collection, *Slouching Towards Bethlehem* (1968), Didion, a fifth-generation

Californian, presented herself in all her gear-shifting sangfroid, the antithesis of those of the New York intelligentsia who didn't even know how to drive, much less command a car with a 427-cubic-inch big-block V-8 under the hood putting out 390 horsepower. Here was the avatar of the LA writer: mobile, commanding, contemporary. The fact that this avatar was a woman wasn't incidental. It was the icing on the cheesecake.

Historically, the narrative of women and cars comes down to one truism: sex sells. From the models at car shows (the original "booth babes") to the porn stars, wrestlers, and burlesque dancers who've graced the covers of *Lowrider* magazine to the Carl's Jr. ads featuring Paris Hilton and model Kate Upton writhing around cars while devouring patty melts, women have been used to peddle a range of male fantasies of virility manifested by and through the car. But what of the car's relationship to the shape and soul of Southern California more broadly?

It is impossible to imagine Southern California without the private automobile. The transformation of earth into real estate in the later part of the nineteenth century dovetailed with the discovery of oil in the region. The internal combustion engine lit that oil on fire inside first thousands and then millions of cars, which themselves allowed for the distinctive spread of development that characterized first the region, then the rest of the planet. If the present era can be construed as Anthropocene, the twentieth century in Southern California constituted an Autopocene, the structuring of urban and suburban development, and of the very landscape itself, around the capabilities (and limitations) of a society on wheels.

Southern California first invented, then promulgated car culture. Its foundation was the freeway system, built horizontally, not vertically, offering a model of the automobile not merely as a simulacrum of freedom but as its ultimate instrument. So, too, did Southern California spawn the affordances required by its automobilized population: oversized service stations, drive-in convenience stores, strip malls, the supermarket. As with horses and trains, the automobile became one of Hollywood's great visual tropes. Whether a panoramic long shot in a road movie or the staccato editing of a chase scene, the cinematic imaginary celebrated the car culture's unities of place, infrastructure, and technology.

In the Roaring Twenties, Southern California saw the highest per capita car ownership in the world. During the Depression, the Duesenbergs of Hollywood's grandees were replaced by jalopies and rickety trucks piloted by impoverished Okies sputtering from the Dust Bowl to pick grapes in the Golden State. During World War II, people like John Steinbeck's fictional Joads, once turned away at the border, were welcomed back as the workforce that rolled Willys jeeps off the production line as fast as they could be shipped to global battlefields. In the postwar boom years, there were the parents steering an endless parade of Chevys and Pontiacs up to their newly built driveways in their interchangeable tract homes in their endlessly sprawling SoCal suburbs. At the same time, those suburbs were policing who was permitted to drive where, making the right to mobility yet another flash point in the region's complicated, and intertwined, histories of race and class.

Moving forward, the story skews younger, with white kids modifying their hot rods and developing the kandy-kolored kustoms about which New Journalist Tom Wolfe rhapsodized. In the barrios of

Southern California, Latinx youths were chopping and channeling their cars, creating a distinct pavement-hugging profile they called "lowriders." By the nineties, the low-slung sleds and hydraulic jacking intersected with hip-hop and the love of rolling in a six-fo' (a modified 1964 Chevrolet Impala). In the twenty-first century, Asian American gearheads in Monterey Park and the other Chinese suburbs tuned up Nissans, Hondas, and Subarus to render them ever faster and more furious. Part of the genius of the *Fast and the Furious*'s car porn is the casting, which offers stars whose ethnicities collapse this contentious, racialized history into a synchronic whole, just like car culture today, with whites, Latinxs, blacks, and Asians all revving into the red zone.

The preceding history leaves out half the drivers in the region, and the complex relationship between dominant car cultures and female drivers. As the nineteenth century turned into the twentieth, there were two types of cars for two types of drivers: hand-cranked gasoline engines that were smelly, tricky, and powerful, sold to men looking to commute to work or travel the open road; and electric engines that started with the press of a button or turn of a key, that were quiet, slow, and range-restricted, marketed to the "woman of the house" for short trips within the bounds of the immediate neighborhood. The relationship between the automobile industry and gender would never be so clear again, with an industry dominated by men consistently mixing its messages over how to sell cars to women, especially the high-performance sports cars the industry loved the most. That is what makes the images of Didion and Angelyne so compelling. Because instead of being used by their Corvettes to build the brand's image, these women used the Corvette to build theirs.

Introduced in 1953, the Corvette was the first, and remains the premier, homegrown sports car, a massive engine torquing four wheels, wrapped in a body that looks good parked at the curb but truly comes alive while gunning down an open stretch of road. After World War II, Hollywood-born, Detroit-based Harley Earl, GM's justly famous director of design, watched as returning servicemen imported the MGs and Jaguars they'd encountered during their time in the European theater. The vets' enthusiasm inspired Earl to push for an American-made competitor. The first generation broke open a market, but the car really came into its own with the C2, or second-generation Corvette, the Stingray. This iteration introduced a slimmed-down body, a big-block engine, a long hood, concealed headlights, a more menacing front end, and a hardtop. Getting the millions of Corvette fans to agree on which iteration of the car is "best" is impossible, but the C2 comes the closest to consensus.

The great literary evocation of the Corvette is *Play It as It Lays*, but over the years the Corvette has had an outsized presence in pop culture. The Beach Boys harmonized about its V-8 engine in "409," the B-side of their 1962 hit, "Surfin' Safari," and two decades later Prince's libidinal "Little Red Corvette" reduced (amplified?) the icon to pure sex. Early sixties TV series *Route 66* was instrumental in establishing the legend, and twenty years later *Stingray* tried to replicate the Corvette-on-the-road formula, but to far less success. The cinema has highlighted the Corvette from the classic 1955 noir *Kiss Me Deadly* to the lamentable *Corvette Summer* of 1977 through the *Fast and the Furious* street-racing franchise (2001–). There's even a metacommentary about the car's staying power as the ultimate in badassery in the 2009 reboot of the *Star Trek* film franchise, when a pre-captaincy, twenty-third-century James Tiberius Kirk spins out a 1965 convertible Stingray on the edge of a cliff before heading off into the farthest reaches of outer space.

Badassery doesn't just invent itself, however. And when it comes to cars, it needs to be baked in before the first model rolls off the line. An iconic car is not just fast; it also has to have something extra—an "it" that digs in deep to the emotions. That's where design comes in. Few consumers can identify the designers who stir their souls. They know the entrepreneurs—from Ford to DeLorean to Musk—but not those responsible for the brands' emotional hooks. Thus it is no surprise that our next subject is someone whose work is as influential as his name is obscure.

Larry Shinoda was a rare hybrid, a designer with racing in his blood. An LA kid, he won the first-ever National Hot Rod Association Nationals in Kansas in 1955. After attending design school back home for one year, he was put forward as a candidate for the Ford Styling Group. Shinoda came in strong, wanted six months to decide if he even liked Detroit (he had his doubts about snow), and demanded Ford pay to ship his dragster out with him. In later years, he recalled saying, "You guys need me more than I need you." Despite an undeniable brilliance in the studio, with an attitude like that, it's no surprise that Shinoda bounced around for a few years before ending up at General Motors.

Shinoda secured his gig designing the C2 because of an illegal street race. He was driving home after work in his Ford Thunderbird when he found himself at a stoplight next to a supercharged Pontiac. The Pontiac driver looked at Shinoda, Shinoda looked at the Pontiac driver, they revved their engines, and then the light turned green. Shinoda smoked the guy off the line and never looked back. The next day, the loser—who happened to be Bill Mitchell, GM's vice president of design—went searching for the driver of the T-Bird and found him in the Chevy bull pen. After getting Shinoda to show him what he'd done to make his car run so fast, Mitchell "almost had a heart attack" because the T-Bird was so perfectly equipped and powerfully tuned. Mitchell pulled Shinoda on the spot for the small team working on the next-generation Corvette.

It was Shinoda who masterminded the transition from the Continental styling of first-generation Corvettes to the Coke-bottle curves and sinuous front end that attracted Didion, Angelyne, and a legion of other fans. Shinoda was adamant that his design work "stake its own uniquely American ground instead of looking to sports car tradition and Europe for inspiration." A quintessential product of Southern California who then worked on the quintessential products of Detroit, Shinoda understood deep in his bones the GM maxim that engineering doesn't sell vehicles; style does. In a multibillion-dollar industry, Shinoda was always regarded as a rebel, a "real car guy," Detroit's ultimate accolade. What that meant was that though he understood sales and market share, what animated him was the smell of gasoline, the hot breath of exhaust, and the adrenaline rush of cornering a tight curve at high speed. In a long and distinguished career, he designed other classic cars, including the 1965 Chevrolet Corvair and the 1970 Boss Mustang for Ford, but it was Shinoda's Corvette that made Shinoda.

That a man born in LA in 1930 to two Japanese immigrant parents should have had a hand in creating something as iconically American as the Stingray is both a testament to his understanding of car culture and a personal triumph over the injustices of history. Shinoda was born into a thriving Japanese American community,

the largest in the United States. At the time, the Little Tokyo neighborhood just east of City Hall was a vibrant enclave of markets, restaurants, Buddhist temples, social clubs, and newspapers, including
the *Rafu Shimpo*, the first Japanese-language paper in the United
States. Young Larry thrived there, an aspiring artist and precocious
motorhead who messed around with cars and rebuilt old engines. If
this sounds like the classic American childhood, greaser division,
history stepped in to change everything.

Japanese Americans, and Asian Americans in general, had not
had it easy in California in the first half of the twentieth century.
Legislators passed laws restricting them from marrying not just
outside their racial classifications but also within; limited their
rights to own property (the residents and businesses of Little Tokyo
were all renters); and embodied a racial hatred that only intensified
after imperial forces attacked Pearl Harbor in December of 1941.
Less than two months later, with hysteria at its highest, the skies of
LA erupted with a fusillade of antiaircraft and .50-caliber machine-
gun fire repelling "another" Japanese assault. In the end, the secretary
of the navy would admit there had been nothing of the kind, just a
case of "jittery nerves," though many people across the Southland
maintained to their dying breath that they saw "something."

Despite being known as a fair-minded reformer, the mayor of
LA, Fletcher Bowron, succumbed to the panic of the moment, as
well as his own racial animus, and pressured the federal government to act decisively "to protect" the West Coast. On February 19,
1942, President Roosevelt signed Executive Order 9066, which
forced 120,000 Japanese and Japanese Americans from their homes
and into what were labeled "internment camps." This order affected

the first-generation immigrants, or issei, who could be either resident aliens or citizens; second-generation nisei, who were American-born citizens; and even third-generation sansei, or the American-born children of American-born parents.

Few voices rose in opposition. One belonged to Clifford E. Clinton, Christian activist and founder of the still-extant Clifton's Cafeteria, who had been a key supporter of Bowron's first winning campaign. "We must avoid the costly mistakes that may follow hysterical action and snap judgment," Clinton protested. His was a voice in a maelstrom, however, and soon afterward families across LA, at the request of their mayor and the order of their president, found themselves stripped of their positions, possessions, homes, and freedoms. So the city, state, and federal governments sent Larry Shinoda, his sister, his mother, and his maternal grandmother to the horse track at Santa Anita to await "relocation," and eventually to Manzanar in the Owens Valley.

Manzanar is Spanish for "apple orchard," and for generations that's what the area was. The land had originally been settled by various Indigenous peoples who'd been driven out by successive waves of newcomers, from the Spaniards to the Yankee cattlemen who displaced the Paiutes after the discovery of gold in the state in the 1840s. By the 1940s, the Owens River water that had nurtured the orchards had long since been diverted to LA by William Mulholland's aqueduct, and all that was left was a bone-dry landscape, bitter cold in the winter, a dust-blown inferno in the summer. By the time the War Department purchased the land, it was all but deserted, making it an ideal location to intern legions of American residents of Japanese descent, three-quarters of them citizens of the country that would make them wait decades for an apology from the Reagan White House for the country's unconscionable wartime actions.

The internees at Manzanar strived to prove their allegiance to their country, even as it was humiliating and imprisoning them. They organized Boy Scout and Girl Scout troops. They formed baseball leagues. They joined the armed forces en masse. The 442nd Infantry Regiment, recruited primarily from the camps, was almost entirely Japanese American and fought with bravery and distinction in the European theater during the war, its combat team one of the most decorated for its size in the history of the U.S. armed forces.

Shinoda did not often publicly discuss Manzanar, but in 1997 he noted that "the barracks had not been finished when we moved in and the roofs had no tar paper, so we slept with towels over our heads, which were dirty by the time we awoke in the morning." Shinoda was acutely sensitive to his family's lack of creature comforts. To that end, he thoughtfully designed appropriately sized chairs for his tiny mother and grandmother, constructing them out of orange crates scavenged from the mess hall, where he worked part time as a cook. His sister, Grace Shinoda Nakamura, recalled her brother's efforts to supplement the camp's decidedly non-Japanese diet: "My brother had the guts and the curiosity to go fishing outside because he could catch fish with his bare hands. He was kind of a marvel."

One of the many challenges for the internees at Manzanar was maintaining their cultural heritage even while their food was being supplied by a government on war footing that neither knew nor cared that fish—much less *raw* fish—was central to their diet. What is surprising is that within twenty years this particular food would establish a foothold in LA and that it would, another two decades later, become a defining feature of the good life in the island on the land that is Southern California.

Two figures were responsible for introducing sushi to America, and they were brought together by a humble cookie. Little Tokyo's dominant supplier of Japanese products, Mutual Supply Co., hired Noritoshi Kanai to come to Los Angeles from Tokyo to rebuild the company's business after the Second World War. Upon moving to the United States, Kanai blossomed as an entrepreneur as well as a manager. He began to personally import honey and sesame cookies from Japan in order to sell them in the American market. At a trade show, Kanai met an enormous man named Harry Wolff Jr., who looked like Santa Claus, though he didn't celebrate Christmas. Impressed by Kanai's hustle, as well as the commercial possibilities the cookies offered, Wolff made Kanai the following proposition: "To be successful in the United States, you have to have a good doctor, a good lawyer, and a good Jewish friend. I am a Jewish broker and I know all the distribution channels, so I'll become your friend and team up with you." The pair wound up selling the cookies together, and did well until Taiwanese bakers undercut the market. Eager for another opportunity to collaborate, Kanai suggested that he and Wolff take a trip to Japan and see what they could drum up.

One night, Kanai took Wolff to their hotel restaurant, which served sushi. Wolff had never had nigiri, the classic dish of freshly cut raw fish hand formed over warm rice. In fact, Wolff, being a pickled herring kind of guy, had had little exposure to raw seafood at all. At the end of their stay, the hotel handed Kanai a whopper of a bill. While Kanai was out hunting down new products, Wolff, a man of considerable appetites, had spent his time sampling an enormous variety of sushi. The two left Japan convinced that there had to be a way to sell Americans on the idea of eating this way.

Once back in LA, they partnered with Little Tokyo's venerable Kawafuku restaurant and in 1964 hired a sushi chef from Japan, employed the chef's wife as the waitress, and transformed Kawafuku's second floor with the addition of a refrigerated counter at which the chef would work, with built-in seating for the patrons. One of the things that had intrigued Wolff in Japan was the dynamic between diner and chef, who was fully visible, as opposed to sequestered behind the kitchen door like the American and European model. Kanai's stroke of genius was coining an idiomatic English expression to describe the setup: they would call it a "sushi bar." As the first dedicated sushi bar in the United States, Kawafuku drew local Japanese Americans and visiting Japanese businessmen. Then it drew the Angelenos who were the latter's business partners. Then culinary adventurers. And then, fatefully, the cuisine's lightness and freshness caught on with Hollywood types, always eager to get in on a wellness trend.

Within two years, the first LA sushi bars opened outside Little Tokyo, including Osho on Pico, adjacent to the 20th Century Fox lot; and Imperial Gardens on Sunset, on the western end of the Strip. Both venues catered to an entertainment crowd—to be even more specific, a Jewish entertainment crowd who, following in the footsteps of omnivore Harry Wolff, traded the assorted smoked-fish tray from Beverly Hills' famed Nate 'n Al deli for platters of toro, unagi, and yellowtail. By the 1980s, sushi was so ubiquitous in LA that it had become a legible cultural signifier. In *Less Than Zero* (1985), the defining novel of Southern California's Gen X debauchery, jaded teens use their fake IDs to order sake at the sushi bar and bitch about their BMWs. In the Brat Pack classic *The Breakfast Club* (1985), even high schoolers in the Midwest understand the class privilege that a princess like Claire Standish (Molly Ringwald) shows when she pulls out a sushi-filled bento box for lunch. Her embrace of West Coast culinary cool was as much a cliché as her nemesis, bad boy John Bender (Judd Nelson), recoiling in horror at the very thought of it.

This divergence between the raw and the cooked, as codified by the great French anthropologist Claude Lévi-Strauss, was central to both LA's embrace of sushi—because it was hip and new and felt transgressive—and the repulsion expressed by Bender and other homespun icons like Louisiana-born Pro Football Hall of Famer turned TV pitchman Terry Bradshaw. Bradshaw was once featured in a commercial set in a sushi bar. When served, he was quizzical: "Sushi? Where I'm from we call that stuff bait!" But just two years after the sushi bar at Kawafuku opened, another restaurant concocted a dish that even a square-jawed athlete from the Deep South could love: the California roll.

The California roll was invented at Tokyo Kaikan, a block from Kawafuku. It combined cooked seafood, originally king crab, and avocado with mayonnaise to simulate the texture of fatty tuna. These ingredients were rolled with the dark seaweed wrapper underneath the rice, creating a spiral-shaped "ura-maki," or "inside-out roll," which solved the problem of diners peeling off the wrapper because they thought it was packaging. There's a tougher question of who exactly to credit for this innovation: the restaurant's corporate owner, Kodaka Daikichiro, who reputedly said, "Why don't you make sushi for the Caucasians?," or the sushi chef himself, Ichiro Mashita, who may have been trying to solve the question of what to serve customers who were disappointed that the rich flavor and mouthfeel of the bluefin tuna to which they'd become accustomed was available only seasonally. Regardless, the team at Tokyo Kaikan conceived the perfect gateway drug to the hard stuff and, what's more, concocted it as an American food in the way that a loaded burrito is an American food, at least as incarnated by Taco Bell and its molten-cheesy brethren.

Within fifteen years, the California roll was joined by the Philadelphia roll, which celebrated the city of its origin by combining cream cheese with smoked salmon, in large measure because even in the City of Brotherly Love, its creator, Japanese-born sushi chef Madame Saito, had a preponderance of Jewish clients who craved nothing so much as bagels and lox. In other words, across the country, the smoked-fish platter—a kosher deli mainstay, itself reimagined as American cuisine—had reached its apotheosis as "Japanese" food. Finally, sushi could be integrated into the deep-fried, high-fat, sweetened and processed pantheon of American cuisine. "Specialty" rolls could be supersized, filled or coated with crunchy, battered tempura, drizzled in sticky-sweet "eel sauce," and even have cheese melted on them—all with the added benefit of incorporating absolutely no raw fish at all. The other thing about a roll is that you can get it cheap and shrink-wrapped from supermarkets and even convenience stores. And any food you can buy at 7-Eleven, well, it's probably meant to be eaten in the comfort of your own car. Thus the California roll's ultimate destiny: like Maria Wyeth's Stingray, to roll "at seventy miles an hour."

It's a testament to something—the fungibility of memory, the grace of forgiveness, the American capacity to embrace talent—that an American kid interned in a bleak camp in the middle of nowhere should somehow be responsible two decades later for creating one of the United States' great contributions to global culture, right up there with apple pie, blue jeans, Elvis, and Facebook on the iPhone, and that the food he was denied at Manzanar, the nigiri and sashimi that defined his culture even as it was being forcibly erased, should within a few decades become an integral part of the American experience (at least on the coasts).

Just before she bought her Stingray, Joan Didion wrote about what having rock stars over for dinner was actually like: "Someone once brought Janis Joplin. . . . Time was never of the essence: we would have dinner at nine unless we had it at eleven-thirty, or we could order in later." And what was served? "We wanted," Didion explains, ". . . sushi."

9 HOT FOOD, COLD WAR

UNTITLED #31 (FREEWAYS) | 1994 | PLATINUM PRINT | 2 ¼ X 6 ¾ INCHES (5.7 X 17.1 CM)

Martial Arts and Culinary Arts, or How Blowback Made Los Angeles the Best Place in America to Fight and Eat

It starts with a one-inch punch. The blow isn't telegraphed. Instead, it explodes as though jet-powered. The volunteer foolhardy enough to be the test dummy flies off his feet into a chair haphazardly dropped behind him. The year is 1964; the place is Long Beach, a hardscrabble port town; and the crowd, well, they know they've just witnessed something historic, and they go berserk.

At the moment fist connects with chest, one world comes into view and another withers away. Southern California was always *on* the Pacific, but to truly become *of* the Pacific it had to experience a series of shocks that rippled out from the American imperium's hot and cold conflicts in Asia during the second half of the twentieth century.

War may not be on the minds of people passing through LA's

Be formless, shapeless, like water.

—Bruce Lee

Home is where you lay your taco.

—Roy Choi

Chinatown when they hit the little plaza where Jung Jing Road meets Sun Mun Way, but fighting just might be. That's because right next to what used to be the infamous eighties punk club Madame Wong's stands a seven-foot-tall statue of the most famous martial artist who ever lived. His body is ridiculously vascular, the skin pulled so taut over his muscles that every rib, tendon, and vein is visible. His right arm is extended in a defensive posture, but the palm is out, ready to strike. His left grips a stick, connected via a short chain to another stick of equal length tucked under his arm. For anyone who has ever watched a kung fu movie, it's not hard to guess that these sticks are nunchuks and that this body belongs to Bruce Lee, martial arts wunderkind, unreluctant sex symbol, and the first Asian global superstar.

It was the veterans of America's Pacific wars, occupations, and peace-keeping missions who brought the martial arts to Southern California, spreading an idiosyncratic and infinitely transmutable mash-up of fighting and philosophy outside the few ethnic enclaves that saw it as an intrinsic part of their culture, as opposed to yet more fodder for the melting pot. Servicemen stationed overseas, especially at the American base in Okinawa, picked up the rudiments of karate and judo. The ones in Korea learned a variety of skills that would only later become known in the United States as tae kwon do, and still others encountered Chinese disciplines that went by various names, including wushu, gung fu, and kung fu. As *Black Belt* magazine noted in 1974, "No group of Americans has done more to promote the . . . martial arts in the United States than Armed Forces personnel."

One such vet was Ed Parker, who picked up a few basic skills on the streets of his native Honolulu and then studied more seriously during his three years in the Coast Guard. After getting out, Parker opened a studio in Utah, but he didn't make an impact on the national level until 1958, when he opened two dojos in Southern California. Parker taught an Americanized karate called kenpo—his Mormon acolytes referred to him as the Joseph Smith of the sport— and Parker's approach won him a new generation of converts. These included police and security professionals, stuntmen, actors like Warren Beatty and Natalie Wood, and the usual contingent of veterans. One of these vets had taken up karate when he was stationed in Germany, and then signed on with Parker in 1960 after mustering out of the army. His name was Elvis Aaron Presley, and the fact that he was the most famous pop star in the world made him the ideal student for the ambitious Parker, who ended up working as the latter's personal bodyguard during the Fat Elvis Graceland years. Even with a poster boy like Elvis, however, Parker couldn't propel his obsession into the broader consciousness.

That's how Parker found himself organizing the Long Beach International Karate Championships in 1964. His first task was upping the wow factor. Enter Bruce Lee, a young guy generating buzz in the Bay Area, then the center of the U.S. martial arts universe. Lee was born in San Francisco in 1940 while his parents were on tour with a Cantonese acting troupe from Hong Kong. They made the decision to move back home just before the protectorate endured its brutal Japanese occupation and the postwar influx of more than half a million refugees from the Chinese Communist Revolution. Though the Lees were upper class, their neighborhood grew rough, and they insisted their son study martial arts for his own protection. Be careful what you wish for, as the saying goes. Before long, the young man became so skilled at street fighting that he had to be sent back to America to keep him out of harm's way. In the United States, Bruce finished high school and took classes at the University of Washington before migrating to the Bay Area. There he kicked up a fuss by opening a studio devoted to his own variant of kung fu, called Jeet Kune Do.

Lee was a troublemaker. Not only did he practice a style of his own making, he taught it to non-Chinese, a redoubled insult to traditionalists. But there was only so much the latter could do, because Lee was that good. His students embraced him precisely because he offered a synthesis of techniques rather than a regurgitation of traditional forms. He emphasized fluid reactions, maximal speed, and minimal telegraphing of intentions, stressing that the point of the martial arts was to win fights by embodying combat realism, as opposed to mastering what Lee derided as the "flowery forms" of the classical approach.

Parker hoped that Lee would live up to his reputation for controversy, and Lee hoped that coming to LA would jump-start Hollywood stardom. Both hopes were fulfilled that day in Long Beach, but not precisely in the ways imagined. What the audience saw when Lee took the stage was a slim young man standing five feet seven inches and weighing 140 pounds. But it was not his appearance that electrified them. It was what he'd trained his body to do. First there were the two-finger push-ups. Dropping down with his feet set shoulder width apart, Lee put one hand behind his back, extended the other, and, using only his index finger and thumb, executed planked push-ups. The fighters in the audience realized the control this took, as well as the hand strength. But the crowd was looking for more than training tips, and Lee's next trick was pure magic. Lee positioned himself face to face with Bob Baker, a man who had no idea what was coming. Looking out at the audience, Lee raised his hand, forming a fist an inch from Baker's chest. Then, with a punch that had no tell whatsoever, Lee closed that one-inch gap, blowing Baker—who had to skip work the next day due to "unbearable" pain—clear off his feet. It was that single, explosive blow that made Bruce Lee a star.

One of the Hollywood students Parker invited to drive down to Long Beach was Jay Sebring. Sebring was a playboy who had been introduced to Parker's studio by his client and friend, the actor Steve McQueen. Sebring was the first celebrity hairstylist for men, and as such had enough cultural capital to open the door at any party. Sebring pioneered the layered shag that Jim Morrison matched with leather pants as he led the Doors to rock-and-roll glory. At Kirk Douglas's request, Sebring did the hairstyles in *Spartacus*, using blow-dryers, hair spray, and scissors instead of clippers. There had been barbers to the stars before, of course, but it had never occurred to any of them they could charge twenty times the price of a normal haircut to people who wanted to change the world, or at least emulate those who did. Sebring was smart. He watched Lee onstage and fully understood the implications, because he knew *it* when he saw *it* and, better yet, had the contacts to promote what he saw. Sebring decided right then and there to bring the young martial artist into his glittering world. He started by introducing him to the celebrities who would become Lee's private students. These included McQueen, rising starlet Sharon Tate, and her director husband, Roman Polanski.

If Sebring's name rings bells, it may be because he was among the victims the night the Manson Family murders took place at 10050 Cielo Drive. When Sebring pleaded for mercy for his friend Sharon, eight and half months pregnant with Polanski's baby, the cultists shot him in the stomach and then stabbed him to death. Before detectives established that it was Manson who'd masterminded the events, Polanski, beside himself with grief, suspected everyone in his orbit. Because of a pair of horn-rimmed spectacles found at the murder house, Polanski even wondered about his martial arts teacher, Bruce Lee, who'd mentioned in passing that his glasses had gone missing. Polanski suggested they go to the optician that same day to pick out a new pair, which would be his gift, ruling Lee out as a suspect only after discovering how different his prescription was from the mysterious horn-rimmed pair (which turned out to be a false clue planted by Manson, who, needless to say, relished messing with people's heads).

Before the killings, Sebring had helped Lee secure a recurring role as Kato, a masked martial artist, in *The Green Hornet*, a comic-book

TV adaptation by William Dozier, best known for producing *Batman*, the 1960s camp classic. Although the short-lived show's fan mail skewed toward Kato, Lee failed to break out as a star in his own right. Yes, he was hired to kick out a light fixture hanging eight feet in the air in 1969's regrettable rendering of Raymond Chandler's private eye in *Marlowe*, and to train a blind detective in the ways of Jeet Kune Do in four episodes of the 1971 TV series *Longstreet*, but Hollywood's recalcitrant racism proved an impenetrable obstacle.

After *The Green Hornet*, Lee pitched a show to be set in the Old West featuring a wandering Chinese warrior, but got nowhere. To make matters worse, soon afterward ABC green-lit a remarkably similar show about a Shaolin monk who flees China for America, where he dispenses frontier justice with his hands and feet. *Kung Fu* became a smash hit and would have been the perfect vehicle for Bruce Lee. But the powers that be chose to cast Hollywood scion David Carradine, an Anglo actor with no martial arts background whatsoever. Feeling ripped off and insulted, Lee abandoned Hollywood.

His return to Hong Kong was triumphant. That single season of *The Green Hornet* played over and over but was known there as *The Kato Show*. Then he starred in three films from Hong Kong studios—*The Big Boss* (1971), *Fist of Fury*, and *The Way of the Dragon* (both 1972)—followed by his one fully realized, Hollywood-financed production, the global megahit, *Enter the Dragon* (1973). For Chinese audiences, these films portrayed a shift from a *wen* physicality of refinement—think of a scholar putting down his books and defeating his foes without breaking a sweat—to a *wu* masculinity emphasizing muscularity and sheer power. In each film there comes a moment when Lee takes off his jacket and shirt, cracks every joint in his body, and then flexes, expanding his upper torso like a cobra's hood. Lee's *wu* display never boded well for his opponents.

As to where this formidable body came from, it was a product of Lee's otherwise unsuccessful sojourn in Southern California. While he was in Hollywood, Lee wasn't just waiting for his star to ascend. He was metamorphosing. First, he radically shifted his diet. Obsessed with the protein powders consumed by bodybuilders, Lee tossed back vitamins. He also incorporated raw juices and organic vegetables, the staples of the new health-food scene emerging in LA. In 1971 the *LA Times* noted that "the organic community has reached its fullest flower in Southern California... in the midst of all the franchised food chains, in the center of technological wilderness, are some 300 health stores, [and] at least 25 organic restaurants." One of these restaurants, well frequented by Lee, was the Source.

The Source's founder was Jim Baker, a six-foot-four decorated Marine Corps veteran of World War II and an expert in jujitsu. In fact, Baker had killed at least two men with his bare hands: the first in a fight over a dog (he was exonerated); the second over a woman (that one he did time for). Homicidal history aside, Baker was in many ways a typical Southern Californian of his generation: born in the Midwest, he fought in the Pacific theater, and then, after the war, set up shop in LA instead of going back home. Baker was exceptional in other ways. He was drawn to the aforementioned protohippie Nature Boys, especially eden "only God and the Infinite should be capitalized" ahbez, whose life changed in 1948 when Nat King Cole made a hit of his song "Nature Boy," an ethereal tune later recorded by musicians as varied as jazz virtuoso John Coltrane and rock's shape-shifter, David Bowie. The song's central message—"The greatest thing you'll ever learn is just to love and be loved in return"—resonated for Baker, containing as it did the crystalline seed of everything from the Beats' panegyrics to "the mad ones" in the fifties, to free-loving hippies grokking each other like Martians in the sixties, to the Jesus Freaks' embrace of the Greco-Christian concept of *agape*, or universal love, during their heyday in the seventies.

Baker, too, was a spiritual seeker, devouring, among other texts, *The Secret Teachings of All Ages*, one of Los Feliz–based theosophist Manly P. Hall's (endless) works. Baker found a personal guide in the athletic, charismatic Indian guru Yogi Bhajan, who introduced America to kundalini yoga, as well as White Tantric Yoga, a sexual devotion of which Bhajan declared himself the one and only living master. But by the late sixties, Baker was approaching fifty, drinking heavily, and feeling left out of the excitement of life on Sunset Strip. He also needed money to support all that seeking. To that end, he and his first wife (he had seventeen, fourteen at the same time—more on that later) founded a string of LA restaurants that hybridized American dining with healthier ingredients. The Source was the most influential—and notorious—of them.

There had been vegetarian, vegan, and even raw-food restaurants in LA going back to the teens. In the same way that the new city was open to spiritual innovation, so, too, were its citizens open to treating food as medicine for the body and soul. The braided influences on this emergent "health food" culture included: nineteenth-century German *Lebensreform*, which advocated for naturopathy and nudism; the desires of the region's older midwestern retirees (the Folks) for miracle cures; and the sheer bounty of California's agriculture.

But there was never a place quite like the Source, which from its founding in 1969 on Sunset Strip pushed past faddists and cultists to capture a dynamic clientele of young people and celebrities like Bruce Lee and Steve McQueen. Baker created an origin myth for the restaurant, revolving around a mystical encounter in the Malibu hills with a fellow hiker who committed $35,000 to Baker, provided that his restaurant embody the "dietary wisdom found in the teachings of Jesus Christ as revealed through the Essene Gospels of Peace." The counternarrative claims that Baker robbed a bank. Whether its funding was divine or criminal, the Source became the source for salads overflowing with carrots, beets, cucumbers, romaine, avocados, alfalfa seeds, red cabbage, tomatoes, sunflower seeds, and pignoli, ideally washed down with herbal mu tea, carob milk, or fresh beet juice.

In an era when fathers were often distant and authoritarian, men who embraced the young were doubly seductive. So it was that Baker built a cult that he called the Source Family. Dressed all in white, his attractive acolytes worked as servers at the restaurant and lived a communal life in a mansion in the Hollywood Hills, becoming ever more enthralled by the man who now called himself Father Yod, claiming to be either God or one of his incarnations. After being confused one too many times with the Manson Family (Father Yod's "spiritual" marriages to fourteen just-post-teenage brides did not exactly clarify matters), the Source Family ended up closing down the restaurant and moving en masse to Hawaii. There Father Yod decided to try hang gliding without taking any lessons. He strapped on his wing, ran off a 1,400-foot-high cliff over the Pacific, plummeted straight down to the shore, broke his back, and died nine hours later. Within two years the community disbanded, and to this day, former members are divided about whether Father Yod left his earthly body on purpose.

Just as diet didn't save Father Yod from the force of gravity, food alone didn't remake Lee's body. That metamorphosis took working out with a group of American martial artists, mostly vets, that Lee had met in Long Beach, among them a marine vet and kickboxing champion named Joe Lewis; a former soldier, Mike "the Animal" Stone; and a former airman named Chuck Norris, who went on to fame in film, television, and internet memes, but only after filming a fight with his old friend Lee at the conclusion of *The Way of the Dragon*, considered one of the great battles in the history of martial arts films. What Lee took from them were bodybuilding techniques that allowed him to add muscle and definition to his body, not only focusing on his biceps and chest but also strengthening and defining the connective tissue, tendons, and ligaments. Joe Weider, the kingpin of American bodybuilding and the great patron of that other LA immigrant Arnold Schwarzenegger, referred to what Lee created as "the most defined body I've ever seen." In fusing kung fu's fluid mechanics with Muscle Beach's bulk and definition, Lee created an entirely new model for the cinematic action body.

Lee's global audiences may not have known *wen* from *wu*, but they revered his athleticism—the lightning-fast flips, balletic throws, and flying kicks, all done while visibly straining every muscle and tendon. Bruce Lee's health food–fueled, weight-trained body separated all action films into a before and after. From the *Matrix* trilogy to superhero franchises, no action hero in Lee's wake can escape his corporeal influence, whether a boxer like *Rocky* (1976), a traveler from the future like Sarah Connor in *Terminator 2* (1991), or the glut of abs-forward superheroes like *Captain America, Thor,* or any other shirtless members of the Marvel Cinematic Universe (2008–).

Lee's body was more than aesthetic or even functional. It was also political. At the tail end of the Vietnam War, in a moment of decolonization and a global burgeoning of ethnic consciousness, the symbolism of a ripped Asian male tearing through his imperial oppressors was searing. Not coincidentally, black and brown audiences were among Lee's most loyal fans. In his book on black films of the seventies, Darius James, the African American performance artist, nominated Bruce Lee as "the greatest blaxploitation hero of all time." Indeed, by the middle of that decade there were more than a few self-styled urban monks wandering the streets of South LA, clad in long silk robes and coolie hats, swirling metal *baoding* balls in their hands. Even Mexico's iconic Virgin of Guadalupe got in on the radicalization of the martial arts. Already a synthetic image incorporating Indigenous imagery into New World Catholicism, the Virgin appeared in California artist Ester Hernandez's politicized 1976 rendering as a militant defender of Chicanx rights, clad in a black-belted robe, her leg extended in a perfect sidekick.

Over the decades, the resistance has leached out of the martial arts body that Lee created, the emphasis shifting from urban warriors to carpooling karate moms, with kung fu movies laying the groundwork for the mixed martial arts, which has come to eclipse boxing as America's favorite combat sport. But for the average MMA pay-per-view subscriber, this is spectacle stripped of history. Whether they know it or not, the booze-addled, adrenaline-soaked fans of America's fastest-growing sport are in the octagon with the ghosts of empire and a few specters of unlikely stardom, such as the brotherhood of veterans who encountered martial arts as they were sent to protect, invade, or occupy Asian lands, channeled through the rough streets of Long Beach and exploded onto the screen by the supernova Bruce Lee. This legacy crystallizes in Southern California, which claims Lee as one of its own by way of not only the Chinatown statue but also—naturally—a star on Hollywood Boulevard, just east of the Highland Metro stop.

Martial arts were not the only thing vets picked up a taste for while in Asia. Servicemen came back from the Pacific theater of World War II and later the Korean War longing for the "exotic" locales they'd left behind. What they were offered was the entirely ersatz postwar tiki scene. Southern California led the nation in the bars and restaurants festooned with carved wooden idols, leafy fronds, and wallpaper depicting naked "native girls," with servers dropping pupu platters laden with imaginary Chinese, Hawaiian, and "island" delicacies, all of this cultural appropriation to be washed down with oversized goblets of rum-based libations. Disneyland opened the Enchanted Tiki Room in 1963, with audio-animatronic graven tikis to entertain visitors waiting in line with the most racist kind of Hollywood pidgin dialogue: "Me Rongo, god of agriculture, my land so good to me, I got time for sport, I fly kite, me Number One kite flyer." The attraction was sponsored by the Dole Food Company and featured a short film on the history of the pineapple. "Polynesia" was never so pseudo.

Except, perhaps, at Beverly Hills' Luau (1953–1978), perched high on Sunset Boulevard, surrounded by a moat, and famed for its blue lagoon. Owned by one of Lana Turner's many ex-husbands, Steve Crane (father of Turner's infamous daughter Cheryl, who at age fourteen stabbed and killed her mother's lover, mobster Johnny

Stompanato), the Luau was renowned for welcoming the underage, especially if they were connected. Candice Bergen, who was both, made sure to always grab the money seat and order a Smoke Cloud, a coconut shell on a bed of dry ice that the bartender would float across the lagoon to the kind of patron particularly thirsty for attention. It was a theatrical moment, she recalled, "like a pond that had caught fire ... a trail of smoke through the entire dining room until it landed on your table and then you couldn't see the person across from you." Taking its cues from LA bandleader Les Baxter's 1952 album *Ritual of the Savage*, a night at the Luau would have been scored to a kitsch-fest of "tropical" rhythms and "tribal" chants meant to evoke sultry breezes and primal passions. While the music played and the palm fronds undulated, diners would down delicacies like rumaki (water chestnuts and calf's liver wrapped in bacon, speared with a toothpick before being broiled into a crisp little ball) and crab rangoon (deep-fried wontons filled with crabmeat and cream cheese, then drizzled in sweet plum sauce).

That LA would embrace an Asian cuisine that wasn't Asian—liver, bacon, and cream cheese?—makes sense given that there had been almost no Asian immigration for decades. Prior to the Chinese Exclusion Act of 1882, immigration from Asia to the western United States had come in waves, leading to backlash and restrictions. The Immigration Act of 1924 created the U.S. Border Patrol and restricted immigration even more, effectively closing off entry into the United States to the vast majority of Asians for another four decades. If vets and their dates wanted to experience "the Orient," they were going to have to do so via American hosts like the pioneering Donn Beach (born Ernest Gantt) of Don the Beachcomber in Hollywood, or Ray Buhen, the Filipino American mixologist who started as a prep guy at Don's, moved to the Luau, and then opened his own place, the Tiki-Ti, in 1961. His son and grandson are still mixing up Cobra's Fangs and Missionary's Downfalls for hipsters and old-timers alike behind the Tiki-Ti's bar on the shaggy border of Silver Lake and Los Feliz.

Tiki exploded in LA, went national, and now survives on nostalgia's fumes. The Asian cuisine that followed, however, is resolutely contemporary. Food truck–obsessed millennials ordering spicy Thai sausage from Sanook Soi 38, Taiwanese pot stickers from Bling Bling Dumpling, or braised–pork belly rice bowls from Cafe Vietnam don't tend to question why this global foodtopia is available to them. In the state that pioneered legalized marijuana, they just want to feed the beast. But everything from *what* they are eating to *how* they are eating it—perched on curbs, grease-streaked plates propped on their knees—is, like martial arts, a direct legacy of the United States' brutal proxy wars across Asia during the second half of the twentieth century.

The intelligence community uses the term "blowback" to describe the unintended consequences of covert actions, the way that past policies create a boomerang effect in the present. Indeed, those who executed America's grand strategies in Asia probably never expected that a generation or two later, the cuisines of the countries they were systematically carpet-bombing would come to define Southern California's flavor profile. Of course, those displaced during the hot parts of the so-called cold wars were able to exert this kind of influence only because of a change in U.S. law. For forty years after 1924's Immigration Act there were racial and ethnic quotas on immigration that favored Europeans and excluded Asians. But the passage of 1965's Immigration and Nationality Act changed everything. Motivated by civil rights idealism and the real-politik of the Cold War, President Lyndon B. Johnson reassured the country that "this bill that we will sign today is not a revolutionary bill.... It will not reshape ... our daily lives or add importantly to either our wealth or our power." But he was profoundly wrong, because 1965 kicked off a demographic restructuring that transformed LA or, better yet, LAX Immigration and Customs, into the next Ellis Island.

The first visible wave of Asian immigrants were refugees from the Korean conflict. In 1950 the communist north invaded the U.S.-allied south, starting a war that killed over two million Koreans, more than half a million Chinese soldiers, and fifty thousand U.S. troops. While North Koreans never escaped the ruthless dictatorship of the Mafia-like Kim family, America's new policies offered opportunities for South Koreans to immigrate to the United States. Seeing the benefits of remittances coming back to Korea, Seoul was encouraging, and California soon became the center of the Korean diaspora.

Korean immigrants filled in the dilapidated parts of East Hollywood, a region between by-then-seedy MacArthur Park to the east and the mansions of Hancock Park to the west. Though Koreatown suffered significant losses during 1992's looting and violence, by the turn of the millennium it was booming. Young patrons rolled from club to club, downing shots of soju—the Korean national drink—and selecting from hundreds of restaurants and pubs: bubbling hot pots here, Seoul-style fried chicken there, and everywhere BBQ joints where patrons grilled their own meats, accompanied by little side dishes known as *banchan*, including kimchi, the fermented cabbage without which no repast can properly call itself Korean.

But back to those club kids hunting for late-night food. If there is one figure to whom they owe a drink (he's partial to Jägerbombs), it's Seoul-born, LA-raised Roy Choi. Choi has had many identities: gambler, drug addict, lowrider, Culinary Institute of America grad, hotel chef. But most significant, he created a Korean-fusion food truck called "The Kogi Truck aka Kogi BBQ aka Kogi aka Kogi Por Vida aka SO damn bomb aka Kojeeeeee," which totally reinvented the entire category.

Food trucks have their origins in two distinct American traditions that emerged after the Civil War, the first being chuck wagons that fed cowboys on cattle drives, complete with stations for prep, service, and cleanup; the second, pushcarts, which peddled pre-made sandwiches, meat pies, and tamales to urban workers. Fast-forward a hundred years—past the 1960s ice cream trucks with their melodic chimes, past the original catering trucks that dished up workaday fare at job sites—and you land on Choi. Like many LA chefs before him, he fused the flavors of the city he knew and loved—Korean and Mexican, in particular—serving short-rib tacos, kimchi quesadillas, and the eponymous "Kogi dogs" to hungry students at UCLA, surfers in Venice, and partiers downtown. What was revolutionary, however, was not necessarily the food itself but the extent to which Choi and his partners built word-of-mouth via the then-new microblogging site Twitter, transforming a modest kitchen on wheels into a geolocative, streetscape-activating, mobile site of production and consumption, rolling from the mountains to the valleys, from the desert to the sea. What Kogi signified above all was being in the know and in the now to the first fully networked generation.

Forty miles southeast of K-town is the next stop on our tour of

Cold War blowback. Westminster is a dusty stretch of Orange County, inland from the adjacent paradises of Huntington Beach and Newport Beach. Westminster developed after World War II to house returning vets and freezing midwesterners who wanted their own little swatch of sunshine, even if it was east of the 405 freeway. But what was once a bedroom community for Anglos was transformed following the Vietnamese refugee crisis of the late seventies. Though President Gerald Ford announced on April 23, 1975, that the Vietnam War was "finished as far as America is concerned," the following decade saw a flood of "boat people," so desperate to escape their country that they fled in rickety flotillas to find their way to the heart of the imperial power that had abandoned them to their fate. By 1980 there were a quarter of a million Vietnamese immigrants in the United States, and by 1990 more than 300,000 in Southern California alone, the highest concentration in the country. By 2010 Westminster was over 40 percent ethnically Vietnamese.

It wasn't entirely surprising, then, to find Vietnamese Americans running for city council on anticommunist platforms—not that there were communists in Westminster, but to prove their bona fides in opposing the still nominally communist government of contemporary Vietnam. Nor that somewhere along the way, Westminster became the best place in the United States to sample the wonders of Vietnamese cuisine: a steaming bowl of pho, noodles floating in an aromatic beef-based soup; the subtle interplay of flavor and texture in a lettuce wrap stuffed with mint leaves, pickled carrot, and daikon shreds; a flash-fried imperial roll, dipped in somebody's great-grandmother's *nuac nom* (fish sauce).

The past is never dead, especially when it comes to family recipes. So it is with Crustacean in Beverly Hills, one of a chain of

Vietnamese-fusion restaurants stretching from the San Francisco Bay Area down to Orange County, run by three generations of women starting with Helene "Mama" An. Inside the restaurant's main kitchen, there is a smaller wooden structure with a locked door, known as the Secret Kitchen. From the outside, it seems like a pure marketing gimmick, coyly leveraging the exoticism of the "Orient" in everything from sex to food. But the real secret of the Secret Kitchen is less mysterious. After fleeing Vietnam and finally achieving success in the cutthroat restaurant world, Madame An found some of her most closely guarded family recipes turning up on competitors' menus. She decided that all subsequent restaurants would include kitchens-within-kitchens that only family members and servers of more than ten years' standing could enter, all others reduced to receiving plated food passed through metal slots in the door. If that level of secrecy seems a trifle paranoid, remember that, like so many Vietnamese refugees, the Ans lost everything after the fall of Saigon. They rebuilt and prospered, but for many others just getting a foot in the door in a new country was difficult.

If that foot had impeccably polished toenails, it was likely due to the intervention of a Hitchcock blonde. Tippi Hedren is best known for her starring roles in *The Birds* (1963) and *Marnie* (1964), which led to an invitation to join a USO tour entertaining U.S. troops, where she met and befriended many South Vietnamese. After the war ended, she devoted herself to resettlement charities, including one dedicated to finding work for Vietnamese refugee women, who often had limited English skills. In 1973 Hedren visited a refugee camp near Sacramento. In the midst of a brainstorming session, the actress and the Vietnamese transplants bonded over something that required neither language nor cultural proficiency. The women had fallen in love with the star's perfectly lacquered nails.

Hedren had come up in the studio system, but even after she left she maintained the rigorous—and expensive—grooming rituals of the Hollywood elite. Hedren saw an opportunity for these refugees to join and perhaps even transform one segment of the multibillion-dollar beauty industry. She asked her personal manicurist—Dusty Coots from the Nail Patch in Encino—to design a curriculum focusing on mani-pedis, as well as on the financial realities of running a business. Twenty women were in that first class; today, 80 percent of the people who work in nail salons in California have Vietnamese heritage. They persevered despite the long hours, demanding clients, and exposure to toxins, driving down the cost of manicures by more than half, transmuting a celebrity's prerogative into an everyday luxury.

From everyday luxuries we turn to an everyday necessity—the humble doughnut—whose ubiquity, at least in the mini-malls of Southern California, is yet more blowback from America's Indochinese adventuring. The protagonist of this story is a Cambodian refugee named Ted Ngoy, who wound up in Southern California along with one hundred thousand of his fellow Cambodians after U.S. military covert operations paved the way for the genocidal Khmer Rouge regime. It was 1975 when Ngoy and his family arrived at Camp Pendleton. Within a month the Torrance church that sponsored them found Ngoy part-time work at a Mobil gas station. One day a coworker offered him a treat from DK's Donuts across the street. It was Ngoy's first doughnut in his new country, and the taste reminded him of the sweet round cakes, or *nom kong*, he'd grown up with. Thereafter, he watched with interest as carload after carload stopped to fuel up on DK's carbs and caffeine. In his halting English, Ngoy approached the store's owners and talked to them about the business, seeing in it a low-cost entry to his American dream. He could begin with a friendly demeanor, the ability to pour coffee quickly, and a willingness to wake before dawn to fire up the fryer. The owners encouraged him to apply to Winchell's University, the managers' training program for the regional Winchell's Donut House chain (its inestimable contribution to humankind being the fourteen-doughnut "dozen"). Ngoy was the first person from Indochina to go through the program, learning the basics of frying, dipping, filling, glazing, and, most important, selling.

As with the nail business, here was a venue where owners and employees could effectively interface with their customers across language and cultural boundaries. Ngoy eventually bought more than twenty doughnut shops—the first, none other than DK's Donuts—and set up hundreds of his countrymen in the business. For one brief, shining moment, he was Southern California's doughnut king. Then he went bankrupt, got divorced, and had to reinvent himself (more than a few times), but that's what makes him a hero of American (and Cambodian) capitalism. He and the legion of deep-frying, sugar-glazing, pink-to-go-box-filling, java-pouring, incredibly hard-working Cambodian families contributed something truly special by salvaging a small bit of classic Americana—the cruller and glazed-doughnut recipes of the transplanted midwestern Folks—not to mention ensuring that SoCal remains the greatest place in our nation to buy a baker's dozen.

The doughnut—like the burger—is one of the great foods to eat when you drive: the right size, the right price, pairs well with coffee. Your food goes in your lap, but the method best suited to LA's stop-and-go (but often just stopped) morning traffic is to put your beverage in a cupholder, which, it should be noted, was invented in LA. Inspired by the trays attached to windows in the city's many drive-ins, in 1950 Jack Fazakerley patented a design for an attachable, flip-down version, which didn't become standard in cars until Chrysler introduced the first minivans in 1983. By 2020 Subaru may have overestimated the hydration needs of the American public, with nineteen cup holders in the Ascent SUV. By contrast, none come standard in the $380,668 Ferrari F12, though a carbon-fiber cupholder is available as a $3,533 option.

If you get back into your car and take the 5 to the 101 through Hollywood on your way west, you will encounter a polyglot collection of blowback cuisines. We start with Thai food and that revitalized stretch of East Hollywood known as Thai Town—the only designated Thai Town in the country, by the way. Though the United States did not fight in Thailand proper, there were actions both acknowledged and covert occurring in all three of its eastern neighbors (Vietnam, Cambodia, and Laos), making allied Thailand a key base for staging incursions. Thais immigrated to Los Angeles in large numbers beginning in the 1960s and extensively in the 1980s, settling all over the city. Their numbers reflect a familiar pattern—there are more Thais in LA than anywhere outside Thailand. Thus it is that pad thai noodles and green papaya salad have become a late-night staple to rival the chili cheeseburger.

As the Cold War in Asia fades into memory, its counterpart in El Salvador, Nicaragua, and Guatemala is disappearing from the public consciousness as well. But in the eighties, the Reagan administration supported right-wing attacks on Indigenous and left-wing antigovernment movements across the Southern Hemisphere, and

U.S.-supported death squads drove generations of Central Americans to the relative safety of Los Angeles, transforming the Westlake district around MacArthur Park—our next stop—into an open-air market for grilled Guatemalan *dobladas* (fried masa turnovers filled with shredded chicken and drizzled with tomato sauce, cabbage, and cheese); Salvadorean *sopa de pata* (tripe soup); and the Nicaraguan version of *gallo pinto*, "painted rooster" (rice, beans, and onions fried in coconut oil to make them extra creamy).

Head west and north of Westlake and Pico Union, and the availability of everything from the *basturma* (cured smoked beef) in Hollywood's Little Armenia to the Russian restaurants of West Hollywood offering *vareniki* and *golubtsi* (Russian- and Ukrainian-style stuffed cabbage) washed down with *mors* (a noncarbonated fruit drink made from lingonberries), to the occasional Uzbek restaurant showcasing *plovs* (the national dish, best described as a lamb-and-rice pilaf) maps out an expanded field of blowback. Heading west, you hit the cultural spine of Iranian Los Angeles.

As Iran destabilized during the 1970s, those with means started to look for bolt-holes throughout the world. Even before 1979's Islamic revolution, enterprising LA real estate agent Mike Silverman took out ads in Tehran-based magazines touting Beverly Hills as a safe harbor with rolling terrain and a gentle climate, just like home. After the revolution, half of Iran's eighty thousand Jews fled, with thirty thousand settling in Los Angeles. Many bought homes in Beverly Hills' Trousdale subdivision, which was later derisively nicknamed the new Persian Gulf. After the revolution, there were more than 300,000 Iranians and Iranian Americans in Southern California. Thus the portmanteau "Tehrangeles," which to this day remains the center of global expatriate Iranian life and a place where you can count on finding *fesenjan* and *zereshk polo*. For those whose Farsi is rusty, this would be a light meal—for an Iranian family, at least—of walnut and pomegranate chicken stew served with barberry rice.

If dessert appeals, there's no better place than Mashti Malone's Ice Cream, one of Southern California's great blowback hodgepodges, situated in a mini-mall just south of Hollywood Boulevard that also houses the offices of the free erotic newspaper the *LA Xpress*. In 1971 the shop opened as Mugsy Malone's, art-directed to showcase the full panoply of Irish clichés, including an emerald-green four-leaf clover on the sign facing La Brea Avenue. Nine years later an Iranian chef named Mashti Shirvani bought the business but couldn't afford a new sign, so he followed the classic immigrant pattern of adaptive reuse, replacing "Mugsy" with "Mashti." The new store offered rose-water sorbet covered with frozen rice noodles (*faloodeh* in Farsi), and saffron ice cream sandwiches rolled in fresh, crushed pistachios, alongside the standard fare of chocolate mint and cookies and cream. It took Mashti "Do I look like a Malone to you?" Shirvani almost forty years to spring for a new sign. As he had come to understand over the intervening decades that branding trumps purity, the name and the shamrock remain unchanged.

The cool cucumber sorbet at Mashti Malone's is as perfect a distillation of blowback cuisine as one can scoop into a bowl. But in the twenty-first century, economic rivalries are coming to take precedence over military ones. The United States' most important competitor is China, and the story of Chinese food in Southern California is one of advances and retreats, racism and triumph, chop suey and little balls of tapioca suspended in milk tea.

Chinese have been in Southern California longer and in greater numbers than any other group from Asia. Their journey starts in the nineteenth century, when they came to California to fish for abalone and mine for gold with the forty-niners, and their numbers increased as they found work tying a continent together by rail. Chinese immigrants provided the backbreaking labor but from the beginning were treated as less than human, their wives and children banned even from entering the country. A few of these men, almost all untrained as cooks, ended up in and around downtown LA's infamous Calle de Los Negros, where they made cheap but tasty food from what they could scrounge in their new home—first to feed their countrymen, then, curious others. This first Chinatown popularized such heavily sauced, stir-fried miscellanies as chow mein, which has its roots in traditional Cantonese cuisine but is an American-Chinese hybrid to the core.

As the community around the Calle grew, so did nativist hostility. In 1871 there was a race riot during which a murderous mob lynched around twenty Chinese men and boys. From the 1860s through the 1920s, local, state, and national laws enacted the racist fearmongering of those opposed to a "Mongolian invasion." In 1874 U.S. senator James G. Blaine defined the struggle in culinary terms: "You cannot work a man who must have beef and bread alongside of a man who can live on rice. . . . The result is not to bring up the man who lives on rice to the beef-and-bread standard, but it is to bring down the beef-and-bread man to the rice standard." American labor leader Samuel Gompers cowrote a pamphlet a generation later that reiterated the metaphor in even more explicitly racist language: "Meat vs. Rice: American Manhood against Asiatic Coolieism— Which Shall Survive?"

In 1931 the city forced out Chinatown's three thousand ethnic

Chinese to make way for Union Station, the last of America's great train depots. The community was in limbo for almost a decade until the establishment of not one but two replacement Chinatowns, both just west of the original. LA's second Chinatown was a short-lived Orientalist enclave called China City. It was opened in 1938 by Christine Sterling. She was the Anglo entrepreneur responsible for saving the city's oldest adobe and original pueblo from redevelopment, through the racially and historically dubious rebranding of Olvera Street into a "Mexican village." The "campesinos" selling sombreros, serapes, and taquitos to tourists were joined a few blocks away by rickshaw-driving, jade-hawking, mandarin-collared "celestials," the faux exoticism of their "Oriental" walled city baked in by an army of studio set designers. These professional fantasists set the tone for the city's third—and current—Chinatown, the first in America to be owned and developed by ethnic Chinese investors.

New Chinatown, as it was called, opened onto Broadway and Hill Streets and was from its inception a fully scripted space, studded with wishing wells, kitschy pagodas, and dragon-festooned gateways welcoming locals and tourists alike in search of a China recognizable from Hollywood films. Here was a distillation of location scouting and set designing that yielded an ersatz platzgeist that eventually became "real," as New Chinatown outlived China City, accumulated its own layers of history, and became the beloved and completely identifiable space it is today. In the late nineteenth and early twentieth centuries, the area housed a large Italian community, so that may justify one final cross-cultural comparison: like Pinocchio, the puppet who wanted to be a "real" boy, Chinatown, built to the specs of filmic imaginaries, became a densely layered part of LA's urban landscape.

New Chinatown's food was tailored to the broadest American tastes, featuring such dubious fare as the eleven varieties of chop suey and "Bar-B-Que sparerib" sandwiches (on toast, an extra nickel) on the menu of the long-defunct Rice Bowl restaurant— which happened to be at the same intersection now occupied by the statue of Bruce Lee. The menus didn't change significantly until new waves of Chinese immigrants began to arrive after 1965—from Taiwan, Hong Kong, and the mainland.

Many of these were educated middle-class professionals, and they arrived armed with plenty of cash. Fred Hsieh knew just what they should do with it. In 1973 he opened Mandarin Realty in the fading business district of Monterey Park, a low-density, middle-class bedroom community filled with aging Anglo vets and their families who wanted to live like they did in *Leave It to Beaver*. But Hsieh had a different vision: he was going to sell the suburban dream to the new, flush immigrants. Why move to dense and over-crowded Chinatown, especially if you spoke Mandarin and the predominant dialect downtown was Cantonese? Why not come to Monterey Park, where there were split-level ranch homes with yards and even pools, low crime rates, freeway access to downtown, and a good school district?

What happened over the next three decades was not simply a demographic transformation—from 10 percent Asian in 1970 to 40 percent in 1980 to 67 percent in 1990—but the birth of something new in the United States: what the geographer Wei Li calls an "ethno-burb." First Monterey Park and then other nearby San Gabriel Valley (SGV) communities like Alhambra and Rosemead began filling with immigrants who had the means to remake their neighborhoods to their own tastes, rather than adapting to existing norms.

Thus the rapid proliferation in the SGV of specialty markets with enormous fresh-fish tanks, bok choy and taro in the produce section, and imported canned goods of all sorts. New restaurants exploded at the same time, with signage and menus in Mandarin, with nary a plate of orange chicken—basically McNuggets in syrup—to be found.

Instead, the SGV offered everything from Western Islamic Uighur lamb and bread dishes to Northern Dalian jellyfish appetizers. Reviewing Shanghai No. 1 Seafood, Jonathan Gold, LA's Pulitzer Prize–winning food journalist, wrote the following about a dish called "braised three strings": "while the construction may be a little alarming on the plate—it really does look like Cousin It, with a mushroom cap for a beret—by the time you disassemble it into slivers of ham and chicken in the serving bowl, in a puddle of ultra-concentrated chicken broth, you probably will have fallen in love." The menu "is not altered to suit the Western palate, and many of its most stunning effects may whiz straight over the heads of diners not actually raised in eastern China." American director Wayne Wang goes even further, claiming that "because of better ingredients and the preservation of the cultural traditions," the food in the SGV is the equal of and sometimes even superior to that in China itself.

All was not bean cakes and egg tarts, however, as many in the SGV came to resent and then resist these cultural and culinary shifts. To quote one older Anglo resident in the 1980s, "Before, immigrants were poor. They lived in their own neighborhoods and moved into ours after they learned English, got a good job, and became accustomed to our ways. Today the Chinese come right in with their money and their ways. We are the aliens." Another complained that "all these Chinese characters on signs . . . it is one bold slap in the face." In 1986 Monterey Park's nativist faction passed Resolution 9004, which declared English the city's official language, amended the sign codes, and encouraged the city's police department to report "illegal aliens" to federal authorities. The resolution was so flawed it had to be withdrawn, but the political rifts exposed in Southern California expanded across the state a few months later with the passage of Proposition 63, the "English is the Official Language of California Amendment," and six years further on with the success of Proposition 187, which banned undocumented immigrants from accessing most state services, including public schools. In fewer than three decades, the fissures uncovered in the SGV had spread wide enough to open the space for a full-blown nativist to ascend to the U.S. presidency.

Yet Fred Hsieh's vision of a Chinese American suburb in the SGV prevailed. Just look at the "boba generation," those second-generation millennials named for a favorite beverage, sweet milk tea with bobbing tapioca balls. Boba came over from Taiwan in the late nineties, starting in a mall in the SGV city of Arcadia. Boba is sweet, infinitely customizable, and, because it's neither alcoholic nor as caffeinated as coffee or energy drinks, acceptable (if not always palatable) to parents. Boba is a liquefaction of all things cute. One of the first of the shops, called Lollicup, became a dominant player, ending up manufacturing 80 percent of the raw tapioca pearls served in America and even opening a "Boba University" in Chino to teach budding entrepreneurs the secret of mixing up the concoction.

In Southern California, what began as a fad turned into a staple, first in any neighborhood with a large Asian population, then spreading to include anywhere where there were Asian and Asian American college students, and then, finally, everywhere. Journalist Clarissa Wei wrote a deeply personal essay about her own teenage milk-tea obsession, when choosing which boba shop to frequent in the SGV was a rite of passage and a marker of identity. The Fung Brothers' comic music video "Bobalife" lays it out: "The flavors are fruity and the straws are big.... Make it tasty, make it tasty... call us the boba generation." Though hardly a rigorous demographic category, the boba generation can be seen as the beneficiaries of decades of struggles to carve political, economic, cultural, and political spaces for Asian American communities in the SGV. These battles, which are ongoing, are reminders of why the screen heroics of a figure like Bruce Lee still resonate. The injustices of global incursions and their descent into the sanctioned savagery of wars both hot and cold, domestic and geopolitical, never just conclude. The English novelist L. P. Hartley opened his 1953 novel *The Go-Between* with the line "The past is a foreign country: they do things differently there." But as we've seen from Long Beach's karate tournaments to Koreatown's hot-pot specialty counters to Cambodians replicating perfect midwestern doughnuts day after day after day, blowback is real, and the different ways immigrants did things *there* morphs over time into the way things are done *here*.

10 THE BILLION-DOLLAR BAY

UNTITLED #40 (FREEWAYS) | 1995 | PLATINUM PRINT | 2 ¼ X 6 ¾ INCHES (5.7 X 17.1 CM)

Ports, Too Much Stuff, TruckNutz, Wife Swappers, and a Gangster in a Yachting Cap

R ow after row of mass-marketed goods—KIT KAT bars, L'eggs pantyhose, Energizer batteries—form an endless regression of capitalist overproduction, a color-coded efflorescence of *stuff*, enough to dazzle even the most jaded sensorium. Eventually, the bits and pieces cohere into a picture: a store, but not just any store, a dream, then a triumph, then a cautionary tale of a store. Born in Los Angeles, 99 Cents Only mirrors the monomania of its founder, one Dave Gold, who worked from 4:00 a.m. to 7:00 p.m. every day to build an empire of some four hundred emporia across the West by stocking stuff he could sell at the same—and, to him, perfect—price of ninety-nine cents. Gold mastered this trick in his parents' liquor store in downtown's Grand Central Market: "Whenever I'd put wine or cheese on sale for $1.02 or 98 cents, it

No loss should hit us, which can be avoided with constant care.
—A. P. Møller

Obviously crime pays, or there'd be no crime.
—G. Gordon Liddy

never sold out. When I put a 99 cent sign on anything, it was gone in no time."

Gold bested the dollar stores around the country because he saw his project less as a salvage operation (discounting the unwanted) than as a showcase of carefully curated items culled from an ever-more-tightly interwoven international economic system. Gold also had taste, his aesthetic the outcome of a marketing algorithm that creates sense and sensibility from the material chaos of the era.

One of the chain's highest-profile outlets is on the 6100 block of Wilshire Boulevard, just west of the LA County Museum of Art and across the street from a complex of contemporary art galleries known (for their address) as 6150. After openings, artists and collectors would put down their wineglasses, bid their good-byes, and head out to the parking lot, which fronts onto Wilshire. From their cars they could look across the wide boulevard into Dave Gold's glowing storefront, whose entire inventory cost less than the painting, sculpture, or photograph they'd just been admiring. One of those artists was determined to capture something of this ironic juxtaposition on the city's Miracle Mile.

German photographer Andreas Gursky's *99 Cent* (1999) is a mural-sized photograph that is both a technical marvel and an economic argument. Painstakingly stitched together from smaller high-resolution photographs that blur the distinction between the real and the hyperreal, the panoramic image is distinguished by its blinding clarity, the subtly amped-up colors contributing to sheer optical overload. A sly critique of consumerism at the turn of the millennium (the more cheap stuff, the better), it was also, at $2.3 million, one of the single most expensive photographs ever sold at auction.

Both the mammoth photograph and the overstuffed store it represents attest to the importance of a Los Angeles industry that churns through billions of dollars a day. It is vital to the region's economy, though its reach is global, and when it shudders to a halt during a strike, you better believe the entire world knows. We are not talking about Hollywood but rather Southern California's ports.

It's always been about water. As the fictional mayor of Los Angeles puts it in *Chinatown*, "Without water the dust will rise up and cover us as though we'd never existed!" The mayor is arguing about constructing a dangerous new dam with Hollis Mulwray, the chief engineer of the city's Department of Water and Power, a character modeled on William Mulholland, the real-life engineer who ushered in twentieth-century Los Angeles via the aqueduct. The water from that (real) aqueduct flowed onto the lawns and into the pools of Southern California's suburban utopia before ending up as run-off in the Pacific, where surfers were learning how to hang ten and carve turns on the waves. Thus it was that water—both fresh and salt—defined the region's famed "lifestyle." At the close of the twentieth century, water regained its alchemical preeminence as the ports became behemoths of global trade.

There are actually two separate entities: the Port of Los Angeles out of San Pedro, which was once a separate town but was consolidated into the larger metropolis more than a century ago; and the Port of Long Beach, which remains an independent city. People in the shipping business make a distinction between the two, but no one else bothers, much less families stepping up the gangplanks onto a Disney cruise ship heading to Mexico.

The scenic way to approach the ports is to head south through the Palos Verdes Peninsula, a spectacular drive reminiscent of Italy's Amalfi Coast, ringed with ludicrously expensive estates blessed with breathtaking views. The only reason besides the views to stop in PV, as it is known to locals, is to visit Lloyd Wright's Wayfarers Chapel, a modern glass building supported by wood and glimmering metallic trussing, nestled into a grove of redwoods on a rocky promontory. Wright (son of Frank Lloyd) designed it for a Swedenborgian congregation that followed a Swedish mystic Christian who proselytized ethical vegetarianism, so there's that connection to the proclivities of contemporary Southern Californians.

Head downhill on Palos Verdes Drive South and before hitting the ports themselves, you can take in the whole harbor from Angels Gate Park, in San Pedro. Other than the view, Angels Gate is known for two things: a colossal bell that the South Korean government donated as a bicentennial friendship gift; and a basketball court that sits on a hilltop slope that from one approach looks like it's perched directly over the Pacific, as if an errant pass would send a ball floating to Hawaii. On the court, you are still above the grit of San Pedro and Long Beach, but the physical environs start to take shape: the boats stacked up in the bay prior to unloading; the monumental cranes on the docks; the spiderwebs of rail and truck routes in and out. Leaving Angels Gate and descending into the maelstrom immerses you in the ports' sensory overload. The funk of diesel fumes melds with the tang of saltwater; the scent of raw sewage escapes the gourd-shaped anaerobic digesters of a water-treatment plant; the metallic squeal of slow-moving trains running over steel rails is punctuated by the squawks of seagulls; light bouncing off the water illuminates the particulate matter that creates those spectacular sunsets. All this combines to make the ports feel less like a part of Los Angeles than a separate fiefdom, albeit one with inconsistent branding.

Bad branding or not, the ports are the present of Los Angeles and will remain vital to its future. LA is both the entry point to twenty-first-century America for Asian immigrants and the pump through which Asia's material manufacturing enters U.S. markets, flooding the country so thoroughly and so efficiently that its citizens now take for granted that the cost of made goods should approach the cost of information—that is, basically free. As the United States shuttered its own manufacturing base in favor of offshoring to Asia, the importance of LA's ports to the nation's economic life has exploded. During a dockworkers' strike in 2014, the ships backing up in the bay were said to cost the country more than a billion dollars a day in losses.

On a clear day, the midspan of the Vincent Thomas Bridge offers the best way to take in the ports' relationship to both the water and the land. Due north, the spires of downtown LA glimmer in the sun, and the rail lines leading to Union Station and points east fan out like tendrils. To the south, there are multicolored shipping containers stacked up on the piers, resembling nothing so much as gargantuan Lego pieces. All over are the cranes that load and unload the containers—towering, spindly things that conjure Transformers or the snow-walking AT-ATs in George Lucas's *The Empire Strikes Back*.

All of this is visible on a clear day, but famously in Southern California, lots of days aren't, the result of the inversion layer, which acts as a lid tightly locked over the skies. In 1542, when the Spanish conquistador and explorer Juan Rodríguez Cabrillo became the first European to sail north past what is now called Long Beach, he called his safe harbor La Bahía de los Fumos, or Smoke Bay, because the air was thick with the fires of the Indigenous peoples he encountered. Celebrated for his courage and reviled for his barbarity, Cabrillo died of gangrene a year later, after struggling with Tongva warriors on Santa Catalina Island, just across from what we now call San Pedro Bay. While the skies haven't changed much in the intervening centuries, the bay's physical environment has been enfolded into a gargantuan, technologized cityscape, the result of one hundred years of massive capital investment and overarching ambition.

There was no guarantee that San Pedro Bay was going to become the region's dominant port. In the late nineteenth century, railroad magnate Henry Huntington made a big push to link his existing transportation network to the "long wharf" he'd established in

Santa Monica Bay. Had he succeeded, Santa Monica, Venice, and even Malibu would be covered with cranes and semis instead of mansions and Maseratis. But rivals defeated Huntington in 1897 and later extended the city limits down to swallow up the independent city of San Pedro, ensuring that the region's burgeoning industries would ship their goods and raw materials from there rather than from Santa Monica Bay.

Because the Midwest and the East Coast remained central to the American economy, rail was more important than shipping to Los Angeles through the thirties. World War II changed everything. The Pacific theater demanded an immediate ramp-up of the West Coast's ports, and Seattle-Tacoma, San Francisco, and San Diego, as well as Los Angeles, saw prodigious increases in the amount of tonnage passing through. But what propelled LA's ascent to the domination of the entire Western Hemisphere was precisely the fact that it wasn't the port of choice after the end of World War II. Instead, it was second tier, prompting its managers to be receptive to new strategies that might move the San Pedro bay ports up the ranks.

After the war ended, a trucking executive named Malcolm McLean masterminded a better way of getting stuff from New Jersey to Texas. Why load a semi, unload the contents into the hold of a ship, and then reload it onto a new truck? What if you could take the trailer off the semi and load it right onto the boat in Newark, then unload the trailer in Houston and drop it, unopened, on a cab there, cutting out the hard work of getting the stuff into and then out of the ships? In April 1956, McLean launched the *Ideal-X*, the first "container" ship. It took a few years, but eventually the containers became standardized, at eight feet wide and eight and a half feet high, in twenty- or forty-foot lengths. Trucks and railcars were modified in turn, creating a fully intermodal transport system, meaning that the containers, also known as boxes, could be filled with raw materials or manufactured goods and delivered via ship, train, or truck without ever disturbing the contents.

It took time to adapt to McLean's innovation, but LA's ports saw themselves as having little to lose and much to gain by shifting to the container model. Much the same thing happened with Maersk, the Danish shipping line that became the ports' most important tenant. The line traces its roots back to a nineteenth-century veteran captain, Peter Mærsk Møller, who personally experienced the epochal shift from sailing ships to steam-powered vessels. In 1904 Peter and his son A.P. founded what became the Maersk Line. By the start of World War II, it was Denmark's largest fleet, so when Nazi forces rolled into Copenhagen in 1940, there was no question that a Wehrmacht officer would march into Maersk's headquarters and demand that the company hand over its ships. The bulk of Maersk's boats was unavailable for use by the Third Reich, however, because A. P. Møller had dispatched them to the United States, where the company was being run by his son, Arnold Mærsk McKinney Møller. While A.P. waited out the war in Copenhagen, son Arnold delivered the Maersk fleet to the Allies, exactly as planned. Outflanking the Nazis reaffirmed A.P. and Arnold's obsession with managing risk in a risky business, and their commitment to "constant care" defined the company as it grew over the next half century into the largest shipping line in the world.

As part of extending its dominance, Maersk made an indelible mark on LA's topography. Like Poseidon striking his trident against the water and raising new lands, the company dredged the bottom of the harbor and constructed five hundred acres out of the sea. Pier 400, completed in 2000, extended Terminal Island in the most ambitious project in the ports' history. The largest terminal in the world devoted to one company, Pier 400 holds the record for the fastest unloading of a standard vessel—its cranes, container yard, on-dock rail and truck gates all designed to function as a single, well-oiled machine. From the moment a boat docks at Pier 400, it takes no more than seven days to get whatever is on it off it, transported to Tuscaloosa or Tucson, and placed on the shelves at Walmart or Target or 99 Cents Only, demonstrating the invisible power that LA exerts on the material abundance of twenty-first-century America.

Like Andreas Gursky, LA-based artist Jason Rhoades was obsessed with the proliferation of goods that global trade brings in its wake. In his sprawling installation *The Black Pussy... and the Pagan Idol Workshop* (2005), Rhoades juxtaposed dream catchers, hookah pipes, beaver-felt cowboy hats, neon "pussy" signs, and other adults-only paraphernalia taken from a seized shipping container. In *Tijuanatanjierchandelier* (2006), he explored the correspondences between two border towns six thousand miles apart (Tijuana, Mexico, and Tangier, Morocco) via an agglomeration of objects stripped of their origins and cultural specificity: generic Moroccan chandeliers; nominally Mexican maracas; debased novelties like TruckNutz, swinging plastic testicles otherwise destined to hang from the trailer hitch of a 4x4. At first glance, gallery-goers might well see the work as "piles of stuff," as Rhoades's mentor, artist Paul McCarthy, facetiously described it. But as the years pass, Rhoades looks ever more attuned to the centrality of those denatured piles of stuff in the lives of twenty-first-century Americans.

Rhoades came to prominence in the post-9/11, prerecession era, a time when President George W. Bush offered the following "solu-tion" to the "problem" of terrorism: "I encourage you all to go shop-ping more." To see what average Americans purchased when they went shopping, the media made various voyeuristic portals available. Two television shows in particular—*Wife Swap* and *Supernanny*—focused a lens onto the domestic spaces of the ultimate consumers of mass culture: families with children.

Wife Swap was not about sex but instead about families "trading" mothers, a neat freak swapping with a slob, a hunter with a vegan; cue the reality-style histrionics and feel-good conclusions. In *Super-nanny*, families at the end of their rope were granted salvation in the form of Jo Frost, a self-trained British child-rearing consultant, who spent each episode establishing new disciplinary procedures for the children in question, as well as their clueless parents. What united *Wife Swap* and *Supernanny*—besides the anxiety-provoking scrutiny of sexual politics within nuclear households—was that much of the action was in epic, open-plan spaces that looked as if toy bombs had gone off in them, leaving behind an unholy profusion of Munchkin Mozart Magic Cubes, Fisher-Price See 'n Says, Star Wars lightsabers, and Legos beyond number—perhaps even some of the fifteen hundred included in Lego's 2014 Maersk-themed kit, a model of the Line Triple-E, then the largest ship in the world. In any case, constructing the Triple-E out of Legos in a family room over-flowing with the bounty of Pier 400 would be just too meta.

Wife Swap and *Supernanny* dramatized the spoils of a prereces-sionary criminal real estate market born of rock-bottom fuel prices and predatory lending practices. In doing so, they exposed a new face of housing in America: deep in exurbia, surrounded either by mostly nothing or by other lumbering structures like themselves, not exactly McMansions, but too hypertrophied to be just "houses." Call them pornographic displacements of volume: so many rooms, so many yards of wall-to-wall carpeting, such high ceilings, no place to sit down. That's what sticks, these cavernous spaces palpably lacking the three or four couches and five or six armchairs needed to furnish the expansive lifestyle they appeared to promote. Instead the swapped wife and the airdropped nanny confronted rooms-cum-chasms, punctuated by a lone sofa, a beanbag chair, the self-referential big-screen TV, and those piles of toys, looking like nothing so much as a G-rated Jason Rhoades installation.

Real estate brokers like to use the term "great room," which sounds straight out of *Beowulf*, or at least a sword-and-sorcery banquet but in fact derives from midcentury-modernist developer Joseph Eichler's insight that after World War II, families wanted to live in ways that were both less structured and more open to interaction. In Southern California—from the San Fernando Valley to Thousand Oaks to Orange County—Eichler built thousands of quintessentially suburban houses, deploying post-and-beam construction, which allows for large, unencumbered interior spaces. Instead of separate kitchens, dining rooms, and living rooms, his homes erased the separations between these formerly distinct zones so that Mom could prepare dinner at her kitchen island while overseeing her on-average 2.4 kids doing homework at the table while trying not to harbor resentment at the sight of Dad kicking back in the La-Z-Boy at the end of his long, hard day at the office.

One of the many midcentury homes to embrace Eichler's great-room concept is a tidy split-level with good freeway access located at 11222 Dilling Street in Studio City, in the Valley, just over the hill from Hollywood. A quick drive-by indicates nothing that might explain why, when the house was up for sale in 2018, the Realtor was able to boast that, with the exception of the White House, 11222 Dilling was the most photographed home in the United States. The Zillow.com write-up, however, explains that this house served as the setting of *The Brady Bunch*, the iconic sitcom that ran on ABC from 1969 to 1974. While the interiors were shot on stage 5 at Hollywood's Paramount Studios, the facade of the Dilling Street house anchored the show's imagining of 1970s suburbia, as experienced by a widower with three boys who married a widow with three girls, all with "hair of gold, like their mother"—in effect, the blandest of blended families, though fans would later learn that the actor who played the lantern-jawed dad was closeted and gay; the eldest TV son lusted after and briefly dated his TV stepmom; and the eldest TV daughter was addicted to cocaine, a seventies LA drug par excellence.

The Brady Bunch remains a pop-culture phenomenon, spawning a short-lived animated series, various reunion shows, two full-blown movie adaptations in the mid-1990s, and that earworm of a theme song, which to its demographic is an enduring signifier of domesticity and California-style self-satisfaction. In 2018 the HGTV network purchased the Dilling Street house in order to perform *A Very Brady Renovation*, as it branded the show devoted to documenting the work. The designers took the existing single-story house and squeezed in an actual second floor in order to have the reno match the original production designers' fiction of two stories connected by a twelve-step staircase (which HGTV had to cut down to eleven in order to fit). Though it's doubtful the execs had ever read French philosopher Jean Baudrillard, his notion that Los Angeles exemplifies the triumph of the simulation over the "real" seems particularly appropriate. So, too, is it somehow fitting that HGTV was founded in 1994, the same year China was granted provisional favored-nation status by the United States, thereby opening the flood of new goods that were funneled through LA's ports and came to land in the great rooms that are the ultimate signifier of every HGTV renovation.

The new goods were layered on top of old ones, and no matter how big the spaces, sometimes even they couldn't contain the super-abundance. For those leery of parting with their surplus stuff, Southern California birthed yet another solution: the storage locker. Glendale-based Public Storage is the largest self-storage company in the business, providing the opportunity to take the excess that overwhelms a house or apartment and to rent a space to store it for as long as the owner is willing or able to pay the monthly fee. It is a business that flourishes in good times, when people accumulate; and also in bad times, when they downsize but are loath to part with their possessions.

Though it might seem that the end point for the surfeit of goods churning through the ports would be the dumpster or the storage unit, following the law of the conservation of matter, there are further ways for these goods to flow back into the economy. In California, if a renter doesn't pay on a storage unit for a period of three months, the facility is legally entitled to put the contents of the unit up for public auction. In the depths of the twenty-first century's Great Recession, A&E remade these manifestations of loss into entertainment. *Storage Wars* (2010– , including various spin-offs) features professional resellers roving through some of Southern California's bleakest regions, bidding against one another for the contents of lockers filled with goods unknown to them, in the hope of benefiting from the misfortunes of others. The squabbling dealers, who have become celebrities in their own right, are the televisual fulfillment of the promise and the pitilessness of stuff.

There's no aesthetic to the storage space as it empties, just a winnowing of sheer junk from the possibly salable. "Knolling," on the other hand, is about the exquisite visual fulfillment that stuff can offer when it's arranged according to a strict algorithm. In 1987 Andrew Kromelow, an art student working as a janitor in the Santa Monica office of architect Frank Gehry, took the tools, pieces of equipment, and myriad bits strewn around the office and organized them at ninety-degree angles. The resulting tableaux engendered a surprisingly deep level of satisfaction among Gehry and his staff. Another young worker in the office, Tom Sachs, began taking pictures of these geometric arrangements from above and continued to do so after establishing a major career in the arts. His genre of flat-lay photography, called "knolling," became a social-media phenomenon, with knollers laying out all manner of stuff following rules Sachs codified and posted in 2009:

1. Scan your environment for materials, tools, books, music, etc. which are not in use.
2. Put away everything not in use. If you aren't sure, leave it out.
3. Group all "like" objects.
4. Align or square all objects to either the surface they rest on, or the studio itself.

Knolling fetishizes order, but when the sheer proliferation of stuff overwhelms, the rich can seek out professional assistance.

Pioneering reality television star Paris Hilton had a friend who helped the hotel heiress deal with her shopping addiction by rearranging closets in her Hollywood Hills mansion. This budding entrepreneur, a natural adept at corralling the frenzy of plenty, described her business model thusly in 2006: "I go to my clients' homes and I help them clean out their closets.... We take whatever they don't want and I sell it for them on eBay." She was, of course, the young Kim Kardashian, whose own closet, once she became more famous, made Paris Hilton look like Marie Kondo, the Japanese organizational expert and messiah of minimalism, whose cri de coeur a decade later to toss or give away all possessions that don't "spark joy" was powerfully emblematic of the proverbial swing of the pendulum, sparking an uptick in donations to thrift stores nationwide (overwhelming them with mountains of unwanted and unsellable stuff). As Los Angeles is the unsheltered homeless capital of the United States, this redistribution of stuff would appear to be a welcome development, though the Los Angeles City Council has enforced the "Kon-Mari" method on the unsheltered homeless by restricting them from keeping more than sixty gallons of stuff with them on the street at any one time. That's the equivalent of a large garbage can, and during sweeps, sanitation workers cart off the excess, backed up by police wielding Tasers.

Battles over stuff are waged constantly, but never so much as on the day after Thanksgiving—Black Friday, the biggest shopping day of the year and the kickoff for the all-important Christmas season. On that day in 2011, a woman walked into an LA County Walmart with a can of pepper spray, which she used on twenty other shoppers, including children. This committed if overzealous citizen of our consumer's republic was accused of wielding the spray to clear a path to the stuff she wanted. As a captain in the LA Fire Department put it succinctly: "She was competitive shopping."

If stuff itself is a lure for vice, the ports as locales—with their transient populations, imports of dubious provenance, and, until the containerization of trade, burly dockworkers wielding baling hooks—redouble the possibilities for violence. Unlike coastal Florida, Southern California was never a haven for pirates, but what it did have were sanctioned gambling ships, which from 1927 to 1939 bobbed off the shores of Long Beach, San Pedro, and Santa Monica, the floating scenes of myriad crimes.

The ships were fully outfitted as casinos, complete with craps, blackjack, sports betting, and forgotten games of chance like faro, a French card game once as popular as poker, and chuck-a-luck, played with three dice tumbling in a cage. Southern Californians would queue up to take a short water-taxi ride to cross a boundary line they didn't really understand, delivering themselves into the hands of gangsters for an evening of entertainment and thrills. The quasi-legality was all part of the fun, as it was decades later in the period before the full legalization of marijuana in California. For twenty years before that, cannabis was available for "medicinal" needs, and there was a certain thrill in the acquisition of a "medical marijuana" card in order to enter "dispensaries" that couldn't open bank accounts (because financial institutions operate under federal law), meaning that every storefront had a hulking and well-armed guard, with the occasional gun battle breaking out just to keep the weed-buying public on its toes. But back in the 1930s, weed was still reefer and assumed to cause madness, while gambling was a more accepted form of adult entertainment, even if the law thought otherwise.

No one was as important to Southern California's water-bound, semilicit gambling trade as Tony "the Admiral" Cornero, the owner and operator of the most important of the floating casinos. A Catholic immigrant from the hardscrabble north of Italy, Cornero had by his early twenties determined that the nativist Protestant midwesterners who'd voted for Prohibition had done him a great favor. It wasn't that hard to figure out that a ship loaded with legal whiskey in Canada was far more valuable the moment it passed into U.S. waters and became contraband. To that end, Cornero established "friendly," if illegal, ports of call from San Francisco down the coast to Southern California, which is not to say Cornero escaped Prohibition unscathed, serving eighteen months at McNeil Island prison, when all he was trying to do, he maintained with altruistic pride, was "to keep 120 million Americans from poisoning themselves" with homemade moonshine.

Experience with an illegal trade that many didn't see as much of a problem and seafaring expertise built over years of rum-running were the perfect prerequisites for Cornero's next hustle after repeal: gambling, just far enough past the three-mile offshore limit to avoid the reach of local, state, and federal authorities. In 1938, Cornero refurbished a retired lumber hauler called *The Star of Scotland*, installing 150 slot machines, a bingo parlor for four hundred, a sportsbetting hall, and a stupendous table-gaming floor. After rechristening her the *Rex*, Cornero moored the boat 3.1 miles off the coast, in "international waters," and opened for business.

The *Rex* was the perfect spot for the high-rolling celebrities who had seen their favorite underground gambling den, the Clover Club on Sunset, closed for a time by LA's reform-minded mayor, Fletcher Bowron, a few months earlier. But the big money was in bringing in regular customers, whom Cornero's employees came to refer to as "squirrels." America never seems to find a median between prohibition and promotion, and so it was for the new enterprise. Two-mile-high letters spelling out "REX" appeared as skywriting above Santa Monica, while newspaper ads described an evening on the *Rex* as "surpass[ing] all the thrills of the Riviera, Monte Carlo, Biarritz and Cannes." Cornero passed out thousands of cards advertising the food ("Cuisine by Henri"), the music ("DANCE to the Rhythm of the REX MARINERS"), and those talismanic three words for insomniacs: "WE NEVER CLOSE." The key element? Continuous water-taxi service to and from the ship for only twenty-five cents a ride. In a country still mired in the Depression, the prospect of an inexpensive evening at sea with music and dancing appealed, so much so that waiters came up with yet another name for those "squirrels" who didn't gamble and barely tipped. They were "seagulls," because "all they ever do is squawk, shit, and fly."

Unlike Prohibition and the war on weed, the laws against gambling—at least at sea—were never lifted. Which meant that Cornero and the other gangsters/gamblers/soldiers of fortune plying their trade continued to come up against two resolute enemies: LA's district attorney, Buron Fitts, and the state's attorney general, Earl Warren. When it came to guts and notoriety, Fitts was every bit Cornero's equal. He started his career as a protégé of the infamous DA Asa Keyes, but after his boss was caught up in the Julian Pete oil stock fraud, Fitts prosecuted his mentor and sent him to jail. Fitts darted in and out of trouble with land deals, a prostitution ring known as the Love Mart, and credible accusations of covering up Hollywood's misdeeds. Yet through corrupt mayoralties and the reform era that followed, he hung in as DA, winning a string of high-profile cases and never shying away from publicity. He once sent an assistant district attorney to Union Station to plant a kiss on film star Mae West, letting her and the assembled press know, "This is from Buron." West—no slouch when it came to putting men in their places and more than a little sympathetic to "racket boy Tony Cornero" (as she called him) in his public battles with Fitts—responded with the immortal quip, "Is that a gun in your pocket, or are you just happy to see me?"

Fitts was a tough, if deeply flawed, foe, but Earl Warren was the very embodiment of the law's righteousness. For Warren, who would go on to become governor of California, then chief justice of the U.S. Supreme Court, the gambling boats were "a great nuisance" that instantiated an existential battle: Can the pursuit of profit and pleasure ever justifiably supersede the law? Warren's position was that states should act regardless of whether jurisdiction was fully established. He and Fitts went at the gamblers from every angle they could think of: shutting down the water taxis, harassing the employees on land before and after their work on board, even raiding the *Rex* on the water. The first time out, the gamblers had been warned and were ready with water cannons. Warren's men backed off, concerned about starting a firefight that might jeopardize the safety of patrons. The next time, the forces of the law managed to board, and in short order confiscated the gambling equipment and hauled Cornero's "associates" to jail. The most famous raid of all on the gambling ships never actually happened. It takes place at the close of Raymond Chandler's *Farewell, My Lovely* (1940), when the private detective Philip Marlowe hires an ex-cop turned boatman to get him out to a fictionalized version of the *Rex*, the knight-errant journeying through air "as cold as the ashes of love" to mete out destiny's fatal arrows in one final showdown.

But back to Cornero. His third act (maybe his fourth, having somehow survived an assassination attempt in 1948, when two Mexican hit men shot him in the stomach) was to ditch his jaunty yachting cap and go inland to Nevada, where he established the Stardust, one of the first luxury casinos on the Vegas Strip. This turned out to be his final act, because after borrowing money from famed mob banker Meyer Lansky (cofounder with Bugsy Siegel of Murder, Inc., and model for *The Godfather*'s Hyman Roth), Cornero collapsed at the Desert Inn's craps tables. Whether he was poisoned remains in dispute. What is indisputable is that postmortem he was repatriated to Southern California's Inglewood Park Cemetery, just high enough on a hill to catch a glimpse of the waters of the bay. In the twenty-first century, Inglewood Park Cemetery overlooks a sprawling sports entertainment complex housing not one but two NFL teams, the Rams and the Chargers, the ghost of Tony Cornero smiling down on them as professional sports embraces gambling in order to reap yet more profits.

Terminal Island sounds like it would be a better resting place for a dead gambler than Inglewood. But the spit of land between the cities of Long Beach and Los Angeles is not a memento mori. Its name pays homage to the Los Angeles Terminal Railroad Company, which built a line there a century ago to move goods from the ports to downtown. Terminal Island encapsulates every aspect of alchemical Los Angeles: earth, fire, air, and water. It is a particularly visible example of the transformation of earth into real estate because, as noted earlier, when there wasn't enough earth for Pier 400, they just made more. As for fire, the ports at and around Terminal Island first became dominant because of oil shipments from the surrounding fields, including Long Beach's famous Signal Hill, which in the 1920s was the site of one of the richest oil strikes in the world. In terms of air, one of the most notorious planes in aviation history took off from Terminal Island. And as for water, well, Terminal Island sits in the middle of the busiest port in the hemisphere.

At the start of the twentieth century, no one cared more about Terminal Island than the residents of Fish Harbor. Upward of three thousand Japanese immigrants (issei) lived in what they called Furusato, roughly translated as "home, sweet home." Their children (nisei) spoke a unique dialect, an amalgam of Japanese and English, and with their parents pioneered albacore fishing and abalone harvesting, leading the way in establishing San Pedro's fishing industry. The coming of the era of air was devastating for Furusato, because within a few months of the bombing of Pearl Harbor and the subsequent transformation of Southern California into an aeronautics powerhouse, Furusato's entire population was interned.

As the era of fire transitioned to air, so, too, did Terminal Island. During World War II, it was remade for military use, which meant building up runways and facilities for the naval air force. But the most famous flight didn't use Terminal Island's runways—it was a water takeoff by the largest plane constructed to date. Of all of the idiosyncrasies that industrialist turned aviator turned movie mogul turned recluse Howard Hughes unleashed on the world, the H-4 Hercules may have been his most idiosyncratic. The bra he engineered for Jane Russell's cleavage in *The Outlaw* (1943) and the mania that had him grow out his hair and nails and watch the 1968 spy thriller *Ice Station Zebra* over and over again may be better known, but the Hercules was a uniquely Hughesian folly. His original intent was to construct a flying boat to replace the transport ships vulnerable to submarine attack. But the only flyable version of the plane was delivered after the war—not to mention millions over budget—and because of metal rationing, Hughes chose the unorthodox strategy of making it out of wood. Livid about the whole fiasco, Congress subpoenaed Hughes to find out how and why the United States had funded this absurdity of an airplane, bigger than a football field.

The Hercules is better known today as the Spruce Goose (even though it was made primarily of cedar). Constructed in the Hughes facility just south of Venice, it was trucked down to Terminal Island, where the plutocratic airman took the throttle for its maiden—and only—flight, around the bay. For decades, the Spruce Goose was warehoused at Pier E, and then in the 1980s it was turned into an unlikely tourist attraction in Long Beach, where it was housed in the world's largest, custom-built geodesic dome. After visitors dwindled, the plane ended up in an aviation museum in Oregon, and a cruise line now leases the dome as a passenger terminal.

One person preternaturally tuned in to Hughes's wavelength was his former employee and fellow pilot George Van Tassel. Van Tassel needed help building an all-wooden construction of his own in Landers, a speck in the desert near Joshua Tree. In 1954, in a prime spot near a small airfield, Van Tassel began work on an acoustically tuned dome, and according to him, Hughes offered material and engineering support to create the "Integratron," designed to extend human life spans by harnessing anti-gravitational forces to bend time. As one might expect from a man whose first book was entitled *I Rode a Flying Saucer* (1952), it was an alien being who gave Van Tassel the plans, via thought transference, naturally. According to Landers lore, Hughes would fly out to the site occasionally, less for the alien visitations than because he loved the pie that Van Tassel's wife, Eva, served in their Integratron-adjacent café.

Landers is little more than one hundred miles east of the coast, so Hughes could have made a quick trip of it from Terminal Island, which one cannot say of those semipermanently housed by the federal government in one of its signature transformations of the ports. In 1938 Washington constructed what is now known as the Federal Correctional Institution, Terminal Island, a low-security prison that houses one thousand inmates. Given the weather and the view, the place picked up a reputation as a cushy Club Fed, and a major corruption scandal in the mid-1980s did nothing to disabuse the public of that notion. But make no mistake about it: FCI Terminal Island is a prison, and it has held some pretty seriously bad men, including Al Capone and LA's two most infamous criminals, gangster Mickey Cohen and cult leader Charles Manson. FCI Terminal Island has also been home to more benign figures, such as *Hustler* publisher Larry Flynt, automaker John DeLorean, and the Grateful Dead's sound engineer, Owsley Stanley, who was in for being one of the biggest producers of LSD in the Bay Area. Stanley was an all-around creative type. Not only an outstanding amateur chemist, Stanley created the band's maximalist public-address system and even designed its dancing bear logo. That the Grateful Dead played a free concert in 1971 at the prison holding their once and future sound guy was, however, not the weirdest juxtaposition during that stoned and mellow decade on Terminal Island.

Speaking of head-spinning, the period that Harvard psychologist turned apostle of LSD Timothy Leary and FBI agent turned

Watergate burglar G. Gordon Liddy spent in the stir together quali-
fies. As a prosecutor in upstate New York in the early sixties, nascent fascist Liddy arrested budding guru Leary for leading a band
of psychonauts as they dropped then-legal LSD, smoked illegal
marijuana and hashish, participated in encounter sessions, and engaged in enough "free love" to raise the hackles of any clean-cut DA
in America. After this campaign of harassment, Leary moved to
California and Liddy headed to Washington. Just over a decade
later, they wound up in Terminal Island together, Leary serving
time for a bewildering series of drug crimes and prison escapes and
Liddy, henchman for Richard M. Nixon (the president who once
called Leary "the most dangerous man in America"), paying the
price for his role as a key, if tragicomic, figure in the Watergate
complex break-in that brought down the president he served.

Another ten years hence, Liddy and Leary teamed up for a tour
of college campuses, a conservative/liberal dog and pony show that
presaged the twenty-first century's penchant for entertainment mas-
querading as politics. They became the highest-paid performers on
that circuit, and their stop in LA was turned into a weird little film
called *Return Engagement* (1983) that is as much a document about
early-eighties demicelebrity (with a cameo by then–bit part actor
Arnold Schwarzenegger) as an analysis of the duo's respective phi-
losophies, such as they were. The scene of the erstwhile "opponents"
sitting with their wives on a balcony at the Chateau Marmont is
utterly indistinguishable from a home video of two middle-aged
couples on vacation, brunching in the sun.

Even on the balcony of a Sunset Strip luxury hotel, however,
what radiates off Liddy and Leary is their mutual desperation to be
the center of attention. Onstage, Leary would remind his audiences

that he had spent more time in the U.S. armed forces than Liddy but less time in prison, the one conscious nod toward their joint stint on Terminal Island. Their legacies live on in odd ways. Liddy, whose half-baked, post-prison, Nietzschean memoir, *Will*, was an eighties bestseller, slithered into right-wing talk radio early, his tough-guy persona still a staple on the AM band and Fox News. Leary's mantra, "Tune in, turn on, drop out," morphed into a sixties mnemonic, and the former Harvard professor's musings on space migration and life extension were featured in *Neurocomics* (1979), a one-off cowritten by the actor Leonardo DiCaprio's father that went nowhere. Liddy, on the other hand, was immortalized in the greatest comic book of the last fifty years, Alan Moore and Dave Gibbons's *Watchmen*, as the amoral "Comedian," a murderous government operative in black leather. Immortality is a funny thing, but Liddy, and even Leary, would have agreed that "once you realize what a joke everything is, being the Comedian is the only thing that makes sense."

There's no making sense of the twenty-first century's addiction to stuff. We are in a prison of our own making, the walls constructed from goods produced anywhere and shipped everywhere. The wonders of a system that can offer such bounty at low cost has to be balanced against the ecological nightmare of an economy built around throwaway consumerism and the transformation of the sea itself into the churning storage locker for the world. Reportage about LA's ports has to contend with "biggests," "bests," "firsts," and "fastests," but no matter how powerful a force, the ports, their largest stakeholders, their workers, and even the surrounding communities cannot do much more than clean up their act, reducing pollution and congestion, which in turn would only accelerate the entire system.

Conflicts about materialism and sustainability are going to have to play out globally at the personal, ethical, social, and political levels. It's far easier to imagine the breakdown of the system as it now exists—that billion-dollar-a-day loss—than to reimagine what manufacturing, trade, and consumption could be in a better world. But that reimagining will need to happen, and a time to ponder it might well be in the early evening, sitting on the basketball court in Angels Gate as the stars emerge to shine over the harbor below.

11 DAYS OF THE DEAD

UNTITLED #41 (FREEWAYS) I 1995 I PLATINUM PRINT I 2 ¼ X 6 ¾ INCHES (5.7 X 17.1 CM)

Frozen Bodies, Real Martyrs, Fake Shemps, and the Quest for Immortality in the City of Angels

here is a frozen creature in Southern California that *will not die*, an Indomitable Snowman straining against his glacial cocoon to claim his rightful place among the superheroes, villains, and shape-shifting chimeras cranked out by entertainment conglomerates from Anaheim to Burbank. This creature is their spiritual godfather, (Walter Elias) Disney on Ice. His body is, of course, not cryogenically preserved beneath Disneyland's *Pirates of the Caribbean*, as urban legend would have it, and was in point of fact cremated and then interred at Forest Lawn cemetery. But no matter. Disney's frozen head is tailor-made for metaphor. Uncle Walt was an animator, bringing to life the insentient and making delightful the impossible. With a wave of his hand, brooms danced and mice sang. But, as noted in chapter 3, playing with mortality is the secret sauce ladled

Who will fight the bear? No one? Then the bear has won.

—Bas Jan Ader

Expect me . . . like you expect Jesus to come back
Expect me . . . I'm coming.

—Tupac Shakur

over his corporate oeuvre. Bambi's mother, Dumbo's father, both of Cinderella's parents, deer, elephant, and human—all dead. Yet mortality's sting isn't as fatal in Disney's realm as it is in our own. Snow White eats a poisoned apple and undergoes a sleeping death, only to be reanimated by "love's first kiss." Disney understood Hollywood's maxim that if something works once, it will work again. Thus *Sleeping Beauty*, where yet another young girl succumbs to the machinations of yet another evil older woman, falls into a state closer to a coma than to sleep, only to be awakened by another one of those kisses. Eros and thanatos were never so colorful, nor so well scored.

Disney's obsessions mirrored those of the region. Southern California was the first place on earth where human bodies were frozen with the specific intention of later being thawed out and then—what?

Cured? Saved? Reanimated? In 1966 the first cryonaut, retired psychologist Dr. James Bedford of Glendale, California, transitioned into the icy unknown. The freezing process was overseen by the president of the Cryonics Society of California, Robert Nelson, an LA-based television repairman later reviled for the "Chatsworth Disaster," concatenating comic atrocities that included the cramming of two, three, or even four bodies into capsules meant for one and the abdication of the moral and financial responsibility to maintain the liquid nitrogen at minus 196 degrees Celsius. Nelson's charges putrefied, as meat—even of the human kind—will do without proper refrigeration. The *Valley News* reported that "the stench near the crypt is disarming, strips away all defenses, spins the stomach into a thousand dizzying somersaults."

Should we be surprised that the man behind this debacle in the San Fernando Valley mortuary turned out to be the creator of the myth of Disney on Ice? In the *Los Angeles Times* Nelson claimed— without offering any corroborating evidence—that in the short interval between Bedford's freezing and Disney's death a few months later, the master's personal secretary had contacted him to inquire about cryonics. "If things had worked out differently," went Nelson's dubious claim, "Walt Disney could have been the first man frozen." There is a poetic logic to rumors of cryogenesis swirling around an animator obsessed with the future. As we saw in chapter 6, Disney worked with rocket scientists to promote space travel, featured a "Tomorrowland" in each of his parks, and oversaw plans for EPCOT, the Experimental Prototype Community of Tomorrow, a utopian city he envisioned as the jewel of Florida's Disney World. Why shouldn't an imagination this capacious have embraced technology to escape death?

So many denizens of the Disney empire can be counted among the undead. Take Mickey Mouse. Copyright on this signature rodent has been extended twice, first in 1976 and again in 1998, with the magnificently named Sonny Bono Copyright Term Extension Act. While Disney's corporate lawyers have done a great job of suing preschools and day-care facilities for putting up unauthorized Donald Duck murals, they are occasionally slapped down for overreach. And when it comes to cultural sensitivity to appropriation, it turns out that entertainment conglomerates could stand to be a bit more woke, especially when dealing with those who have gone to their eternal rest.

In 2013, as a then-untitled Pixar film went into production, Disney set to work pre-protecting the corporation's intellectual property. The animators were tackling a new subject, Mexican folklore, and so on May 1 the corporation's lawyers filed an application with the U.S. Patent and Trademark Office to trademark "Día de los Muertos," as well as "Day of the Dead." There are places in the United States where this lawyerly hubris would not have had much impact, but Southern California wasn't one of them. It's not just the Mexican and Mexican American populations in the region; it's the fact that even non-Latinx residents understood that what the House of Mouse was attempting fell somewhere between trademarking a religious sacrament and invading the Yucatán Peninsula.

Día de los Muertos, a holiday consecrated to venerating the dead, dates back to the pre-contact period. Its best-known North American variant developed in Mexico, melding Indigenous and Catholic idioms. Traditions include decorating cemeteries and creating *ofrendas*, or altars, commemorating family and friends who have passed on. The *ofrendas* can be as simple or ornate as their builders wish, often lit with candles, covered in the Aztec marigolds known as *cempasúchil*, and embellished with skulls made of sugar. An *ofrenda* usually has two or more levels. At the bottom are the "down-to-earth" elements, such as small chairs and woven mats, so the souls of the departed can rest. The middle level holds candles, food, and especially drink, tequila or mescal in particular. The top displays photos or other keepsakes of loved ones, to keep them in memory. Families in the United States practiced Día de los Muertos at home until the seventies, when LA pioneered public celebrations that have expanded across the country, transforming the holiday into a cross-cultural, ecumenical celebration. In the new millennium, Día de los Muertos—packaged and merchandized as Day of the Dead—has become, like Halloween, another opportunity to stoke the desire for carnival, which translates into spending money, this time not on "sexy nurse" or Iron Man costumes but on those evoking the dapper skeletons La Catrina and El Catrín.

Given the Día/Day's new ubiquity, the audacity of Disney's legal team came off as particularly offensive. Nor, of course, would it be the first time the powerful attempted to strip the people of ownership of something no one had previously assumed could be owned. Cartoonist Lalo Alcaraz, for one, was furious. He created a poster for an imaginary film titled *Muerto Mouse*, which starred a Godzilla-sized, skeletal Mickey rampaging through the city's streets, with the tagline "It's coming to trademark your *cultura*!" Twitter mobs and the churning online outrage machine sprang into action, generating petitions signed by more than twenty thousand people and garnering mainstream media attention. As CNN observed in its coverage, Disney might do well to note that, its claim to ownership aside, the Día/Day had been listed, as far back as 2003, among UNESCO's "Masterpieces of the Oral and Intangible Heritage of Humanity."

But Disney didn't become the most influential entertainment conglomerate in the world without learning something about "community outreach" and crisis management. Its PR department set to work calming the Twitterverse, reining in the lawyers, and transforming the embarrassment into a triumph of multicultural marketing. One of its masterstrokes was to invite into its realm stakeholders and critics, including Alcaraz, as "cultural advisers." When "The Untitled Pixar Movie About Día de los Muertos" was released as *Coco* in 2017, the outrage had dissipated and the lawyers' cold hearts, one presumes, were warmed by the film's Academy Award for Best Animated Feature and the almost $1 billion in revenue generated worldwide.

Another of these cultural advisers was the master *altarista* Ofelia Esparza. A lifelong resident of East LA, Esparza learned the art of constructing an altar from the women in her family, a tradition she passed on to her own daughter, the artist Rosanna Esparza Ahrens. In 2018 they created the *El Pueblo de Nuestra Señora la Reina de Los Ángeles* altar, which is on permanent display at the LA County Museum of Natural History. The *El Pueblo* altar is more than a dozen feet wide and features almost three hundred images and objects representing the city, ranging from Simon Rodia's Watts Towers to Jesse Valadez's famed Gypsy Rose lowrider to a small Mickey Mouse Disneyland souvenir, festooned with sugar skulls and skeletons.

Just to the right of Mickey is an image of a stamp that the U.S. Postal Service issued on April 22, 2008. The face on the stamp may not register instantly, but the name, "Rubén Salazar," and the legend, "during Chicano protest rally in East Los Angeles," might take some people back. During the sixties and seventies, Salazar was the most important Latino journalist in the United States and for many their first introduction to what became known as El Movimiento, or the Chicano civil rights movement. Without the memory of Rubén Salazar, the Day of the Dead as we know it—not to mention Disney's *Coco*—might not exist.

Salazar was the first Mexican American to hold a full-time position at the *LA Times* as a reporter, and while he was always concerned with border issues and immigration, throughout the fifties and early sixties he maintained fairly centrist views. But in the later part of the decade, Salazar held two important positions, as a columnist for the *Times*, and news director for KMEX, the first Spanish-language television station in Southern California. Salazar was there as the political consciousness of Mexican immigrants and Mexican Americans crystallized under the pressure of endemic racism, law-enforcement harassment, chronically underfunded schools, and the Vietnam War's toll on the community's youth, who suffered terrible casualties during the United States' Southeast Asian incursions.

African Americans' struggle for civil rights was a paradigm for many other battles: women's liberation, the battle for gay rights, the American Indian Movement for Indigenous peoples, and, throughout the Southwest, a movement of and for Mexican immigrants and Mexican Americans that identified itself with the idea of *chicanismo*. The term "Chicano" was originally a derogatory word for people who, while living in the United States and originally from Mexico, were not "fully of" either country. However, in the sixties, activists seized upon the term. With his dual affiliation, Salazar was able to introduce Chicano activism to his Anglo-dominant readership at the *Times*, while giving those same activists television time on KMEX, in Spanish no less, to speak directly to their community, not all of whom were ready to embrace Chicano as a label or a politics.

On February 6, 1970, Salazar wrote a now-famous *Times* column, "Who Is a Chicano? And What Is It the Chicanos Want?" In a region "where the country's largest single concentration of Spanish-speaking live," Chicanos are the people who "have no one of their own on the City Council." As for what they want, Salazar was direct: "They want to effect change. Now." For LA's police, notorious for intelligence operations aimed at "subversives," and for LA's county sheriffs, responsible for patrolling (and, in those days, "controlling") the unincorporated Mexican-immigrant and Mexican American part of the county known as East LA, Salazar was the enemy—less a reporter than a mouthpiece for the young demonstrators whom they saw as insurrectionaries, if not full-blown communists or anarchists. Law-and-order fetishists saw Salazar as less of a neutral observer than the head of a fifth column supported by the Westside's feckless, self-loathing left-wingers, whom LAPD chief Ed Davis sneeringly referred to as "swimming-pool communists" rather than the more commonly disparaging "limousine liberals."

The 1968 Chicano high school walkouts were a watershed. Kids demonstrating against the separate and entirely unequal treatment they received in East LA schools suffered brutally at the hands of the sheriff's deputies. Television, including Salazar's KMEX, covered the way they were roughed up for pointing out that at high schools like Roosevelt and Garfield there was only one college counselor per four thousand students, though there were more than enough military recruiters to hit up any Latino who wanted out of the neighborhood, even if by way of Vietnam or Cambodia.

The student walkouts were followed by ever-larger demonstrations in LA and around the country, the largest on August 29, 1970, in East LA. Organized by the National Chicano Moratorium Committee, the antiwar protest drew more than twenty thousand people, who marched down Whittier Boulevard to the green knolls of Laguna Park. What started out peacefully quickly escalated into what can only be called a police riot, with sheriff's deputies sweeping through the crowds, shields up and batons bashing. The most controversial incident was in a dark little bar called the Silver Dollar, at the corner of Whittier and La Verne. The sheriffs stormed the place after receiving an anonymous tip that something was going down inside. Despite the fact that a photographer for the Chicano Movement's paper, *La Raza*—surprised by the near-instant massing of law enforcement around this otherwise quiet space—was there shooting pictures of the action, what happened next is still one of the most debated tragedies in Los Angeles history. What is undisputed is that Deputy Thomas Wilson fired a tear-gas canister designed to pierce walls through the bar's open door, and that hours later authorities announced they had discovered Rubén Salazar dead on the Silver Dollar's floor.

Salazar had stepped inside for a beer in part because he was concerned that he was being followed. One didn't have to be much of a conspiracist to see this as the intentional murder of a journalist. As a foreign correspondent for the *Times*, Salazar had survived a stint in war-torn Saigon and served as chief of bureau in Mexico City during its worst social unrest since the revolution, yet he ended up lying in a pool of blood on Whittier Boulevard. There were contradictory reports from the very start, some claiming a bullet to the head, later ones coalescing around the tear-gas canister delivering the lethal blow. There was a coroner's inquest into his death, and also a secret federal grand jury investigation, but neither identified enough concrete evidence to bring anyone to trial. Whether accidental casualty or victim of a targeted assassination, Salazar became a martyr to the Chicano cause. His body was displayed at Bagües & Sons Mortuary in Boyle Heights, and they handled the viewing as if it were a state funeral.

His memory still resonates. Laguna Park is now Rubén F. Salazar Park. He is featured in murals everywhere from *The Wall That Speaks, Sings and Shouts* in LA to Lincoln Park in El Paso, Texas. Chicano music giant Lalo Guerrero closed his corrido "La Tragedia Del 29 De Agosto" with "*Que no haya muerto en vano Rubén Salazar*," a plea that the martyr should not have died in vain. In Frank Romero's wall-sized painting *Death of Rubén Salazar* (1986), a stylized phalanx of deputies shoot projectiles-cum-fireworks over the roof of the Silver Dollar, just next door to a movie theater whose marquee reads "La Muerte de Rubén Salazar."

Romero was a member of Los Four, who were among the first Chicanx artists to show at the LA County Museum of Art. He was also associated with Self Help Graphics & Art (SHG), an Eastside institution founded in the early seventies by the Franciscan nun Karen Boccalero. It was there that the most enduring yet least recognized tribute to the martyred journalist began. Two years after Salazar's death, and as the white-hot moment of the Chicano movement cooled, SHG decided to do something public that drew upon their own *cultura* but that would make an impact on the city and beyond. They invited *altaristas* to build *ofrendas* and folks in the neighborhood to parade in costume through the streets, thereby staging the first modern, public iteration of Day of the Dead in the United States—all to commemorate Rubén Salazar.

If *Coco*'s millions of viewers don't realize that they are participating, however tangentially, in a celebration of a martyr who spoke truth to power, don't blame Hunter S. Thompson. Thompson was the living embodiment of Salazar's realization late in his career that "neutral" reporting covered up as much as it revealed, and his growing feeling that "newsroom objectivity may result in untruth." Objectivity was never one of Thompson's faults, and when he covered Salazar's death for *Rolling Stone* in the April 21, 1971, issue, his long-form journalistic attack bore the title "Strange Rumblings in Aztlan." A series of all-cap subheads demonstrated just where Thompson was going to take his readers:

THE... MURDER... AND RESURRECTION OF RUBEN SALAZAR BY THE LOS ANGELES COUNTY SHERIFF'S DEPARTMENT . . . SAVAGE POLARIZATION & THE MAKING OF A MARTYR... BAD NEWS FOR THE MEXICAN-AMERICAN . . . WORSE NEWS FOR THE PIG... AND NOW THE NEW CHICANO... etc.

How a Kentucky-born good ol' boy like Hunter S. Thompson ended up writing one of the defining pieces of New Journalism about the making of a Chicano martyr hinges on another unlikely connection—to the writer, lawyer, fabulist, and all-around hell-raiser Oscar "Zeta" Acosta, Thompson's avowed "brother" and "partner in crime." Like Salazar, Acosta had roots in Mexico by way of El Paso, but unlike Salazar, who was born into the bourgeoisie, Acosta was a defiant son of the working class. Acosta lived a life that packed in at least twice as much action as the thirty-nine years he was allotted would seem to have allowed. He was a high-school rebel, a member of the air force band, a Baptist missionary to Indigenous peoples, a public defender in Oakland, a cook in Aspen, El Movimiento's most visible attorney, the author of two vital works of Chicanx literature, *The Autobiography of a Brown Buffalo* (1972) and *Revolt of the Cockroach People* (1973), and a famous literary character in his own right.

If readers of Thompson's most celebrated book, *Fear and Loathing in Las Vegas* (1971), are having trouble identifying Acosta, his prodigious consumption of drugs, alcohol, and adrenaline might provide a clue, even if, as per Thompson, he's characterized as having Samoan rather than Mexican ancestry. Acosta is the model for the fearsome Dr. Gonzo, Thompson's comrade in the "extremely dangerous." The book opens with the two of them screaming toward Las Vegas to cover a motorcycle race in the desert, the trunk of their rented red Chevy convertible filled with "two bags of grass, seventy-five pellets of mescaline, five sheets of high-powered blotter acid, a salt shaker full of cocaine, and a whole galaxy of multicolored uppers, downers, screamers, laughers... and also a quart of tequila, a quart of rum, a case of Budweiser, a pint of raw ether and two dozen amyls." And that's only the fourth paragraph.

"Dr. Gonzo" was the name Thompson chose for his friend. "Zeta," on the other hand, Acosta chose for himself. Zeta was a nom de guerre cobbled from the detritus of pop culture: Ismael Rodríguez's 1959 epic film *La Cucaracha*, featuring the fictional General Zeta, who combined elements of two heroes of the Mexican Revolution, Emiliano Zapata Salazar and Francisco "Pancho" Villa; the Greek-French filmmaker Costa-Gavras's 1969 political thriller *Z*; and the masked hero Zorro, a pulp staple of hundreds of stories, films, radio serials, comic books, and TV shows. Attired in what he called his "name mask," Zeta created a role for himself in real life as a defender of the oppressed and a champion of his people. Zeta's social conscience was forever battling with demons, including racial insecurity; externalized misogyny (he once went on a tear about meeting the Manson Family girls in court and how much he wanted to sleep with them); a bad case of fame whoredom (he carried a briefcase emblazoned with huge letters spelling out "ZETA" and, after posing for her just once, claimed the well-known Annie Leibovitz as "my official photographer"); and an ever-expanding appetite for stimulants, depressants, and hallucinogens of every kind (the Chevy's pharmacopia may have been a Thompsonian exaggeration but, from other reports, not that far off given Zeta's predilections). His accomplishments in the courtroom included defending (in numerical order): the "Biltmore 6," arrested for starting a fire during Governor Ronald Reagan's visit to downtown LA's Biltmore Hotel; the "Eastside 13," who had planned the student walkout; and the "St. Basil 21," who protested the Catholic Church's concentration on building sanctuaries rather than caring for the poor. His most public act was running for the office of LA County sheriff against incumbent Peter J. Pitchess, a law-enforcement legend. Zeta campaigned on a radical, even anarchist, police-abolitionist platform. Law-enforcement officers, he wrote in *The Revolt of the Cockroach People*, are "the violent arm of the rich, and I would get rid of them.... Do Your Own Thing! *Justicia y Libertad*!" As Rubén Salazar noted in the *LA Times*, it wasn't surprising that Zeta lost by over a million votes; what was amazing was that he garnered more than one hundred thousand.

Yet for all these accomplishments, Acosta aka Zeta is best known as a sidekick, and to a *gabacho* like Thompson no less (the latter being Zeta's preferred term, rather than "Anglo" or "gringo"). In "The Banshee Screams for Buffalo Meat," his conflicted eulogy for Zeta, Thompson goes on the defensive. As to why he would take the activist and literary Zeta and disguise him behind yet another name mask, Dr. Gonzo, Thompson claimed the "only reason for describing him in the book as a 300-pound Samoan instead of a 250-pound Chicano lawyer was to protect him from the wrath of the L.A. cops and the whole California legal establishment he was constantly at war with. It would not serve either one of our interests, I felt, for Oscar to get busted or disbarred because of something I wrote about him. I had my reputation to protect."

That reputation is built around the notion that Thompson was the sole creator of what has come to be called gonzo journalism, in which, to quote Thompson, "the writer must participate in the scene, while he's writing it," creating a "style of reporting based on William Faulkner's idea that the best fiction is far more true than any kind of journalism." The self-reflexive participatory impulse is present in Thompson's breakout project, *Hell's Angels: The Strange and Terrible Saga of the Outlaw Motorcycle Gangs*, first published in 1967, but the staccato and baroque cadences, the mix of the real and the hallucinated, and the sense that the gas pedal is floored while the volume is cranked up to eleven, all those hallmarks and tics we associate with Thompsonian gonzo find their fullest flower in 1971, with "Strange Rumblings in Aztlan," and ever so much more so in *Fear and Loathing in Las Vegas*—in other words, *after* Thompson engaged with Acosta, and *after* the latter had fully embraced *chicanismo*, becoming the Brown Buffalo known as Zeta.

When Zeta finally saw a prepublication copy of *Fear and Loathing in Las Vegas*, he threatened to sue in order to keep the book from being published. Zeta was upset about how he was portrayed but utterly despondent that his style had been appropriated. "My God! Hunter has stolen my soul. He has taken my best lines and used me. He has wrung me dry for material." In 1973 *Playboy* magazine published a letter from Zeta contesting the way that it credited "Mr. Hunter S. Thompson as the creator of Gonzo Journalism, which you say he both created and named.... Well, sir, I beg to take issue with you. And with anyone else who says that." Zeta might take some perverse posthumous pleasure that searching for "gonzo journalism" pulls up barely half a million hits on Google, while its scuzzy descendant "gonzo porn," in which the director participates in the scene while filming it, generates one hundred million.

In the end, Zeta more or less blackmailed *Rolling Stone* to publish both the *Autobiography* and *Revolt* through its Straight Arrow Books division and to feature a picture of both Thompson *and* Zeta on the book jacket of *Fear and Loathing*. Since then, Oscar Acosta aka Zeta aka Dr. Gonzo—"one of the most depraved and degenerate figures in American literature," as Thompson described him—has been portrayed in two films, *Where the Buffalo Roam* (directed by Art Linson, 1980), as Carl Lazlo, Esquire, played by the Emmy-winning actor Peter Boyle; and in Terry Gilliam's cult 1998 adaptation of *Fear and Loathing*, featuring Oscar winner Benicio del Toro as Dr. Gonzo. The "real" Zeta has not fared as well. When the Modern Library published a twenty-fifth-anniversary collection that included *Fear and Loathing in Las Vegas* and "Strange Rumblings in Aztlan," they sliced him right out of the original jacket photo, and history.

It is both fair and sad to say that Zeta ended up excising himself from history as well. After *The Revolt of the Cockroach People* came out in 1973, he left LA, which he'd once described as "the most detestable city on earth," and decamped for Mexico. In 1974 he simply disappeared. The rumors are rife: his heart gave out; he was ambushed in a drug deal gone bad; he was assassinated by a U.S. government black-ops team; he boarded a boat to Puerto Vallarta that simply never arrived. There's something poetic about sailing into oblivion, as Bas Jan Ader proved a year after Zeta's disappearance when the Dutch-born, LA-based conceptual artist attempted to cross the Atlantic alone in a thirteen-foot boat and was never seen or heard from again. The Chicano poet Raúl Salinas wrote after Zeta's death, "Is he a hero, a myth? Who knows him? I guess it depends on who you ask.... I am sure the closer you get to Los Angeles, the stronger the memory."

Even though we might wish it otherwise, we often remember the powerful better and longer than we do the legends of those who fight them. So it is that LA offers far more lasting memorials to Richard Nixon and Ronald Reagan, two Angelenos who rose to power specifically because they promised to wield the cudgel of law and order against the incursions of the "counterculture," that is, what and whom Salazar and Zeta were perceived to represent. Nixon's presidency from 1969 to 1974, followed a mere seven years later by Reagan's, from 1981 to 1988, can be identified as the two decades in which Southern California's political influence over the nation was at its height. Both men claimed to speak for the forgotten and the voiceless, but their "silent" majorities were not at all silent when it came to denouncing any challenge to their status. Organizing that majority into a reliable, reactionary voting bloc required money,

which Southern California plutocrats—including aerospace's Howard Hughes, publishing's Walter and Lee Annenberg, retailing's Alfred and Betsy Bloomingdale, and manufacturing's Earle and Marion
Jorgensen—were more than happy to supply. What all these very
rich people shared was a certainty that the "other" had to be battled
tooth and claw (Nixon's preferred feral style) or, alternatively, via
sunny guile (the Reagan approach).

These divergent styles are immortalized in Nixon's and Reagan's
respective presidential libraries. No other metropolitan area can
boast of the presence of two presidential libraries, Nixon's in Orange
County's Yorba Linda, Reagan's in Ventura County's Simi Valley, two
of the most reliably conservative bastions in Southern California.
Presidential libraries are compelling because they straddle the line
between celebration and history. The British warehoused notable
kings beneath Westminster Abbey, the French created a secular
mausoleum for national heroes in the Panthéon, and, since 1924,
V. I. Lenin has been on display in Red Square, outlasting the USSR
itself. For more than half a century, the trend in the United States
has been to entomb presidential corpses in presidential libraries.
But their primary purpose is to house official papers and, second-
arily, to provide gathering places for the faithful. In Nixon's case,
the presentation of legacy has been particularly complicated. After
resigning the presidency under threat of impeachment in 1974,
Nixon boarded a plane for La Casa Pacifica in San Clemente, his
Western White House, to receive a pardon from his second VP (his
first had resigned for tax fraud), to watch Watergate co-conspirators
like G. Gordon Liddy go to jail, and to write his memoirs. The first
of those came out in 1978, and the long and laborious road back
to something like respectability began. A dozen years later the

president and his wife, Pat, presided over the opening of the Richard Nixon Library and Birthplace on land that once belonged to his family. Privately funded by the same plutocrats who had backed his political career, the new institution faced a crucial question: How to craft a narrative of the immoral, the illegal, and the unethical?

For more than two decades, the Nixon Library muted these issues, diverting attention to Nixon's diplomatic achievements. The place is littered with bronze statues of the man interacting with other bronze statues—Prime Minister Churchill, President Charles de Gaulle, and, naturally, Chairman Mao Zedong to celebrate the "opening" of China. The statues are life-size and placed on the ground, which unintentionally diminishes them, making you understand why Napoleon was always immortalized atop a horse. After two decades of this institutionalized amnesia, a mandate from the federal government forced a reckoning with the difficult historical realities, and the story of Nixon's fall is now told with greater detail and accuracy. But the new exhibits on Watergate and the resignation did not sit well with Nixon partisans, who resigned as docents and board members and drafted hundred-page letters of complaint. Perhaps they were mollified by a statue added more recently, in the newly re-created Lincoln Study. In this incarnation, Nixon reclines on an easy chair, feet propped on an ottoman, a pen in one hand, a legal pad in the other. The scale and lighting humanize him, showcasing him in his role as lifelong student of history, one of the best writers to emerge from the office, even if he did so in extremis, forever the embattled Nixon *Agonistes*.

The scale of that statue, and even of the library itself, surrounded as it is by an inauspicious suburban panoply of car washes, dry cleaners, and fast-casual restaurants, contrasts with the full-on monumentalism of Reagan's spread, located in the hills, atop a winding road, at 40 Presidential Drive, the number less geolocative than symbolic, Reagan having been the fortieth POTUS. The Gipper left office after two full terms, and his reputation has only grown. He is, without a doubt, twenty-first-century Republicans' favorite twentieth-century president. That means his scandals—including the failed arms-for-hostages deal known as Iran-Contra—get little coverage, and glossed over are the inconvenient facts about his private life. No mention of Alzheimer's. No sign of his son's ballet dancing (a career that prompted AIDS activists to spread rumors that Ron Reagan was gay). His first wife, the actress Jane Wyman, is given less wall space than that devoted to a "Just Say No" antidrug board game sponsored by second wife, Nancy. What the library does offer in abundance, however, is pharaonic ambition. It is the country's largest, and in 2004 it added a ninety-thousand-square-foot glass pavilion housing the actual Air Force One that flew American presidents from Lyndon Johnson to George H. W. Bush around the globe. Nixon died before the pavilion opened, but one wonders how he would have felt looking at the very same plane that took him back to California after his resignation.

If thoughts of Tricky Dick invariably pull us over to the dark side, the Great Communicator's blithe "morning in America" demeanor, so inspiring to his admirers, so infuriating to his detractors, is imbued with the evergreen radiance that celebrity occasionally confers on those it touches. It should come as no surprise that Reagan's library was the first to embrace three-dimensional holography. As of 2018, the first exhibit visitors encounter is a tableau of the dead president reanimated and redimensionalized. Here he is forever fixed in time—on a whistle-stop tour, in the Oval Office, at his beloved Rancho del Cielo in Santa Barbara, his holographic golden retriever, Victory, trotting at his cowboy boot–shod holographic feet. To create this thanapoptic spectacle, the producers composed the soundtracks out of spliced fragments drawn from the huge archive of Reagan's recorded speeches. Then they found an actor whose face and body were close enough matches to make the digital suturing appear realistic. During the lengthy shoot, the actor wore one of Reagan's own belt buckles, an actual saddle from the ranch serving as decor. The million and a half dollars invested in this endeavor, however, did not mitigate its *unheimlich* creepiness.

Reagan isn't even Southern California's most famous resurrected icon. That distinction belongs to Tupac Shakur, the rapper, poet, and actor who turned up at the Coachella Valley Music & Arts Festival in 2012 to perform with fellow hip-hop legends Snoop Dogg and Dr. Dre. When a shirtless Tupac bounded onstage and bellowed, *"What the fuck is up, Coachellaaaaa!"* the audience erupted into cheers, delighting in Tupac's return from the dead. They couldn't care less that this victim of West Coast rap's most famous unsolved murder had died sixteen years earlier, three years before the very first Coachella. For that matter, Tupac wasn't even "really" a hologram, being instead a version of a "Pepper's Ghost," an optical effect dating back to the nineteenth century in which an image is projected onto angled pieces of glass, which then reflect it back onto the stage, creating an illusion of embodiment for the audience.

Many of the same people involved with the Tupac show later worked on the Reagan hologram. No matter that Reagan wasn't exactly a rap fan, being a Great American Songbook kind of guy, or that Tupac once lamented of eight years of Republican rule, "under Ronald Reagan, an ex-actor who lies to the people, who steals money, and who's done nothing at all for me." However divided in life, the Teflon President and Makaveli (as Tupac came to call himself after reading Machiavelli's *The Prince* in prison) are now united in virtuality. In Los Angeles, a city committed to forestalling death and fetishizing immortality, their differences are ignored as both are reborn as twenty-first-century avatars of the 3-D afterlife.

In the previous century, however, the afterlife was two-dimensional rather than three. The flat stars on the Hollywood Walk of Fame should have cemented the fame of their holders, but as it turns out, even concrete can't keep oblivion at bay. Those five-pointed, pink terrazzo stars have been around since 1960, but even their design highlights the planned obsolescence of notoriety. Verna Felton's star for her television work features a boxy set with two aerials sticking out the top; Jane Froman's for accomplishment in music has an icon of a turntable arm superimposed over a record platter; and Ben Alexander's radio work is memorialized with a bulbous directional microphone. For the young, not only are these names utterly obscure, but their images are inscrutable runes from the archive of dead media tech. Only the most ancient of these symbols—the intertwined masks of comedy and tragedy that have represented the theater since ancient Greece—will be recognizable a century from now.

In Hollywood, it's a tragedy twice over when an actor dies in the middle of shooting a comedy. This predicament causes a rift in the aether. In the case of hilariously awful filmmaker Ed Wood, and his hilariously awful 1959 masterpiece, *Plan 9 from Outer Space*, the director/producer faced a dilemma. He was able to cast his picture in part because he'd promised the actors they would get to work with horror legend Bela Lugosi. The Hungarian émigré could claim to have originated two of Hollywood's hardiest undead subgenres—

the vampire movie and the zombie picture—with *Dracula* in 1931 and *White Zombie* the following year. But by the 1950s, Lugosi was on his fifth wife, suffering from an addiction to Demerol, and even bad roles were few and far between. The dilemma for *Plan 9*, however, was that its fading star died before principal filming even began. A director more concerned with ethics or aesthetics might have found this an insurmountable problem, but Wood was undeterred. He had some footage of Lugosi from another project that he simply threw into *Plan 9*, and to fill in for the deceased, he hired his wife's chiropractor. Wood instructed him to hunch down and pull a cape over his face, as the back doc was younger and taller, and looked nothing like the famed actor. The impersonation was not entirely convincing (okay, not even close), but no one goes to Wood's oeuvre for seamless naturalism.

It took decades for Hollywood to come up with a name for this kind of substitution, and appropriately, it happened during production of yet another low-budget horror film, 1981's *The Evil Dead*. When director Sam Raimi was a kid during the sixties, he had enjoyed Three Stooges comedy shorts on television. But he noticed that in a few of them, Stooge Shemp Howard did not look anything like Shemp Howard. Raimi started watching specifically for what he called "Fake Shemps," but only later did he get the full story. Shemp had been a Stooge early on in the thirties but left the troupe to do his own thing. He rejoined them after his more famous brother Curly suffered a debilitating stroke in 1946, but in 1955 Shemp himself suffered a fatal heart attack after leaving the fights at Hollywood Legion Stadium. The problem for the remaining Stooges was they still owed four more pictures to the notoriously tightfisted Columbia Pictures management. To fulfill their contract, they brought in a longtime collaborator to play "Shemp," whom they usually shot from the back. Raimi reveled in calling the body doubles and stunt people in his films "Fake Shemps." That name, or just "Shemps," spread through the industry and is now the term of art. But the Shemps are analogue doubles in a world that now offers the potential for a different kind of immortality, the endless multiplicity of the digital.

Actual film clips have been sutured together for decades to create impossible pairings, from Woody Allen's 1983 mockumentary *Zelig* to Robert Zemeckis's Academy Award–winning *Forrest Gump* in 1994. In the early nineties, two famous Diet Coke commercials deployed digital compositing to create spaces where that moment's celebrities (Elton John and Paula Abdul) mingled with figures like jazz great Louis Armstrong, who had died in 1971, and comedian Groucho Marx, who had likewise departed to the hereafter in 1977. This kind of digital modeling, along with ever-more-lifelike animation techniques, blur the lines between the real and the artificial as generations of the dead are now being resurrected. After Bruce Lee's son, Brandon, died in a freak accident during the filming of 1993's *The Crow*, the producers pulled out the full panoply of tricks to complete the picture, from a Fake Shemp to computer-generated imagery (CGI). Two decades later, Johnnie Walker Scotch commissioned a television advertisement for the Chinese market featuring a full CGI Bruce Lee, interspersed with "real" footage and stills. CGI Bruce paces through the Hong Kong night, declaiming how "legends are made." The fact that Lee didn't drink alcohol is less disconcerting than the realization that these techniques are fast escaping the uncanny valley, and that the distance between us, the living, and them, the dead, is closing fast, at least when there's money to be made.

Southern California's cemeteries are big business, and like the entertainment industry that surrounds them and supplies their best-known clients, they must innovate or die. In 1917 Hubert Eaton, who vaingloriously referred to himself as the "Builder," created in Glendale's Forest Lawn what he saw as "a place for the living," with art rather than relics, a "spiritual" rather than a "religious" space: "I shall endeavor to build Forest Lawn as different, as unlike other cemeteries as sunshine is unlike darkness, as Eternal Life is unlike death." English visitors including Aldous Huxley and Evelyn Waugh could contain neither their contempt nor their guffaws at Eaton's antiseptic necropolis with its bowdlerized art and flag-waving patriotism, but the regular Folks of Southern California ate it up. Until Disneyland opened, it was Southern California's most popular tourist attraction and the place Walt Disney's parents most wanted to see when they came to LA to visit—and where, as noted above, Walt himself chose to be interred.

Another cemetery favored by the entertainment elite was Hollywood Memorial Park, which backed directly onto the Paramount Studios lot. Among the notables laid to rest there are director Cecil B. DeMille, actress/singer Judy Garland, and Mel Blanc, the voice of Bugs Bunny, whose headstone is inscribed THAT'S ALL FOLKS. It was also the final stop for gangster Bugsy Siegel, but that's a longer, bloodier story that pauses along the way at the safe beneath his regular table at the Formosa Café, a mile and a half west on Santa Monica Boulevard. Siegel was hardly the only shady character associated with the place. Jules Roth, its owner from 1939 to 1997, was a crook who sailed around the world on the company yacht, a head-scratching extravagance he supported by embezzling $9 million from the endowment-care fund intended to maintain the grave sites in perpetuity. In 1974 the crematorium literally collapsed around the body of singer "Mama" Cass Elliot, and by the nineties the cemetery itself went bankrupt.

When Tyler and Brent Cassity, two brothers from the Midwest, moved to LA to take over in 1998, there was much to be done. They immediately rebranded Hollywood Memorial Park as Hollywood Forever and committed millions to renovations. But they weren't interested in mere upgrades. Like Eaton, the "Builder" behind Forest Lawn, their plan was to reinvent the category. One of their schemes was the creation of LifeStories video headstones, online tributes to the dead that resembled nothing so much as the "montages" that SoCal kids were feted with at bar mitzvahs, *quinceañeras*, and sweet sixteens. In promoting LifeStories, the Cassitys declared that the "ultimate way in this town to cheat death is to become famous" and that at "least with the tribute your memories are preserved forever." Well, not exactly forever: the cemetery discontinued this service as DIY smartphone memorials became ubiquitous.

More lasting has been the importation of actual films into the resting places of the people, famous and not, who made them. Since 2002, Hollywood Forever has been hosting open-air summer screenings that draw up to four thousand Angelenos, who come to picnic on the grass, smoke weed, and enjoy the show. These evenings have reinvigorated the nineteenth-century tradition of treating cemeteries as spaces to commune with the living as well as the dead. But for many, the real draw is the stars glittering overhead.

Stars.

From the inception of the movie business in Los Angeles, the city has crafted infernal engines to produce "more stars than there are in heaven," to quote the MGM Studios tagline. But mystics and string theorists tell us that there are at least as many heavens as there are stars. The connections made here from Mickey to Coco to Zeta to Tupac to Mama Cass are inspired as much by the city's platzgeist as by any trail of evidence, drawing less from the causalities so dear to the discipline of history than from the esoteric correspondences central to alchemy. In the more than one hundred years since the first movie cameras started rolling, the city has advanced through the four alchemical elements: from earth to fire to air to water. And yet for all this, the city remains forever tied to the fifth element, the quintessence, or aether, in and out of which Hollywood manufactures dreams.

Alchemy's great work had as its goal producing a philosopher's stone that could perform miracles: the first, transmuting base metals into gold, and the second, granting immortal vitality. That fame could create infinite riches and everlasting youth remains one of the city's animating fantasies. But as the sense of Los Angeles's history deepens, drawing from all its elements and not just that elusive fifth one, the city that has been at the edge of forever can break through the screen and open itself both to multiplicities and multitudes.

Conclusion TEARS IN RAIN

UNTITLED #42 (FREEWAYS) I 1995 I PLATINUM PRINT I 2 ¼ X 6 ¾ INCHES (5.7 X 17.1 CM)

To call Los Angeles the city at the edge of forever is simultaneously to acknowledge its existence at the western edge of the continent and to honor its position as a place that produces dreams and fantasies for the whole globe. The speculative thrives in Southern California, from the real estate boosters who point to raw tracts of land and conjure sprawling developments, to any number of other dreamers, talking with their hands, conjuring a future "something" out of thin air. There would have been no Hollywood film business if not for these magicians of the aether, because to convince bankers that raw plots and unexposed strips of celluloid would make millions for them requires a particular skill set that Los Angeles has incubated for generations.

Great cities offer lifelong educations. They are too big, too dense,

Connections need not really exist, but without them
everything would fall apart.

—Robert Menasse

too much to process in their totality, so we parse them through personal experience, via the stories we hear from neighbors and politicians, and by what artists create in and about them. As Brooklyn's
great poet Walt Whitman put it, we all contain multitudes, so when
people come together in as unlikely a place as the newly watered
desert of Southern California to build a city as quickly and rapa-
ciously as they did Los Angeles in the twentieth century, there are
going to be a multitude of multitudes.

All that multiplying gets us into the realm of large numbers, and
the machines we've built to handle what we now call "data." It's
been my day job to think about how data manifests itself as culture,
having staked out a career as a critic and theorist of what used to be
known as new media but has emerged simply as the way we live

now. Thinking about how technology and culture come together segued more easily than you might expect into a longer investigation into the place where I was doing that thinking. So it was that I started to reimagine Los Angeles itself, coming up with ways to understand it, to map it, to make it cohere, at least for me. What I was searching for was a way to avoid the city's clichés that have gone viral, and, as discussed in the first chapter, to construct a platzgeist, that is to say, a compelling sense of place.

I found that the metaphors imported from alchemy made sense here, and even more as they were mixed and remixed chapter by chapter. The stories about architecture engage with the earth that the structures are built on, the dirt that was transmogrified into real estate. That real estate was made accessible by the fire igniting the pistons in the cars that linked all those far-flung homes. The air above became the dominant element from just before World War II to the end of the Cold War because the industries producing planes, rockets, and satellites superpowered the region's economy. A desert metropolis demanded water and grew into a global trading capital by exploiting and expanding its ports. And then there was that fifth element, aether, because Los Angeles is where we craft our ever-more-essential—whether we want them to be or not—models of fame and celebrity. The digital communication technologies that connect the global populations of the twenty-first century have not challenged so much as fully exported the city's constructs of glamour and notoriety to the rest of the world and, with them, the region's alchemical nature. As mentioned in chapter 1, almost a century ago Don Ryan claimed that LA aspired to Los Angelicize the entire world. Those aspirations have been fulfilled and then some, and if that process sounds straight out of science fiction, perhaps it is.

I was certainly one of those Los Angelicized as if taken over by aliens. When I was a kid living in New York, I was a fanatic for things emerging from Southern California without having the slightest notion of their origin points. So it was that my favorite episode of my favorite television show was a direct influence on this book. That show was *Star Trek*, and that episode was "The City on the Edge of Forever." It doesn't really matter what it was about—a time portal, Hitler, a knit cap to cover pointy Vulcan ears, etc. What matters is that the idea of a city that forever faced the unknown resonated. At the time I had no idea that the coauthor of that episode was the sci-fi great Harlan Ellison. I didn't know that Ellison had a bit part in an essay that ignited sixties New Journalism—Ellison's the smart-ass who stands up to a bullying icon in "Frank Sinatra Has a Cold" by Gay Talese (the same Gay Talese who later chronicled the sexual revolution at Sandstone). I didn't know that Ellison was a New Journalist himself, writing for the independent *LA Free Press* out of the very coffeehouse that was the epicenter of the Riot on Sunset Strip. I didn't know that Ellison was almost as famous for his irascible temper and litigiousness as he was for his powers of imagination. By the time I was almost finished with this book, I knew all this and more, and was half looking forward to the inevitable lawsuit from him, even though he certainly knew you can't copyright a title. Sadly, though, he passed away a year before I finished. Decades before, he'd written that "the winds of the city carry alchemical magic," and this book certainly echoes that assertion. If alchemy, around which so much of the book has been organized, is protoscientific, then speculative fiction can be seen as postscientific.

Three of the central themes of speculative media—time travel, interstellar voyaging, and lifelike robots—are the least likely aspects of the genre to ever "come true." How these themes intersect in one of the most iconic films ever made about a Los Angeles that doesn't exist demonstrates the usefulness of speculative thinking about the city.

Some events are meta, others are megameta. Seeing Ridley Scott's 1982 film *Blade Runner* at the Hollywood Forever cemetery in 2019 may have established a new category of meta-megameta. The film centers on a policeman from a squad of "blade runners" who track down runaway lifelike androids called "replicants" in order to "retire" them, an act indistinguishable in physical and moral terms from murder. *Blade Runner* opens with rolling credits that set the parameters of this world, then a title card situating the place and the time: LOS ANGELES, NOVEMBER 2019. The next shot is one of the film's most iconic, a vision of the city as a tightly packed, rain-swept, dark-toned apocalypse lit by shooting jets of fire. The crowd at Hollywood Forever, in that very year, erupted at the sight of the title card, laughing in recognition of the disjunction between the exceptionally pleasant evening (complete with a free-food promotion sponsored by an internet delivery service) and the hellscape unfolding in front of them.

The three impossibles of speculative fiction were all present. Here were the replicants created by the Tyrell Corporation—"more human than human," as per the company's motto—who worked on "Off World" colonies advertised on floating blimps. We're never sure how far "off world" these places are, but the lead renegade replicant, an Aryan-looking supersoldier named Roy Batty, tells the blade runner that he has "seen things you people wouldn't believe, attack ships on fire off the shoulder of Orion," which is a constellation more than five hundred light-years away from Earth. Not to get all geeky here, but given that the replicants are designed to have very short lives with built-in "termination" dates, the only way for these impossible constructs to make their impossible interstellar journeys would be via impossible time travel.

And yet there was a certain poignancy to watching all of these impossibilities projected onto the wall of a mausoleum on a perfect LA evening. To begin with, the presenters of the film honored the actor who played Batty, Dutch action stalwart Rutger Hauer, who had died earlier that year, his actual death matching the fictional termination date of his most famous character. Hauer as Batty famously improvised much of his climactic death scene, which takes place on the roof of a dilapidated building just as the sun breaks through the film's ubiquitous and sulfurous rain clouds.

The final sequences of the film were shot on location at the Bradbury Building, a sui generis masterpiece completed in 1893. In addition to *Blade Runner* and its cameo role in the noir classics *Double Indemnity* and *DOA*, the Bradbury Building serves as the main set of "Demon with a Glass Hand," which many consider the best episode of the fifties television sci-fi anthology *The Outer Limits*. Intriguingly enough, that episode is about time travel, interstellar voyaging, and lifelike robots and, in yet another twist, was written by Harlan Ellison.

Esther McCoy, the architectural historian and critic who was Rudolph Schindler's assistant at the Kings Road house and whom we last encountered rhapsodizing about the Eames LCW chair, was the first to make the story of the Bradbury as compelling as anything filmed there. She tells us that Lewis Bradbury, a magnate from the mining business, commissioned Sumner Hunt, a respected architect, to design a multistory commercial building for him at the corner of Broadway and Third Street. Bradbury wasn't happy with Hunt's designs but did like his assistant, a young draftsman named George Wyman. Wyman, deeply influenced by the then-common belief in spiritualism, used a Ouija board to ask his dead brother if he should accept Bradbury's offer and take on the project, even if it meant betraying Hunt. The specter replied: "Take the Bradbury Building. It will make you famous."

Wyman was not just a spiritualist; he was also an aficionado of Edward Bellamy's pioneering work of speculative utopian fiction, *Looking Backward: 2000–1887*, a Rip Van Winkle–esque tale about a man who wakes up more than a century into his future. Among other marvels (including a pretty good approximation of broadcasting), the time traveler is taken to a building that appears to him like "a vast hall full of light." And that is precisely what Bellamy fan Wyman decided to create for his new patron. While the front of the Bradbury Building is clad in a handsome enough Romanesque facade, it's the interior that justifies its fame. Stepping through the modest doors on Broadway, visitors enter an airy, five-story latticeworked triumph with a skylight illuminating the interior courtyard above it. The elevator alone looks like the inspiration for every steampunk illustration ever drawn. The combination of brick, marble, and ironwork is simultaneously substantial and weightless, and to stand in its atrium is to be temporally suspended in a present layered between a lost past and a future that never was. McCoy's story, now legend, about the building only enriches the experience, with its indebtedness to phantasms, ectoplasmic interventions, and sci-fi imaginaries.

There is another story here, though. John Crandell, a landscape architect and independent historian of downtown LA architecture, notes that McCoy's primary sources included Wyman's daughters, Louise and Carroll, who might well have embellished the family legacy. Also interviewed was Carroll's son—Wyman's grandson—who verified what his mother and aunt told McCoy, adding that he had in his possession the very Ouija board that had summoned the spirit of his grandfather's late brother. What kind of person keeps an almost-hundred-year-old Ouija board around the house, though? Well, perhaps it will become clearer if the grandson is revealed to be none other than a figure last seen in chapter 6, Forrest J. Ackerman, the creator of fandom and cosplay as we know it, and literary agent for famous science fiction authors like Ray Bradbury (no relation, alas, to the Lewis Bradbury who commissioned the building).

So here we have a fantastic story about a fantastic building, which itself relies on the testimony of the man who coined the term "sci-fi" for speculative literature. Both Wyman and Hunt went on to design more buildings, but only Hunt's garnered much attention, including the great, adobe-inspired Southwest Museum in Mount Washington, northeast of downtown. Whatever the truth, the legend of the Bradbury Building, not to mention its decayed state in the early eighties, made it the perfect location for the climax of *Blade Runner*.

The film gives a sense of what the center city felt like in the eighties, at least to a recent arrival like me. Every day after 5:00 p.m., it was as though a neutron bomb had gone off, decimating the population but leaving the buildings standing. Drawing from this postapocalysm, Ridley Scott worked with the visual futurist Syd Mead to create a style they called "retro-deco." They infused their filmic world with the idea that the future would accrete up and around the past without ever fully replacing it. That pastiched look was so successful that it's been almost impossible for speculative media to escape its influence. Retro-deco may have forecast 2019 LA, but by the twenty-first century, no one would mistake the film's blighted urban landscape for the thriving neighborhoods now re-branded as DTLA. The Bradbury itself sits across the street from the reinvigorated Grand Central Market, which has become a model of the twenty-first-century food hall, appealing to consumers with money to spend on artisanal cheeses and craft beers. So at least that part of the film's prophesizing proved overblown.

And yet the vision of the city as an ecological wasteland under a punishing acid rain seems closer than ever, if only because a city still reliant on gas-burning cars (LA created the Autopocene, after all); watered by sources hundreds and sometimes thousands of miles away; prone to devastating and ever-worsening wildfires; built atop a desert landscape crisscrossed by some of the most famous earth-quake faults in the world, which sits next to a sea that is inexorably rising, cannot help but cause even the blithest Southern Californian to worry. The triumph of Los Angeles in the twentieth century, its rise to global prominence via a will to power, and the unlikely con-nections and improbable truths laid out in this book are as much at risk as anywhere else on the planet.

So even as Los Angeles continues to work to convince the rest of the world to love it as much as it loves itself, the warning offered by Roy Batty of a future that hasn't befallen the city—yet—still resonates. The doomed replicant tells the conflicted blade runner that everything that has happened to both of them, and by implication to us all, can be lost "like tears in rain." It is the responsibility of those who live in and love this planet's great cities to ensure that the edge of forever is a plane and not an abyss.

ACKNOWLEDGMENTS

For all its critiques, this book is a love letter to the place where my dreams came true. Over the years, I've had the good fortune to have had jobs that allowed me to indulge obscure interests and unlikely obsessions. Many of those show up, either directly or obliquely, in these pages. The fact that Paul Slovak, my editor, did not just accept but embraced my approach to Los Angeles and its histories—alchemy, connectionism, and the like—was just one more stroke of luck. From the moment I walked into his office, I knew this was who I wanted to work with. Thanks as well to editorial assistant Allie Merola, copy editor Hilary Roberts, and designer Meighan Cavanaugh.

The manuscript would never have made it to Paul's desk were it not for my extraordinary agent, Joe Spieler. Joe valued my voice, championed the book at every turn, and will forever have my gratitude.

Catherine Opie was generous enough to offer permission to use her Freeway Series photographs. They are included to convey the idea of connectivity and metaphor, and their formal beauty is matched only by their incisive intelligence about the city that we both call home.

The first two chapters were published in slightly different form in

The Believer, and the enthusiasm that editor Heidi Julavits showed was an early sign that these ideas might garner a wider audience. Doug Sery, good friend and my decades-long editor at the MIT Press, pushed for me to expand my reach with this project even though it meant he wouldn't be publishing it.

I was honored to be the Dana and David Dornsife Fellow at the Huntington Library in 2015–16. Thanks to Steven Hindle, W. M. Keck Foundation Director of Research, and William F. Deverell, director of the Huntington–USC Institute on California and the West. Asif Siddiqi was kind enough to let me tag along on a visit to SpaceX in Hawthorne. Daniel Immerwahr reminded me of why it's good to have colleagues who are polymaths. The Tuesday lawn bowling sessions when the Huntington's grounds were closed to the public are a memory I'll not soon forget.

A Vectors fellowship at the University of Southern California supported turning "Gidget on the Couch" into a short film. Thanks to USC's Tara McPherson, designer/producer Dmitri Siegel, director Matt Nourse, and cameraman Quetzal Aguilar. The resulting project, online at http://vectors.usc.edu/projects/index.php?project=96, includes a scene where I walk down Surfrider Beach in Malibu with the real Gidget, Kathy Kohner Zuckerman—a true perk. Mieke Gerritzen and Koert van Mensvoort produced a multimedia performance of "The Factory Model of Desire" as part of their *Biggest Visual Power Show* at the historic Million Dollar Theater, which gave me my first, and so far only, opportunity to perform on Broadway (LA's Broadway, but still).

At the Art Center College of Design's Media Design program, first with Norman Klein, and then with Tim Durfee, I ran a series of Dialectical Bus Tours of Southern California that prompted some of the thinking that evolved into this book. My thanks to Richard Hertz, Andy

Davidson, and Anne Burdick for supporting these mobile investigations. When I moved to UCLA, I encountered equal enthusiasm from colleagues in the Design Media Arts department and, with Rebeca Méndez, cotaught a hybrid seminar/studio on rebranding Los Angeles. At UCLA, I joined a diverse and brilliant group of scholars in the Digital Humanities and Urban Humanities programs. Special thanks to Johanna Drucker and Todd Presner for their collegiality and friendship. Other longtime friends and supporters of this project from academia include Ken Goldberg, Lev Manovich, Jeffrey Schnapp, Caroline Jones, Peter Galison, and Geert Lovink. My research assistant, Peter Sebastian Chesney, is a brilliant young historian trained at UCLA, and his unflagging energy and willingness to look at the manuscript through different critical lenses was of immense benefit.

Jeff Strauss, Jeff Elmassian, and Dean Parisot (among other carnivores) indulged a shared passion for LA's historic steakhouses. Many evenings in LA and Palm Springs were spent with Laura Morton and Jeff Dunas talking about Southern California's flora, fauna, and photography. I have benefited greatly from Mike Fatula's wise counsel. I appreciate the enthusiasm shown the project by friends including Louise Sandhaus, Didi Dunphy, Jim Barsness, Deborah Michel, Tom Rosch, Andrew Fayé, Dan Harries, Steve Mamber, Steve Tiger, and David Gow. Douglas Hepworth, as always, had my back and held my beer.

My mother, Katharine Daly, was fiercely supportive of this book, as she has always been of all my work. I miss my late father, Marvin Lunenfeld, and wish he could have read this. My daughters, Maud and Kyra, generously shared their Los Angeles with me over the years, and it's been wonderful to welcome Kyra's husband, George Carstocea, into our SoCal clan.

Finally, there's my wife, Susan Kandel. She's published six sterling mystery novels set in Southern California. On joint research forays, we shared taco crawls through East LA, immersed ourselves in the Integratron's sound baths, explored the docks on Terminal Island, and ferreted out gangsters' hideaways in the San Bernardino Mountains. Susan is my inspiration, cheerleader, editor of last resort, and co-conspirator. Words cannot express what I, much less this book, owe her.

NOTES

Introduction: Welcome to LA

3 "A place belongs forever": Joan Didion, *The White Album* (1979; repr., New York: Farrar, Straus and Giroux, 1990), p. 146.

5 scratch the phony tinsel: Variations on this quote have been attributed to actor and pianist Oscar Levant in the early sixties and to radio personalities Henry Morgan and Ed Gardner in the late forties.

6 "Steve, Jake, and Mexicali Rose": Daniel Mark Epstein, *Sister Aimee: The Life of Aimee Semple McPherson* (New York: Harvest, 1994), p. 297.

6 some thirty thousand: Matthew Avery Sutton, *Aimee Semple McPherson and the Resurrection of Christian America* (Cambridge, MA: Harvard University Press, 2007), p. 103.

6 "That's my story": Epstein, *Sister Aimee*, p. 313.

Chapter 1: The Alchemical City: Drive-By Punditry, Location Scouts, and a User's Guide to Elemental Los Angeles

8 "There it is. Take it": Catherine Mulholland, *William Mulholland and the Rise of Los Angeles* (Berkeley and Los Angeles: University of California Press, 2000), p. 4.

9 "The solution, once revealed": Raymond Chandler, "Casual Notes on the Mystery Novel" (1949), in *Raymond Chandler Speaking*, Dorothy Gardiner and Katherine Sorley Walker, eds. (Berkeley and Los Angeles: University of California Press, 1997), p. 65.

10 Los Angeles County had a population: Population statistics in Southern California are highly debatable and fungible, especially before the twentieth century. County numbers are better than city ones, and Indigenous people were usually undercounted. That said, the first U.S. census of newly conquered Los Angeles County resulted in a count of 3,530. Cambridge University Press's

Historical Statistics of the United States, which takes multiple sources into account, offers the following for the metropolitan area of Los Angeles: 101,454 in 1890; 170,298 in 1900; 504,131 in 1910. https://hsus.cambridge.org. All URLs were checked and live as of June 16, 2019, unless otherwise noted.

11 three most important and influential studies: Carey McWilliams, *Southern California: An Island on the Land* (1946; repr., Layton, UT: Gibbs Smith, 1973); Reyner Banham, *Los Angeles: The Architecture of Four Ecologies* (1971; repr., Berkeley and Los Angeles: University of California Press, 2009); Mike Davis, *City of Quartz: Excavating the Future in Los Angeles* (London and New York: Verso, 1990).

13 "Every great burst": Peter Hall, *Cities in Civilization* (New York: Pantheon, 1998), p. 3.

13 "city with the aspirations": Don Ryan, *Angel's Flight* (New York: Boni and Liveright, 1927), p. 82.

13 The rest of the world: The classic study of LA's automobile-centric design strategies is Richard W. Longstreth, *City Center to Regional Mall: Architecture, the Automobile, and Retailing in Los Angeles, 1920–1950* (Cambridge, MA: MIT Press, 1998).

14 "people with brains": Eve Babitz, *Eve's Hollywood* (1972; repr., New York: New York Review Books, 2015), p. xi.

15 (self-loathing and misogynistic) joke: Thomas Leitch, "Hitchcock and His Writers: Authorship and Authority in Adaptation," in Jack Boozer, *Authorship in Film Adaptation* (Austin: University of Texas Press, 2008), p. 70.

15 "the most important person": Daniel Bernardi and Julian Hoxter, *Off the Page: Screenwriting in the Era of Media Convergence* (Berkeley and Los Angeles: University of California Press, 2017), p. 27.

15 "Millions are to be grabbed": Pauline Kael, "Raising Kane," in Pauline Kael, Herman J. Mankiewicz, and Orson Welles, *The Citizen Kane Book: Raising Kane and the Shooting Script* (1971; repr., New York: Limelight Editions, 1984), p. 9.

15 known colloquially as the "Folks": David Fine, *Imagining Los Angeles: A City in Fiction* (Reno and Las Vegas: University of Nevada Press, 2004), p. 57.

17 the bitter-screenwriter narratives: Fine maintains that the city's literature is "largely the work of men who came here to work as screenwriters." Fine, *Imagining Los Angeles*, p. x.

18 both an experimental protoscience and a spiritual system: E. J. Holmyard, *Alchemy* (1957; repr., New York: Dover, 1990), p. 16.

20 only a short time in the 1920s: Steven J. Ross, "How Hollywood Became Hollywood: Money, Politics, and Movies," in Tom Sitton and William Deverell, *Metropolis in the Making: Los Angeles in the 1920s* (Berkeley and Los Angeles: University of California Press, 2001), pp. 255–56.

21 reputed to be richer than Rockefeller: Stephen Birmingham, *California Rich: The Lives, the Times, the Scandals, and the Fortunes of the Men & Women Who Made & Kept California's Wealth* (1980; repr., Guilford, CT: Lyons Press, 2016), p. 157. See also Margaret Leslie Davis, *Dark Side of Fortune: Triumph*

and Scandal in the Life of Oil Tycoon Edward L. Doheny (Berkeley and Los Angeles: University of California Press, 1998).

22 At the height of wartime production: To give a sense of the enormity of the U.S. investment in "Fortress California," peak aircraft employment in LA during World War II was 228,400, and U.S. military spending on aircraft by June 1945 was $7 billion. Arthur C. Verge, "The Impact of the Second World War on Los Angeles," in "Fortress California at War: San Francisco, Los Angeles, Oakland, and San Diego, 1941–1945" (special issue), *Pacific Historical Review* 63, no. 3 (August 1994).

23 the brutal deportation: George Sanchez points out that the mass repatriation campaigns during the Depression in the 1930s reduced the Mexican population of Los Angeles by a third and set the template for the postwar deportation of the *braceros*. George Sanchez, *Becoming Mexican American: Ethnicity, Culture and Identity in Chicano Los Angeles, 1900–1945* (Oxford, UK, and New York: Oxford University Press, 1993), p. 210.

23 epochal transfer of wealth: Gerald D. Nash, *The American West Transformed: The Impact of the Second World War* (Bloomington: Indiana University Press, 1985), p. 17.

Chapter 2: Gidget on the Couch: Freud, Dora (No, Not That Dora), and the Secret Austro-Hungarian Roots of Surfing

29 "If all American literature": Tim Appelo Amazon.com review (n.d.). https://www.amazon.com/dp/B001QTV4OU?_encoding=UTF8&isInIframe=1&n=133140011&ref_=dp_proddesc_0&s=digital-text&showDetailProductDesc=1#iframe-wrapper.

29 "If I had a couple bucks": "Gidget Makes the Grade," *Life*, October 28, 1957, p. 114.

30 "You're breathing, aren't you?": Kathy Kohner Zuckerman, quoted in Deanne Stillman's introduction to Frederick Kohner, *Gidget* (1957; repr., New York and Berkeley: Penguin, 2001), p. xii.

33 "I was so jazzed up": Kohner, *Gidget*, p. 149.

34 "Malibu is the exact spot on earth": Paul Gross cited in "Malibu," an entry in Matt Warshaw, *The Encyclopedia of Surfing* (Orlando, FL: Harvest/Harcourt, 2005), p. 359.

34 the mysterious and gifted Miki Dora: The indispensable biography is David Rensin, *All for a Few Perfect Waves: The Audacious Life and Legend of Rebel Surfer Miki Dora* (New York: HarperCollins, 2008).

37 "Bad omens," he wrote: Mickey Dora, "The Crackerjack Conspiracy," *Surfer* 10, no. 2 (May 1969), reprinted in Chris Mauro and Steve Hawk, eds., *The Best of Surfer Magazine* (San Francisco: Chronicle Books, 2007), p. 18.

37 "that moment when the sea gods": C. R. Stecyk III and Drew Kampion, *Dora Lives: The Authorized Story of Miki Dora* (Santa Barbara, CA: T. Adler Books, 2005), p. 24.

38 forging plane tickets: Nat Young, *Church of the Open Sky* (Melbourne: Michael Joseph/Penguin Books Australia, 2019), pp. 32–33.

38 full-on racism and conspiracy-mongery: Rensin, *All for a Few Perfect Waves*, p. 318.

39 *kaiserlich-königlich*: Robert Musil, *The Man Without Qualities*, vol. 1, *A Sort of Introduction and Pseudo Reality Prevails*, trans. Sophie Wilkins and Burton Pike (1930–1943; repr., New York: Vintage, 1996), p. 29.

42 house for radicals: Robert Sweeney and Judith Sheine, *Schindler, Kings Road, and Southern California Modernism* (Berkeley and Los Angeles: University of California Press, 2012).

42 "as if there had never been": Reyner Banham, "The Master Builders" in *A Critic Writes: Selected Essays by Reyner Banham*, selected by Mary Banham et al. (Berkeley and Los Angeles: University of California Press, 1996), p. 172.

43 Pauline Schindler's decade-long attempt: Susan Morgan, "Not Another International Style Ballyhoo: A Short History of the Schindler House," in *Schindler Lab*, ed. Anthony Carfello, Sara Daleiden, and Kimberli Meyer (Los Angeles: MAK Center for Art and Architecture, 2015), https://schindlerlab.org/history/#_edn2.

Chapter 3: The Factory Model of Desire: Walt Disney, Hugh Hefner, and the Transformation of Sex, Death, and Boredom in America

47 "The sex of the millennium": Germaine Greer, *The Whole Woman* (New York: Alfred A. Knopf, 1999), p. 191.

47 "If anything is more": Carl Hiaasen, *Team Rodent: How Disney Devours the World* (New York: Random House, 1998), p. 12.

48 This was the world: Two sources used for details on Disney's life are Michael Barrier, *The Animated Man: A Life of Walt Disney* (Berkeley and Los Angeles: University of California Press, 2007), and Neal Gabler, *Walt Disney: The Triumph of the American Imagination* (New York: Alfred A. Knopf, 2006).

49 "I'm sometimes frightened": Sergei Eisenstein, *Eisenstein on Disney*, ed. Jay Leyda, trans. Alan Upchurch (Calcutta: Seagull, 1986), p. 2.

49 "the Disney method": Walter Benjamin, cited in Miriam Hansen, "Benjamin and Cinema: Not a One-Way Street," in *Walter Benjamin: Critical Evaluations in Cultural Theory*, vol. 2, *Modernity*, ed. Peter Osborne (London and New York: Routledge, 2005), p. 357.

50 an Arkansas woman: Steven J. Tepper, *Not Here, Not Now, Not That! Protest over Art and Culture in America* (Chicago: University of Chicago Press, 2011), p. 30.

51 Hugh Hefner had a warm, supportive mother: Much of the biographical detail about Hefner's life is drawn from Steven Watts, *Mr. Playboy: Hugh Hefner and the American Dream* (Hoboken, NJ: John Wiley & Sons, 2008).

52 "We like our apartment": Hugh Hefner, "Editorial," *Playboy* 1, no. 1 (1953), p. 3.

53 "Lest We Forget" and "The most successful sex object": Watts, *Mr. Playboy*, p. 286.

53 research on human needs: Abraham Maslow, "A Theory of Human Motivation," *Psychological Review* 50, no. 4 (1943): pp. 370–96.

54 concept of "weenie-tecture": Jesse Schell and Joe Shochet, "Designing Interactive Theme Park Rides," *IEEE Computer Graphics and Applications* 21, no. 4 (July–August, 2001): p. 11.

56 "a Bunny... does not": From the *Bunny Manual*, excerpted in John Robertson, *50 Years of the Playboy Bunny* (San Francisco: Chronicle Books, 2010), p. 60.

56 In a 1970 paper, Japanese roboticist: Masahiro Mori, "The Uncanny Valley," trans. Karl F. MacDorman and Norri Kageki, *Energy* 7, no. 4 (1970): pp. 33–35.

58 *The Girls Next Door:* The series aired on E! Entertainment Television from 2005 to 2010.

58 "breast implant illness": Stephanie Petit, "Crystal Hefner Removes Her Breast Implants Because They 'Slowly Poisoned Me,'" *People*, July 20, 2016, https://people.com/celebrity/hugh-hefners-wife-crystal-hefner-removes-breast-implants/.

Chapter 4: Riots Goin' On: Jazz on the Stem, Pop on the Strip, and What Happens When Cops Try to Crush Culture

60 sets the record for baskets: John Einarson, *Forever Changes: Arthur Lee and the Book of Love* (London: Outline Press, 2010), p. 46.

61 the Columbia Records building: Einarson, *Forever Changes*, p. 50.

61 "They came in and flooded a community": Bill Parker, interviewed by Bill Stout on "CBS Presents: Riot or Revolt," originally aired on December 7, 1965. See https://www.c-span.org/video/?327579-1/reel-america-watts-riot-revolt-1965, with Parker's comments at 32:00.

61 Bobby doesn't get the gig: Andrew Hultkrans, *Forever Changes*, 33⅓ (New York and London: Bloomsbury, 2003), p. 44.

63 Committee of Twenty-Five: Kevin Starr, *Golden Dreams: California in an Age of Abundance, 1950–1963* (Oxford, UK, and New York: Oxford University Press, 2009), p. 154.

64 stories about black workers: R. J. Smith, *The Great Black Way: L.A. in the 1940s and the Lost African American Renaissance* (New York: Public Affairs, 2006), p. 71.

65 "The mental corrosion of race prejudice": Chester Himes, *The Quality of Hurt: The Early Years, the Autobiography of Chester Himes* (1972; repr., New York: Thunder's Mouth Press, 1995), p. 76.

65 "a jewel done with loving hands": Douglas Flamming, *Bound for Freedom: Black Los Angeles in Jim Crow America* (Berkeley and Los Angeles: University of California Press, 2006), p. 287.

66 the swinging scat: Slim Gaillard, "Cement Mixer (Putti Putti)" (1945).

66 "the loneliest and most brutal": Jack Kerouac, *On the Road* (1957; repr., New York: Penguin, 1991), pp. 86, 88, and 112.

67 Start at the top: There is no definitive biography of Chief Parker, and he never wrote an autobiography. Sources about his life and legacy include his own book on law enforcement, *Parker on Police*, ed. O. W. Wilson (Springfield, IL:

Charles C. Thomas, 1957); Gerald Woods, *The Police in Los Angeles: Reform and Professionalization* (New York and London: Garland, 1993); and Joe Domanick's studies *To Protect and to Serve: The LAPD's Century of War in the City of Dreams* (New York: Pocket Books, 1994), and *Blue: The LAPD and the Battle to Redeem American Policing* (New York: Simon & Schuster, 2015).

69 actor/producer Jack Webb: Eric Schaefer, "Dragnet," in *Encyclopedia of Television*, 2nd ed., ed. Horace Newcomb (London and New York: Routledge, 2004), pp. 758–59.

69 It remained racist: Glenn Souza, "Perspective on LAPD: A Simple Time, in Black and White: In the '50s, Racism Was an Enforcement Tool Passed Down from a Chief Who Was a God to a Legion of Fuhrmans," *Los Angeles Times*, October 12, 1995, https://www.latimes.com/archives/la-xpm-1995-10-12-me-55977 -story.html.

70 Los Angeles burned twice: Abraham H. Miller offers a comparison of the LAPD responses in 1965 and 1992 in "The Los Angeles Riots: A Study in Crisis Paralysis," *Journal of Contingencies and Crisis Management* 9, no. 4 (December 2001): pp. 189–99.

70 Parker's "arrogant racism": "Editorial: Chief Parker's Time Is Past," *Los Angeles Times*, April 19, 2009, http://articles.latimes.com/2009/apr/19/opinion/ed -parker19.

70 "the last white spot": "Parker Declares City Is White Spot of Nation," *Los Angeles Times*, August 9, 1950, cited in John Buntin, *LA Noir: The Struggle for the Soul of America's Most Seductive City* (New York: Three Rivers Press, 2009), pp. 162 and 369.

71 the LAPD's growing hysteria: Mina Yang, "A Thin Blue Line Down Central Avenue: The LAPD and the Demise of a Musical Hub," in *California Polyphony: Ethnic Voices, Musical Crossroads* (Urbana and Chicago: University of Illinois Press), pp. 60–79.

71 "All the stars": Clora Bryant et al., eds. *Central Avenue Sounds: Jazz in Los Angeles (1921–1956)* (Berkeley and Los Angeles: University of California Press, 1998), pp. 63 and 273.

71 McVea's novelty hit: Jack McVea and others, "Open the Door, Richard" (1946)

73 an instruction manual: Roger McGuinn and Chris Hillman, "So You Want to Be a Rock'n'Roll Star" (1967).

74 public space for private view: Davis, *City of Quartz*, p. 226.

74 "For What It's Worth": Stephen Stills, "For What It's Worth" (1966).

74 clashed with kids in caftans: Sources include Domenic Priore, *Riot on Sunset Strip: Rock'n'Roll's Last Stand in Hollywood* (London: Jawbone Press, 2007), and Mike Davis, "Riot Nights on Sunset Strip," *Labour/Le Travail* 59 (Spring 2007): pp. 199–214, http://www.lltjournal.ca/index.php/llt/article/view/5499.

76 "LA cops are idealists": Jim Morrison, quoted in *The Doors: In Their Own Words*, ed. Andrew Doe and John Tobler (London: Omnibus Press, 1988), p. 90.

76 "essentially about the counterculture's right": Dave McBride, "Counterculture," in *A Companion to Los Angeles*, eds. William Deverell and Greg Wise (Malden, MA: Wiley-Blackwell, 2010), p. 337.

76 "The Old School Hollywood supper clubs": Harvey Kubernik and Scott Cala-
   mar, *Canyon of Dreams: The Magic and the Music of Laurel Canyon* (New
   York and London: Sterling, 2009), pp. 110–11.
77 After the riot: Randy Benjamin and Ron Tennes, "S.O.S." (1966).
79 I'm talking about N.W.A.: Two journalistic accounts are Gerrick D. Kennedy,
   *Parental Discretion Is Advised: The Rise of N.W.A and the Dawn of Gangsta
   Rap* (New York: Atria Books, 2017), and Ben Westhoff, *Original Gangstas:
   The Untold Story of Dr. Dre, Eazy-E, Ice Cube, Tupac Shakur, and the Birth of
   West Coast Rap* (New York: Hachette, 2016).
80 a tale of revenge and justice: Andre Young, Lorenzo Patterson, O'Shea Jackson,
   "Fuck Tha Police" (1988).
81 He had a Handycam: Summer Harlow, "Live-Witnessing, Slacktivism, and
   Surveillance: Understanding the Opportunities, Challenges and Risks of
   Human Rights Activism in a Digital Era," in *The Routledge Companion to
   Media and Human Rights*, ed. Howard Tumber and Silvio Waisbord (London
   and New York: Routledge, 2017), p. 318.

Chapter 5: Space Port Alpha: Libertarians, Libertines, and the Ineffable Lightness of Southern California's High Tech

85 "Extremism in defense of liberty": The *Washington Post*'s transcript of Goldwater's speech to the 1964 Republican National Convention is available at
   https://www.washingtonpost.com/wp-srv/politics/daily/may98/goldwate
   rspeech.htm.
85 "I can honestly say": Barbara Williamson with Nancy Bacon, *An Extraordinary
   Life: Love, Sex and Commitment* (Bloomington, IN: Balboa Press, 2013), p. vii.
86 so many naked bodies: The best-known source for the story of Sandstone is
   Gay Talese, *Thy Neighbor's Wife* (New York: Doubleday, 1981); also Tom Hatfield, *Sandstone Experience* (New York: Crown, 1975).
87 "I got into [a turbulent stall]": Ben R. Rich and Leo Janos, *Skunk Works: A Personal Memoir of My Years at Lockheed* (New York: Little, Brown, 1994), p. 135.
87 "there are bold pilots": Tony LeVier with John Guenther, *Pilot* (New York:
   Harper & Brothers, 1954), p. xi.
87 roughly five decades: See Peter J. Westwick, ed., *Blue Sky Metropolis: The
   Aerospace Century in Southern California* (San Marino, Berkeley, and Los Angeles: Huntington Library and University of California Press, 2012).
89 "better off than were": Ernie Pyle, "Tide of 'Aviation Okies' at Flood in California," *Milwaukee Journal*, May 8, 1941, p. 27.
90 "hypocrisy is the homage": François, Duc de La Rochefoucauld, *Reflections; or
   Sentences and Moral Maxims*, ed. and trans. J. W. Willis Bund and J. Hain
   Friswell (London: Simpson Low, Marston, 1898), p. 27.
90 secrecy central to military aerospace: Mihir Pandya, "The Vanishing Act:
   Stealth Airplanes and Cold War Southern California," in Westwick, *Blue Sky
   Metropolis*, pp. 105–26.
91 "What you just saw": Rich and Janos, *Skunk Works*, p. 131.

91 The whole place was run: This section draws from both Rich and Janos, *Skunk Works*, and Clarence L. "Kelly" Johnson with Maggie Smith, *Kelly: More Than My Share of It All* (Washington, DC: Smithsonian Books, 1985).

92 Keep It Simple, Stupid: Johnson, *Kelly*, p. 161.

93 "matter what your father could do": M. G. Lord, *Astro Turf: The Private Life of Rocket Science* (New York: Walker, 2005), p. 210.

93 early classic of Southern California libertarian thought: John Whiteside Parsons, "Freedom Is a Two-Edged Sword" (1950) in *Freedom Is a Two-Edged Sword and Other Essays* (Phoenix, AZ: New Falcon, 1990), pp. 9–44.

94 the emergence of "suburban warriors": Lisa McGirr, *Suburban Warriors: The Origins of the New American Right* (Oxford, UK, and Princeton, NJ: Princeton University Press, 2001).

94 "It is difficult": Upton Sinclair, *I, Candidate for Governor: And How I Got Licked* (Berkeley and Los Angeles: University of California Press, 1994), p. 109.

95 Reagan reshaped the Republican Party: See Rick Perlstein, *The Invisible Bridge: The Fall of Nixon and the Rise of Reagan* (New York: Simon & Schuster, 2014).

95 "it is not actionable": Cecilia Rasmussen, "Divine Order's Tale Smacks of Cult Fiction," *Los Angeles Times*, May 23, 1999, https://www.latimes.com/archives /la-xpm-1999-may-23-me-40217-story.html.

95 "a $25,000 home": McWilliams, *Southern California*, p. 265.

96 a "buxom showgirl": Talese, *Thy Neighbor's Wife*, p. 166.

98 "a telocratic, synergistic, large-scale community": Hatfield, *Sandstone Experience*, p. 22.

99 "We believe that with the improved": John Williamson, "Sandstone Statement of Purpose" (Los Angeles, 1969), on Barbara Williamson's blog, http://hstrial -jwilliamson8.homestead.com/Microsoft_Word_-_Purpose.pdf. Accessed January 6, 2016.

99 "the perfect mate": Williamson and Bacon, *An Extraordinary Life*, p. 26.

99 I was on a sales appointment: Barbara Williamson, "Embracing an Alternate Lifestyle," *Free Love and the Sexual Revolution* (blog), July 1, 2014, http:// www.barbarawilliamson.org/embracing-an-alternate-lifestyle/.

100 "undoubtedly the most liberated": Talese, *Thy Neighbor's Wife*, pp. 539 and 186.

101 Just a few of the boldfaced names: These names come from Barbara Williamson's *An Extraordinary Life*, as well as contemporary accounts. How much credence one can give to the guest list for an orgy is anyone's guess.

102 "systems analysis served as": David Jardini, "Out of the Blue Yonder: How RAND Diversified into Social Welfare Research," *RAND Review* 22, no. 1 (Fall 1998): p. 4. For more on how RAND's systems research developed during the Cold War, see Alex Abella, *Soldiers of Reason: The RAND Corporation and the Rise of the American Empire* (Boston: Mariner/Houghton Mifflin Harcourt, 2008), pp. 57–58.

103 "other products of the modern world": Frank S. Meyer, "Libertarianism or Libertinism?" in *In Defense of Freedom and Related Essays* (1969; repr., Indianapolis: Liberty Fund, 1996), pp. 183–86.

104 "merged back into the culture": William Yardley, "John Williamson, 80, Co-Founder of Retreat Known for Sex," *New York Times*, May 4, 2013, sec. A, p. 24,

http://www.nytimes.com/2013/05/05/us/john-williamson-dies-at-80-founded-sandstone-retreat.html?_r=0.

104 "hadn't been for aircraft": Steve Pace, *The Projects of Skunk Works: 75 Years of Lockheed Martin's Advanced Development Programs* (Minneapolis: Voyageur Press, 2016), p. 68.

104 Toniann labeled the fastest teen: "Pasadena Lass Gains Speed Title in Talley Equipped Sonic Fighter," *Oxnard Press Courier*, June 4, 1963, p. 4, https://newspaperarchive.com/oxnard-press-courier-jun-04-1963-p-4/.

106 gas masks at the ready: Barry Miles, *Zappa: A Biography* (New York: Grove Press, 2004), p. 8.

106 Floyd Delafield Crosby: David Crosby and Carl Gottlieb, *Long Time Gone: The Autobiography of David Crosby* (New York: Doubleday, 1987), p. 9.

106 leader of the Mamas and the Papas: John Phillips with Jim Jerome, *Papa John: An Autobiography (of the Mamas and the Papas): A Music Legend's Shattering Journey Through Sex, Drugs, and Rock 'n' Roll* (New York: Doubleday, 1986), p. 68.

107 shot himself in the head: Although "Coon Dog" Connor's death was officially ruled an accident, Ben Fong-Torres maintains that "few people outside the coroner's office believed the story" in his *Hickory Wind: The Life and Times of Gram Parsons* (1991; repr., New York: St. Martin's Press, 1998), p. 31.

107 Rear Admiral Morrison: Stephen Davis, *Jim Morrison: Life, Death, Legend* (New York: Gotham Books, 2005), p. 55, and William Grimes, "Obituary: George S. Morrison, 89, Admiral in Tonkin Gulf and Singer's Father," *New York Times*, December 8, 2008, p. B14, https://www.nytimes.com/2008/12/09/us/09morrison.html.

109 Fifty years later: Leonard Kleinrock, "The First Message Transmission," ICANN blog (October 29, 2019), https://www.icann.org/news/blog/the-first-message-transmission.

110 the alt-space business: Tim Fernholz, *Rocket Billionaires: Elon Musk, Jeff Bezos, and the New Space Race* (Boston: Houghton Mifflin Harcourt, 2018), p. 150.

110 Libertarianism is the civic religion: Journalists and political scientists have been analyzing Silicon Valley's ideologies for decades. See just two examples: Paulina Borsook, *Cyberselfish: A Critical Romp Through the Terribly Libertarian Culture of High Tech* (New York: PublicAffairs, 2000), and Noam Cohen, *The Know-It-Alls: The Rise of Silicon Valley as a Political Powerhouse and Social Wrecking Ball* (New York: New Press, 2017).

Chapter 6: Einstein's Bathtub: Science, Art, Magic, and Mayhem from Pasadena to the Moon

112 Sigmund Freud said: Freud was reworking a comment he attributed to Napoleon—"Geography is destiny"—that historians doubt that the Frenchman ever actually uttered. Sigmund Freud, "The Dissolution of the Oedipus Complex," in *The Standard Edition of the Complete Psychological Works of Sigmund Freud, Volume XIX (1923–1925): The Ego and the Id and Other Works* (1924; repr., London: Hogarth Press and Institute of Psychoanalysis, 1961), p. 178.

113 "One man's 'magic'": Robert Heinlein, *Time Enough for Love* (1973; repr., New York: Ace, 1988), p. 250.

113 "Freedom is a two-edged sword": Parsons, "Freedom Is a Two-Edged Sword," in *Freedom Is a Two-Edged Sword and Other Essays*, p. 11.

114 This was, of course, Albert Einstein: Sources include Albrecht Folsing, *Albert Einstein: A Biography*, trans. Ewald Osers (1993; repr., New York: Penguin, 1997), and Walter Isaacson, *Einstein: His Life and Universe* (New York: Simon & Schuster, 2007).

115 "Here in Pasadena it is like Paradise": Folsing, *Albert Einstein*, p. 636.

116 "They are cheering me": David R. Topper, "1931: Einstein's First Visit to Caltech," in *How Einstein Created Relativity Out of Physics and Astronomy*, Astrophysics and Space Science Library, vol. 394 (New York: Springer, 2013), p. 138.

116 "Einstein, creator of some": Abraham Pais, *Einstein Lived Here* (Oxford, UK: Oxford University Press, 1994), p. 138.

116 The respective "looks": Leo Braudy suggests that there was something of the iconicity of Chaplin's Little Tramp character in Einstein's presentation of self in the interactive project *Three Winters in the Sun: Einstein in California* (book and DVD-ROM) (Los Angeles: USC-Annenberg Center for Communication, 2005).

116 "I hight Don Quixote": Jack Whiteside Parsons, "Untitled," *Oriflamme*, vol. 1, no. 2 (Pasadena: Agape Lodge, 1943), n.p.

117 Jack Parsons was raised: The indispensable biography is George Pendle, *Strange Angel: The Otherworldly Life of Rocket Scientist John Whiteside Parsons* (Orlando, FL: Harcourt, 2005). See also John Carter, *Sex and Rockets: The Occult World of Jack Parsons* (Port Townsend, WA: Feral House, 1999).

118 around campus as the Suicide Squad: Carter, *Sex and Rockets*, p. 18.

120 a hedonistic, syncretic utopia: Hugh B. Urban, "The Beast with Two Backs: Aleister Crowley, Sex Magic and the Exhaustion of Modernity," *Nova Religio: The Journal of Alternative and Emergent Religions* 7, no. 3 (2004): p. 10.

120 resell in California at a profit: Lawrence Wright, *Going Clear: Scientology, Hollywood, and the Prison of Belief* (New York: Vintage; 2013), p. 58.

121 allowed to do the almost unthinkable: Pendle, *Strange Angel*, p. 55.

121 The young man's full Prussian name: Sources include Michael Neufeld, *Von Braun: Dreamer of Space, Engineer of War* (New York: Vintage, 2008) and Bob Ward, *Dr. Space: The Life of Wernher von Braun* (2005; repr., Annapolis, MD: Naval Institute Press, 2009).

122 "just the place for you and your friends": Michael Bar-Zohar, *The Hunt for German Scientists* (New York: Hawthorn Books), p. 21.

122 Mittelbau-Dora concentration camp: Neufeld, *Von Braun*, p. 194.

123 Operation Paperclip, an American military: Ward, *Dr. Space*, p. 59.

123 sent down the memory hole: Neufeld, *Von Braun*, p. 239.

124 a series of intricately illustrated articles: J. P. Telotte, "Disney in Science Fiction Land," *Journal of Popular Film and Television* 33, no. 1 (2005): p. 14.

125 "I have devoted my life to amassing": Forrest Ackerman, quoted in Patti Perret, *The Faces of Science Fiction: Photographs by Patti Perret* (New York: Bluejay Books, 1984), p. 31.

125 Boys' Scientifiction Club: Deborah Painter, *Forry: The Life of Forrest J. Ackerman* (Jefferson, NC: McFarland, 2011), p. 27.

126 "hate the hell out of gadgets": Alec Nevala-Lee, *Astounding: John W. Campbell, Isaac Asimov, Robert A. Heinlein, L. Ron Hubbard, and the Golden Age of Science Fiction* (New York: Dey Street Books/HarperCollins, 2018), p. 246.

126 "as perfect a piece of science fiction": Nevala-Lee, *Astounding*, p. 117.

126 Myrtle R. Jones (better known as Morojo): Eric Leif Davin, *Partners in Wonder: Women and the Birth of Science Fiction, 1926–1965* (Lanham, MD: Lexington Books, 2006), p. 87.

127 Communist Party cells: C. Todd White, *Pre-Gay L.A.: A Social History of the Movement for Homosexual Rights* (Urbana and Chicago: University of Illinois Press, 2009), p. 19.

127 The inspiration behind its name: In 1953 Hay began delivering a lecture on his research into homosexuality under the title "The Feast of Fools" and in it gives a description of "Les Mattachine." Harry Hay, "The Feast of Fools," in *Radically Gay: Gay Liberation in the Words of Its Founder*, ed. Will Roscoe (Boston: Beacon Press, 1996), p. 112.

128 playing the organ: Pendle, *Strange Angel*, p. 150.

128 "Everyone was going to be a 'clear'": Pendle, *Strange Angel*, p. 272.

130 "cracked but not broken": Jeff Guinn, *Manson: The Life and Times of Charles Manson* (New York: Simon & Schuster, 2013), p. 58.

131 "Valentine Michael Manson": Ed Sanders, *The Family* (1971; repr., Boston: Da Capo Press, 2002), pp. 30 and 315.

131 Manson used Heinlein's language: Louis Filler, *Vanguards & Followers: Youth in the American Tradition* (1978; repr., New Brunswick, NJ, and London: Transaction, 1995), p. 182.

131 to "creepy-crawl": Guinn, *Manson*, p. 289.

132 "Can you ever live without the game": The afterlife of "Look at Your Game, Girl," including the version by Guns N' Roses, is discussed in Guinn, *Manson*, p. 396.

132 Beausoleil wrote the score: Bill Landis, *Anger: An Unauthorized Biography of Kenneth Anger* (New York: HarperCollins, 1995), p. 237.

133 new "magick lantern": Alice L. Hutchison, *Kenneth Anger: Demonic Visionary* (London: Black Dog, 2004), p. 189.

133 Marjorie Elizabeth Cameron Parsons Kimmel: Sources include those mentioned for Jack Parsons, as well as Spencer Kansa, *Wormwood Star: The Magickal Life of Marjorie Cameron* (Oxford, UK: Mandrake, 2010).

133 "some guy had fallen down": Kansa, *Wormwood Star*, p. 141.

134 one of her erotic drawings: Alice L. Hutchison, "Scarlet Woman on Film: Inauguration of the Pleasure Dome and the Wormwood Star: Kenneth Anger, Curtis Harrington, Marjorie Cameron, and Los Angeles Alternative Film and Culture in the Early 1950s," in *Alternative Projections: Experimental Film in Los Angeles, 1945–1980*, ed. David E. James and Adam Hyman (Bloomington: Indiana University Press, 2015), p. 98.

134 Parsons had earlier written a poem cycle: John W. Parsons and Marjorie Cameron, *Songs for the Witch Woman* (Somerset, UK: Fulgur, 2014). This volume has Parsons's poems illustrated by Cameron's drawings.

135 "Always pass on what you have learned": *Return of the Jedi*, 1983, directed by Richard Marquand, screenplay by Lawrence Kasdan and George Lucas.

136 "as man is, God once was": This distillation of Mormon thought has been attributed to Lorenzo Snow, the fifth president of the Church of Jesus Christ of Latter-day Saints.

136 the wispy tendrils of hair: John C. McDowell, *The Gospel According to Star Wars, Second Edition: Faith, Hope, and the Force* (Louisville, KY: Westminster John Knox Press, 2017), p. 24.

137 Physicists at Caltech: In 2016, on the hundredth anniversary of Einstein's predictions about the existence of gravitational waves, the Caltech-coordinated Laser Interferometer Gravitational-Wave Observatory (LIGO) confirmed their existence.

137 circular impact crater: Pendle, *Strange Angel*, p. 307.

Chapter 7: What Makes Men Happy: Student-Professor Liaisons, Modern Seating, the Story of Civilization, and How Every House Is Haunted

141 "We just did whatever was necessary": Ray Kaiser Eames, interviewed by Ruth Bowman for the Archives of American Art, Smithsonian Institution, Venice, CA, July 28 and 31 and August 20, 1980, n.p., https://www.aaa.si.edu/download_pdf_transcript/ajax?record_id=edanmdm-AAADCD_oh_212044.

141 "Who did the housework": Will and Ariel Durant, *Will & Ariel Durant: A Dual Autobiography* (New York: Simon & Schuster, 1977), p. 338.

142 four in ten Southern Californians: Fynnwin Prager et al., *The "Go-Virtual Initiative": Using Flexible Workplace Practices to Reduce Traffic Congestion, Increase Economic Development, and Provide More Access to Affordable Housing Choices in the South Bay Region of Los Angeles County* (San Jose, CA: Mineta Transportation Institute and San Jose State University, 2019), p. 18.

144 Take the Beverly Hills manor: Donald Bogle, *Bright Boulevards, Bold Dreams: The Story of Black Hollywood* (New York: Ballantine Books, 2006), p. 65.

145 "the doors of Opportunity": W. E. B. Du Bois, *The Souls of Black Folk: With "The Talented Tenth" and "The Souls of White Folk"* (1903; repr., New York: Penguin, 2018), p. 7.

145 When designing homes in Flintridge: Karen E. Hudson, *Paul R. Williams: Classic Hollywood Style* (New York: Rizzoli, 1994), p. 10.

145 training himself to sketch: Hudson, *Paul R. Williams*, p. 11. An abridgement of a 1937 Paul R. Williams essay where he discussed his inverted drawing technique appeared in *Ebony*, November 1986, pp. 148–54.

146 a business named Craig Ellwood: Sources include Neil Jackson, *California Modern: The Architecture of Craig Ellwood* (New York: Princeton Architec-

tural Press, 2002); Neil Jackson, *Craig Ellwood* (London: Laurence King, 2002); and Esther McCoy, *Craig Ellwood. Architecture* (1968; repr., Los Angeles: Hennessey & Ingalls, 1997).

146 thirty-two of the best Italian suits: Jackson, *California Modern*, p. 177.

149 "We spent our wedding night": Durant, *Will & Ariel Durant*, p. 54.

150 "abide there till the Reaper": Durant, *Will & Ariel Durant*, p. 225.

150 "They fitted in there": In his autobiography, *Another Life: A Memoir of Other People* (New York: Simon & Schuster, 1999), Michael Korda discusses his decades of work with the Durants, but these quotes come from an interview promoting the book on C-SPAN's *Booknotes* program, July 7, 1999. Michael Korda, interviewed by Brian Lamb, 27:41, https://www.c-span.org/video/?124611-1/another-life-memoir-people (video and transcript).

150 "He's a monk": Jim Hicks, "Books: More History from the Will Durants: Spry Old Team Does It Again," *Life*, October 18, 1963, p. 89.

151 exploded in rage: Korda, *Another Life*, p. 101.

152 "the least bookish person": Victoria Daley, "Almost a Business: Some Rare Bookshops in Los Angeles, 1920–40," in *Paperback L.A. Book 1: A Casual Anthology: Clothes, Coffee, Crushes, Crimes*, ed. Susan LaTempa (Altadena, CA: Prospect Park Books, 2018), p. 31.

152 "The Declaration of Interdependence": Will and Ariel Durant, "Chapter XIX: Interdependence, 1945," in *Will & Ariel Durant*, pp. 232–44. Also available at http://will-durant.com/interdependence.html.

153 "a stream … sometimes filled with blood": Hicks, "Books: More History from the Will Durants," p. 92.

154 "all is for the best": Voltaire, *Candide: Or Optimism*, trans. Theo Cuffe (1759; repr., New York: Penguin, 2005), pp. 15–16.

154 "Who will dare to write": Will and Ariel Durant, *The Lessons of History* (New York: Simon & Schuster, 1968), p. 41.

154 "into the American public domain": Pravrajika Vrajaprana, "Vedanta in America: Where We've Been and Where We Are," *Prabuddha Bharata*, February 2000, https://vedanta.org/2000/monthly-readings/vedanta-in-america-where-weve-been-and-where-we-are/.

154 found the Durants in prison: Malcolm X and Alex Haley, *The Autobiography of Malcolm X: As Told to Alex Haley* (1964; repr., New York: Ballantine Books, 1992), p. 178.

155 Conceived as a modern dwelling: See Marilyn and John Neuhart, *Eames House* (Hoboken, NJ: John Wiley & Sons, 1994), and James Steele, *Eames House: Charles and Ray Eames Architecture in Detail* (London: Phaidon, 1994).

156 "It was all theatre": Richard Martin, "Lie Back and Think of LA," *Apollo*, October 2015, p. 90, https://www.apollo-magazine.com/california-dreaming-reconsidering-the-work-of-charles-and-ray-eames/.

157 Charles grew up in Missouri: The definitive source is Pat Kirkham, *Charles and Ray Eames: Designers of the Twentieth Century* (Cambridge, MA: MIT Press, 1995).

158 **"Dear Miss Kaiser"**: Veronica Kavass, *Artists in Love: From Picasso & Gilot to Christo & Jeanne-Claude: A Century of Creative and Romantic Partnerships* (New York: Welcome Books, 2012), p. 86.

158 **"the darling of young architects"**: Esther McCoy, "Charles and Ray Eames" (1975), in *Piecing Together Los Angeles: An Esther McCoy Reader*, ed. Susan Morgan (Los Angeles: East of Borneo Books, 2012), p. 184.

159 **"essentially an artistic or philosophical enterprise"**: Charles Eames, quoted in Paul Schrader, "Poetry of Ideas: The Films of Charles Eames," originally published by *Film Quarterly* in 1970, and reprinted in Daniel Ostroff, ed., *An Eames Anthology: Articles, Film Scripts, Interviews, Letters, Notes, Speeches by Charles and Ray Eames* (New Haven, CT: Yale University Press, 2015), p. 289.

159 **"afford to have something"**: "Modern Living: The Anti-casting Couch," *Time*, January 5, 1970, p. 37.

160 **Herman Miller, the company**: Herman Miller, "Resolving the Problem of the Power Nap," n.d., https://www.hermanmiller.com/products/seating/lounge-seating/eames-chaise/design-story/.

160 **credible allegations**: Kirkham, *Charles and Ray Eames*, p. 76. Art historian Judith Wechsler speaks of her affair with Charles Eames in Jason Cohn and Bill Jersey's PBS *American Masters* documentary *Charles & Ray Eames: The Architect and the Painter* (2011).

162 **"Glimpses of the U.S.A."**: Kirkham, *Charles and Ray Eames*, p. 323.

163 **"Domestic Bliss: Angelina Jolie and Brad Pitt at Home"**: Steven Klein's restaging of Julius Shulman's famous photograph of Case Study House #6 was published in *W*, July 2005; it is the fourth image at https://www.wmagazine.com/gallery/brad-pitt-angelina-jolie/all.

164 **the tabloids reported it anyway**: "Brad and Angelina: Real Estate Tells the Truth," *Janet Charlton's Hollywood*, September 5, 2007, http://www.janetcharltonshollywood.com/brad-and-angelina-real-estate-tells-the-truth/. A longer report was posted on September 9, 2007, at http://www.bergproperties.com/blog/brad-pitt-reportedly-offered-8m-for-the-5883-square-foot-former-will-and-ariel-durant-estate-in-los-angeles-los-feliz-neighborhood-actor-was-rebuffed-/.

164 **"Happiness lies in the old-fashioned"**: Will Durant, "What Makes Men Happy?" *The Rotarian* LXXVII, November 1950, p. 9.

Chapter 8: California Rolls: Cars, the Women Who Drive Them, the Men Who Design Them, Avocados, and a Stop in Manzanar

167 **"I live my life a quarter mile at a time"**: *The Fast and the Furious*, 2001, directed by Rob Cohen, screenplay by Gary Scott Thompson, Erik Bergquist, and David Ayer.

167 **"I'm glad you have a TV'"**: Karen Tei Yamashita, *Tropic of Orange* (Minneapolis: Coffee House Press, 1997), p. 125.

168 **"as a riverman runs a river"**: Joan Didion, *Play It as It Lays* (1970; repr., New York: Farrar, Straus and Giroux, 2005), p. 16.

168 The movie is a family affair: Tracy Dougherty, *The Last Love Song: A Biography of Joan Didion* (New York: St. Martin's Press, 2015), p. 325.
169 "a yellow so bright": Abby Aguirre, "Joan Didion Remembers the Day Julian Wasser Took Her Portrait," *Vogue*, June 2014, https://www.vogue.com/article/joan-didion-and-julian-wasser-on-his-portraits-of-her.
169 "There's a point": Joan Didion, interviewed by Linda Kuhl, "Joan Didion: The Art of Fiction No. 71" (1978), in *Conversations with Joan Didion*, ed. Scott F. Parker (Jackson: University of Mississippi Press, 2018), p. 42.
169 "What do you think a celebrity is?": Joshua Paul Gamson, "Introduction: Explaining Angelyne," in *Claims to Fame: Celebrity in Contemporary America* (Berkeley and Los Angeles: University of California Press, 1992), p. 1.
170 Top Hat Café: Lana Turner, *Lana: The Lady, the Legend, the Truth* (New York: E. P. Dutton, 1982), p. 26.
170 "I can feel myself getting": Gamson, "Introduction: Explaining Angelyne," p. 2.
171 A young redheaded girl: Gary Baum, "The Mystery of L.A. Billboard Diva Angelyne's Real Identity Is Finally Solved," *Hollywood Reporter*, August 2, 2017, https://www.hollywoodreporter.com/features/angelyne-la-billboard-diva-30-years-1025678.
171 "Although I act": Natalie Alcala, "20 Questions with Hollywood Billboard Queen, Angelyne," *Racked: Los Angeles*, July 22, 2014, https://la.racked.com/2014/7/22/7585553/angelyne-exclusive-interview.
171 "We've had Gray": Mark Baldassare and Cheryl Katz, *The Coming Age of Direct Democracy: California's Recall and Beyond* (Lanham, MD: Rowman & Littlefield, 2008), p. 82.
172 the original "booth babes": Margery Krevsky, *Sirens of Chrome: The Enduring Allure of Auto Show Models* (Troy, MI: Momentum Books, 2008).
173 So, too, did Southern California spawn: See Jeremiah B. C. Axelrod, *Inventing Autopia: Dreams and Visions of the Modern Metropolis in Jazz Age Los Angeles* (Berkeley and Los Angeles: University of California Press, 2009).
173 the right to mobility: Genevieve Carpio, *Collisions at the Crossroads: How Place and Mobility Make Race* (Berkeley and Los Angeles: University of California Press, 2019), p. 21.
175 the C2, or second-generation Corvette: Randy Leffingwell, *Corvette Sixty Years* (Beverly, MA: Motorbooks, 2012), p. 67.
176 "You guys need me more": Gary D. Smith, "Larry Shinoda, Part 1," *Dean's Garage* (November 17, 2009). http://www.deansgarage.com/2009/larry-shinoda-part-1/.
177 "almost had a heart attack": Yoav Gilad, "Expelled from Design School, Larry Shinoda Designed an Icon," *Petrolicious*, December 1, 2014, https://petrolicious.com/articles/expelled-from-design-school-larry-shinoda-designed-an-icon.
177 "stake its own uniquely American ground": Comments from Larry Shinoda's acceptance speech during his induction into the National Corvette Museum's Hall of Fame in 1998, https://www.corvettemuseum.org/learn/about-corvette/corvette-hall-of-fame/larry-shinoda/.

177 engineering doesn't sell vehicles; style does: Jerry Burton, "The Struggle over the Sting Ray," *Car and Driver*, July 2002, http://www.caranddriver.com /features/the-struggle-over-the-sting-ray-feature-split-window-controversy -page-3.

177 1965 Chevrolet Corvair and the 1970 Boss Mustang: Mike Mueller, *Corvette: 1968–1982* (Osceola, WI: MBI Publishing Concepts, 2000), p. 27.

178 embodied a racial hatred: Carey McWilliams, "What About Our Japanese Americans?," a pamphlet prepared for the American Council of the Institute of Pacific Relations and published by the Public Affairs Committee, 1944, http://content.cdlib.org/view?docId=hb329004sw&brand=calisphere&doc. view=entire_text.

178 a fair-minded reformer: Abraham Hoffman, "The Conscience of a Public Official: Los Angeles Mayor Fletcher Bowron and Japanese Removal," *Southern California Quarterly* 92, no. 3 (Fall 2010): pp. 243–74.

179 "We must avoid the costly mistakes": Scott Kurashige, *The Shifting Grounds of Race: Black and Japanese Americans in the Making of Multiethnic Los Angeles* (Princeton, NJ: Princeton University Press, 2008), pp. 125–26.

180 apology from the Reagan White House: In 1982 the Commission on Wartime Relocation and Internment of Civilians acknowledged that the Roosevelt administration's policies were driven by "race prejudice, war hysteria and a failure of political leadership." *Personal Justice Denied: Report of the Commission on Wartime Relocation and Internment of Civilians* (Washington, DC: U.S. Government Printing Office, 1982), p. 18.

180 "the barracks had not been finished": Jerry Burton, "Larry Shinoda: Looking Back at a Legend," *Hagerty*, February 26, 2018, https://www.hagerty.com/ar ticles-videos/articles/2018/02/26/larry-shinoda-looking-back-at-a-legend.

180 "My brother had the guts": "Grace Shinoda Nakamura Interview," Whittier, California, January 25, 2012, Densho Digital Archive, Densho Visual History Collection, 2012. http://ddr.densho.org/media/ddr-densho-1003/ddr-densho -1003-8-transcript-20f2fcd04c.htm.

181 "To be successful in the United States": William Shurtleff and Akiko Aoyagi, *History of Soy Sauce (160 CE to 2012)* (Lafayette, CA: Soyinfo Center, 2012), p. 2253 [*n.b.* this page number is *not* a misprint; there's apparently a lot to the history of soy sauce], http://www.soyinfocenter.com/pdf/153/Sauc.pdf. Accessed January 9, 2016.

182 first dedicated sushi bar: Sasha Issenberg, *The Sushi Economy: Globalization and the Making of a Modern Delicacy* (New York: Gotham Books, 2007), p. 88.

183 "Sushi? Where I'm from": Commercial for "10-10-220" featuring Terry Bradshaw and Doug Flutie, 2000, https://www.youtube.com/watch?v=XdPWzyF cXWU. Bradshaw was fully in on the joke, of course, and discusses the filming of this commercial as an acting job: "I have learned to play" this "character Terry Bradshaw . . . a well meaning southern boy who might be a little light on the details." Terry Bradshaw with David Fisher, *It's Only a Game* (New York: Simon & Schuster, 2001), p. 54.

183 invented at Tokyo Kaikan: There are conflicting accounts of who spawned the
California roll, with claimants from as far away as Vancouver, but, then again,
it's not called a Canada roll.

184 a loaded burrito is an American food: David Kamp, *The United States of Arugula: The Sun-Dried, Cold-Pressed, Dark-Roasted, Extra Virgin Story of the
American Food Revolution* (New York: Broadway Books, 2006), p. 316.

185 "Someone once brought Janis Joplin": Joan Didion, "The White Album," in
The White Album (1979; repr., New York: Farrar, Straus and Giroux, 1990),
pp. 25–26.

Chapter 9: Hot Food, Cold War: Martial Arts and Culinary Arts, or How Blowback Made Los Angeles the Best Place in America to Fight and Eat

187 "Be formless, shapeless": Bruce Lee's most famous aphorism is cited in Matthew Polly, *Bruce Lee: A Life* (New York: Simon & Schuster, 2018), p. 285.

187 "Home is where you lay your taco": Roy Choi, Reddit Ask Me Anything (AMA),
2015, https://www.reddit.com/r/IAmA/comments/2jwvon/iama_roy_choi_i
_make_korean_bbq_tacos_and_worked/clftv0k/.

188 "No group of Americans": Bud Buonocore, "The GI Budoka," *Black Belt*, February 1974, p. 47, quoted in Sylvia Shin Huey Chong, *The Oriental Obscene:
Violence and Racial Fantasies in the Vietnam Era* (Durham, NC: Duke University Press, 2011), p. 178.

188 his Mormon acolytes: "Mormon Martial Arts, Part III: BYU, Bruce Lee, and
the King," *New West*, March 2, 2006, https://newwest.net/main/article/mor
mon_martial_arts_part_iii_byu_bruce_lee_and_the_king. Accessed March
10, 2017.

190 the "flowery forms": Polly, *Bruce Lee*, p. 174.

190 One of the Hollywood students: Charles Russo, *Striking Distance: Bruce Lee
and the Dawn of Martial Arts in America* (Lincoln: University of Nebraska
Press, 2016), pp. 121–22.

191 Sebring pleaded for mercy: Jeff Guinn, *Manson: The Life and Times of Charles
Manson* (New York: Simon & Schuster, 2013), p. 250.

191 Before detectives established: That Bruce Lee, Jay Sebring, Charles Manson,
and even Joan Didion (godparent to the same child as Roman Polanski, Sharon Tate's husband) were so easily connected to one another—via one or at
most two degrees of separation—is the sign that at a certain stratum, Los Angeles remained a small town for a very long time.

191 Polanski suggested they go: Polly, *Bruce Lee*, p. 267.

192 known there as *The Kato Show*: Polly, *Bruce Lee*, p. 292.

192 a *wu* masculinity: Daryl Joji Maeda, "Nomad of the Transpacific: Bruce Lee as
Method," *American Quarterly* 69, no. 3 (September 2017): p. 755.

193 "the organic community": Mary Reinholz, "Yin and Yang a la Carte," *West* (the
Sunday magazine of the *Los Angeles Times*), February 14, 1971, pp. 6 and 8.

193 One of these restaurants: Interview by the author with Source Family archivist/historian Isis Aquarian, Los Angeles, July 15, 2018.

193 Marine Corps veteran: Isis Aquarian, *The Source: The Untold Story of Father Yod, Ya Ho Wa 13 and the Source Family* (Los Angeles: Process, 2007), p. 24.

193 "only God and the Infinite": Marla Matzer Rose, *Muscle Beach: Where the Best Bodies in the World Started a Fitness Revolution* (New York: LA Weekly Books/ St. Martin's Press, 2001), p. 103.

194 "the mad ones": Jack Kerouac, *On the Road* (1957; repr., New York: Penguin, 1991), p. 5.

194 German *Lebensreform*: Gordon Kennedy, *Children of the Sun: A Pictorial Anthology from Germany to California 1883 to 1949* (Ojai, CA: Nivaria Press, 1998), pp. 8–9.

195 "dietary wisdom found in the teachings": Aquarian, *The Source*, p. 31.

196 That metamorphosis took working out: Bob Wall described the community: We "lived in L.A. and we got together all the time, and there were a lot of other guys that were at our level and a lot of them had black belts. We had a lot of guys that worked out with us; boxers, wrestlers, street fighters, Thai fighters, jiujitsu guys, you know . . . and we were sharing . . . knowledge." Jeffrey Bona, "Interview with Bob Wall," posted January 10, 2011, http://cityonfire.com/fea ture-bob-wall-interview/ (date of interview supplied by interviewer in email to the author dated June 16, 2018).

196 "the most defined body": Mike Mentzer, introduction to John Little, "Warm Marble: The Lethal Physique of Bruce Lee," 1996, https://www.mikementzer .com/blee.html.

197 "the greatest blaxploitation hero": Darius James, *That's Blaxploitation! Roots of the Baadasssss 'Tude* (New York: St. Martin's Griffin, 1995), p. 14.

198 "Me Rongo, god of agriculture": "Disneyland Enchanted Tiki Room—Original Show," by user ru42, https://www.youtube.com/watch?v=fhApjPASb64.

199 "like a pond that had caught fire": Andy Lewis, "If These Menus Could Talk: The History of L.A. Power Dining Revealed," *Hollywood Reporter*, July 22, 2015. https://www.hollywoodreporter.com/features/menus-could-talk-history -la-810280.

199 the U.S. Border Patrol: Kelly Lytle Hernandez, *Migra! A History of the U.S. Border Patrol* (Berkeley and Los Angeles: University of California Press, 2010), p. 26.

199 Ray Buhen, the Filipino American mixologist: Glenn R. Carroll and Dennis Ray Wheaton, "Donn, Vic and Tiki Bar Authenticity," *Consumption Markets & Culture* 22, no. 2 (2019): pp. 166–67.

200 The intelligence community: Chalmers Johnson, *Blowback: The Costs and Consequences of American Empire* (New York: Holt Paperbacks, 2004), p. xi.

201 this bill that we will: Lyndon B. Johnson, "Remarks at the Signing of the Immigration Bill," *The International Migration Review*, no. 1 (Spring 2011): 200–204, p. 201.

204 known as the Secret Kitchen: Vu H. Pham, "Secret Kitchen": An Amalgam of Family, Fortune and Fusion Food in Asian American Cuisine," *Amerasia Jour-*

nal 32, no. 2 (2006): pp. 21–34. See also Eddie Lin, "Behind the Scenes: The Mysterious Story of Crustacean's 'Secret Kitchen,'" *Los Angeles*, May 19, 2014, http://www.lamag.com/digestblog/behind-the-scenes-the-mysterious -story-of-crustaceans-secret-kitchen/.

205 Hedren saw an opportunity: Tippi Hedren, *Tippi: A Memoir* (New York: William Morrow, 2016), pp. 168–71.

205 an everyday luxury: Miliann Kang, *The Managed Hand: Race, Gender, and the Body in Beauty Service Work* (Berkeley and Los Angeles: University of California Press, 2010), p. 44.

206 Ngoy eventually bought: Paul R. Mullins, *Glazed America: A History of the Doughnut* (Gainesville: University Press of Florida, 2008), p. 89.

207 carbon fiber cupholder: This price was for the 2013 model. https://jalopnik .com/ferrari-will-charge-you-3-533-for-a-carbon-fiber-cupho-898949796.

207 a polyglot collection: Cuisine from the Philippines is rising in twenty-first-century Los Angeles but has yet to achieve the ubiquity of the others I have been describing. As well, the fact that the Philippines was a territory of the United States from 1898 to 1946 meant that immigration laws and patterns differed significantly. See E. San Juan Jr., "Filipino Immigrants in the United States," *Philippine Studies* 48, no. 1 (First Quarter 2000): pp. 121–25.

208 real estate agent Mike Silverman: Email dated May 10, 2018, to the author from Steven M. Price, author of *Trousdale Estates: Midcentury to Modern in Beverly Hills* (New York: Regan Arts, 2017).

208 "the new Persian Gulf": Michael Gross, *Unreal Estate: Money, Ambition, and the Lust for Land in Los Angeles* (New York: Broadway Books, 2011), p. 434.

209 "Do I look like a Malone": Hilary E. Macgregor, "The Sweet Life," *Los Angeles Times*, July 9, 2002, https://www.latimes.com/archives/la-xpm-2002-jul-09-lv -mashti9-story.html.

210 Calle de Los Negros: Scott Zesch, *The Chinatown War: Chinese Los Angeles and the Massacre of 1871* (Oxford, UK, and New York: Oxford University Press, 2012), p. 13.

210 "You cannot work a man": Anita Mannur, "Asian American Food-scapes," *Amerasia Journal* 32, no. 2 (2006): pp. 1–2.

210 "Meat vs. Rice": Samuel Gompers and Herman Gutstadt, "Meat vs. Rice: American Manhood against Asiatic Coolieism—Which Shall Survive?" (San Francisco: American Federation of Labor, 1902), archived at https://babel.ha thitrust.org/cgi/pt?id=ucl.32106007093054;view=1up;seq=17.

211 ethnic Chinese investors: After a search, native-born USC graduate and Department of Water and Power engineer turned developer Peter Soo Hoo negotiated to buy a large plot of land from the Santa Fe Railway and sold shares to twenty-eight other Chinese Americans. See Josi Ward, "'Dreams of Oriental Romance': Reinventing Chinatown in 1930s Los Angeles," *Buildings & Landscapes: Journal of the Vernacular Architecture Forum* 20, no. 1 (Spring 2013): p. 32.

212 Rice Bowl restaurant: Josh Kun, *To Live and Dine in L.A.: Menus and the Making of the Modern City* (Los Angeles: Angel City Press/Library Foundation of Los Angeles, 2015), p. 120.

212 But Hsieh had a different vision: Timothy Fong, *The First Suburban China-town: The Remaking of Monterey Park, California* (Philadelphia: Temple University Press, 1994), p. 29.

212 calls an "ethnoburb": Wei Li, *Ethnoburb: The New Ethnic Community in Urban America* (Honolulu: University of Hawaii Press, 2012).

213 "While the construction may be": Jonathan Gold, "Jonathan Gold Reviews Shanghai No. 1 Seafood Village," *LA Weekly*, February 2, 2012, https://www.laweekly.com/jonathan-gold-reviews-shanghai-no-1-seafood-village/.

213 "because of better ingredients": Margy Rochlin, "Q & A with *Soul of a Ban-quet*'s Wayne Wang: Cecilia Chiang + Why the Best Chinese Food in the World Is in the SGV," *LA Weekly*, April 6, 2013, http://www.laweekly.com/restaurants/q-and-a-with-soul-of-a-banquets-wayne-wang-cecilia-chiang-why-the-best-chinese-food-in-the-world-is-in-the-sgv-2896973.

213 "Before, immigrants were poor": Jon C. Teaford, *The Metropolitan Revolution: The Rise of Post-Urban America* (New York: Columbia University Press, 2006), p. 227.

214 Monterey Park's nativist faction: "Sample Ballot and Voter Information Pam-phlet, City of Monterey Park, General Municipal Election, Tuesday, April 8, 1986," compiled and prepared by Pauline Y. Lemire, City Clerk.

215 a deeply personal essay: Clarissa Wei, "How Boba Became an Integral Part of Asian-American Culture in Los Angeles," *LA Weekly*, January 16, 2017, https://www.laweekly.com/how-boba-became-an-integral-part-of-asian-american-culture-in-los-angeles/.

215 "The flavors are fruity": "Bobalife," Fung Brothers ft. Kevin Lien, Priska, and Aileen Xu, 2013, https://www.youtube.com/watch?v=zccNQPH7Xe0.

Chapter 10: The Billion-Dollar Bay: Ports, Too Much Stuff, TruckNutz, Wife Swappers, and a Gangster in a Yachting Cap

216 "Whenever I'd put wine": Shan Li, "Dave Gold Dies at 80; Entrepreneur Behind 99 Cents Only Chain," *Los Angeles Times*, April 26, 2013, https://www.latimes.com/local/obituaries/la-me-dave-gold-20130427-story.html.

217 "No loss should hit us": Ove Hornby, *With Constant Care: A. P. Møller: Ship-owner 1876–1965* (Copenhagen: Shultz, 1988), p. 2.

217 "Obviously crime pays": Staff, "Liddy Believes That Crimes Pays," *Buffalo News*, March 15, 1991, https://buffalonews.com/1991/03/15/liddy-believes-that-crime-pays/.

218 one of the single most expensive photographs: Noah Horowitz, *Art of the Deal: Contemporary Art in a Global Financial Market* (Princeton, NJ: Princeton University Press, 2011), p. 45.

218 "Without water the dust": *Chinatown*, 1974, directed by Roman Polanski, screenplay by Robert Towne.

219 Lloyd Wright's Wayfarers Chapel: Erik Davis, *The Visionary State: A Journey Through California's Spiritual Landscape* (San Francisco: Chronicle Books, 2006), pp. 59–60.

220 a billion dollars a day: Joseph Bonney, "Putting a Price on a Port Strike," *Journal of Commerce*, February 15, 2013, https://www.joc.com/port-news/longshore man-labor/international-longshoremen's-association/putting-price-port -strike_20130215.html. In this article, Beacon Economics' Jock O'Connell challenges the billion-dollar figure: "It's a made-up number, a statistical fiction. It's a conveniently large, round number that people can grab onto. But when you start peeling the onion, it's impossible to justify. It's the equivalent of saying it's a gazillion dollars. If you said a gazillion, people would laugh at you, but a billion sounds reasonable. The same billion-dollar figure is trotted out regardless of the time, place or duration of the strike."

221 snow-walking AT-ATs: George Lucas categorically denies that the AT-AT walkers were inspired by shipping cranes, saying, "That is definitely a myth." Peter Hartlaub, "Nah, Dude, They Weren't Cranes, They Were Garbage Trucks," *SFGate*, June 25, 2008, https://www.sfgate.com/bayarea/article/Nah-dude-they -weren-t-cranes-they-were-garbage-3279459.php.

222 trucking executive named Malcolm McLean: Marc Levinson, *The Box: How the Shipping Container Made the World Smaller and the World Economy Bigger*, 2nd ed. (Princeton, NJ: Princeton University Press, 2016).

223 While A.P. waited out the war: Hornby, *With Constant Care*, p. 163.

224 Pier 400, completed in 2000: Bill Sharpsteen, *The Docks* (Berkeley and Los Angeles: University of California Press, 2011), p. 26.

224 "piles of stuff": D. Edward Martin, "Jason Rhoades: Installations, 1994–2006," *Art[Memo]*, n.d. but assumed to be 2017, http://artmemomagazine.com /jason-rhoades-installations-1994-2006/.

225 "I encourage you all": George W. Bush, "Presidential Press Conference," White House, December 20, 2006, https://georgewbush-whitehouse.archives.gov /news/releases/2006/12/20061220-1.html.

225 Lego's 2014 Maersk-themed kit: See https://shop.lego.com/en-US/product /Maersk-Line-Triple-E-10241.

226 Instead of separate kitchens: Paul Adamson and Marty Arbunich, *Eichler: Modernism Rebuilds the American Dream* (Layton, UT: Gibbs Smith, 2002), p. 13.

227 the most photographed home: Frank Lovece, "'Brady Bunch' House Is Up for Sale for Nearly $2 Million," *Newsday*, July 19, 2018, https://www.newsday .com/entertainment/tv/brady-bunch-house-sale-1.19939580.

227 the triumph of the simulation: Jean Baudrillard, *Simulations*, trans. Paul Foss, Paul Patton, and Philip Beitchman (New York: Semiotext(e), 1983), p. 25.

229 "Scan your environment for materials": Lauren Fritts, "Knolling: The Art of Material Culture," *Art Education* 72, no. 1 (January 2019): pp. 50–58.

230 "I go to my clients' homes": Kim Kardashian, first interview on the E! network, April 2006. Video embedded at https://www.eonline.com/news/590484/kim -kardashian-says-she-would-totally-do-a-reality-show-in-first-ever-e-interview -watch-now.

230 woman walked into an LA County Walmart: Andrew Blankstein and Jack Leonard, "Woman in Wal-Mart Pepper Spray Attack Was 'Competitive Shop-

ping,'" *Los Angeles Times*, November 25, 2011, https://latimesblogs.latimes
.com/lanow/2011/11/pepper-spray-wal-mart-competitive-shopping.html.

232 "to keep 120 million Americans": Jeer Witter, "The Wild Reign of Captain
Tony and His Floating Casinos," *Los Angeles*, March 1965, https://www.lamag
.com/askchris/tony-cornero-and-the-ss-rex/.

233 newspaper ads described: Ernest Marquez, *Noir Afloat: Tony Cornero and the
Notorious Gambling Ships of Southern California* (Santa Monica, CA: Angel
City Press, 2011), p. 47.

233 They were "seagulls": Marquez, *Noir Afloat*, p. 50.

234 "This is from Buron" and "Is that a gun in your pocket": Julia Bricklin, *Blonde
Rattlesnake: Burmah Adams, Tom White, and the 1933 Crime Spree That Ter-
rorized Los Angeles* (Guilford, CT: Lyons Press, 2019), p. 30.

234 "racket boy Tony Cornero": Mae West, *Goodness Had Nothing to Do with It: The
Autobiography of Mae West* (Englewood Cliffs, NJ: Prentice-Hall, 1959), p. 204.

234 "a great nuisance": Earl Warren, *The Memoirs of Earl Warren* (New York:
Doubleday, 1977), p. 132 (editor's note).

234 Warren's men backed off: Warren, *Memoirs of Earl Warren*, p. 135.

235 "as cold as the ashes of love": Raymond Chandler, *Farewell, My Lovely* (1940;
repr., New York: Vintage Books, 1992), p. 255.

235 This turned out to be his final act: Alan Balbonifor, "Tony Cornero," *Las Vegas
Review-Journal*, February 7, 1999, https://www.reviewjournal.com/news/tony
-cornero/.

236 Furusato's entire population: Jeanne Wakatsuki Houston and James D. Houston, *Farewell to Manzanar* (New York: Houghton Mifflin, 1973), offer the
most famous portrait of life on Terminal Island before the internment.

237 Livid about the whole fiasco: Charles Barton, *Howard Hughes and His Flying
Boat* (Vienna, VA: Charles Barton, 1998), p. 12.

237 as the Spruce Goose: Donald L. Barlett and James B. Steele, *Howard Hughes:
His Life and Madness* (1979; repr., New York: W. W. Norton, 2004), p. 118.

237 it was an alien being: Sasha Archibald, "Mass Effect," *Cabinet*, Spring 2014,
http://www.cabinetmagazine.org/issues/53/archibald.php.

238 the Grateful Dead played a free concert: Robert Greenfield, *Bear: The Life and
Times of Augustus Owsley Stanley III* (New York: Thomas Dunne Books,
2016), p. 137.

238 Speaking of head-spinning: Timothy Leary and G. Gordon Liddy, like Owsley
Stanley, were famous white inmates from the upper middle class. In this they
differed radically from California's huge prison population, which was and remains, as Ruth Wilson Gilmore points out, dominated by the "working or
workless poor, most of whom are not white." *Golden Gulag: Prisons, Surplus,
Crisis, and Opposition in Globalizing California* (Berkeley and Los Angeles:
University of California Press, 2007), p. 15.

239 As a prosecutor: Liddy tells his version of the raid in *Will: The Autobiography
of G. Gordon Liddy* (1980; repr., New York: St. Martin's Press, 1991), pp.
147–164.

239 "the most dangerous man in America": Bill Minutaglio and Steven L. Davis, *The Most Dangerous Man in America: Timothy Leary, Richard Nixon and the Hunt for the Fugitive King of LSD* (New York: Twelve, 2018), p. xiii.

240 "once you realize": Alan Moore and Dave Gibbons, *Watchmen Chapter II* (New York: DC Comics, 1986), p. 13.

Chapter 11. Days of the Dead: Frozen Bodies, Real Martyrs, Fake Shemps, and the Quest for Immortality in the City of Angels

243 "Who will fight the bear": Bas Jan Ader, "Quotations of Bas Jan Ader, Comments by Bill Leavitt" (n.d.) http://www.basjanader.com/dp/Leavitt.pdf.

243 "Expect me... like you expect": Tupac Shakur, "Outro" on *Better Dayz* (2002), the fourth of his albums to be released posthumously.

244 "the stench near the crypt": David Walker, "Valley Cryonic Crypt Desecrated, Untended," *Valley News*, June 10, 1979, p. 11.

244 "If things had worked out differently": Bob Nelson with Kenneth Bly and Sally Magana, *Freezing People Is (Not) Easy: My Adventures in Cryonics* (Lanham, MD: Lyons Press, 2014), p. 117.

245 Copyright on this signature rodent: Lawrence Lessig, *Free Culture: How Big Media Uses Technology and the Law to Lock Down Culture and Control Creativity* (New York: Penguin, 2004), pp. 134–35.

245 the corporation's lawyers filed an application: Isabel Millán, "'¡Vámonos! Let's Go!': Latina/o Children's Television," in *The Routledge Companion to Latina/o Popular Culture*, ed. Frederick Luis Aldama (London and New York: Routledge, 2016), p. 54.

245 It's not just the Mexican and Mexican American: The use of "Mexican," "Mexican American," "Chicano/a/x" and "Latino/a/x" in this book is informed by Sanchez, *Becoming Mexican American*, p. 277.

245 covered in the Aztec marigolds: Regina M. Marchi, *Day of the Dead in the USA: The Migration and Transformation of a Cultural Phenomenon* (New Brunswick, NJ: Rutgers University Press, 2009), p. 150, note 10.

246 As CNN observed in its coverage: Cindy Y. Rodriguez, "Day of the Dead Trademark Request Draws Backlash for Disney," CNN.com, May 11, 2013, https://www.cnn.com/2013/05/10/us/disney-trademark-day-dead/index.html.

247 One of its masterstrokes: Griselda Nevarez, "Cartoonist Lalo Alcaraz to Work on Pixar's Day of the Dead Film 'Coco,'" NBCNews.com, August, 23, 2015, https://www.nbcnews.com/news/latino/cartoonist-lalo-alcaraz-work-pixars-coco-n413771.

247 almost $1 billion in revenue: Nancy Tartaglione, "'Coco' Sweet with $800M Milestone at Worldwide Box Office," *Deadline*, May 1, 2018, https://deadline.com/2018/05/coco-crosses-800-million-global-box-office-disney-pixar-1202380459/.

247 In 2018 they created: Beige Luciano-Adams, "The Ofrenda at the Heart of the Natural History Museum's New Permanent Exhibition," *LA Weekly*, June

14, 2018, https://www.laweekly.com/the-ofrenda-at-the-heart-of-the-natural -history-museums-new-permanent-exhibition/.

248 **But in the later part of the decade:** Mario T. Garcia, "Introduction," in Rubén Salazar, *Border Correspondent: Selected Writings, 1955–1970*, ed. Mario T. Garcia (Berkeley and Los Angeles: University of California Press, 1998), p. 29.

249 **"Who is a Chicano?":** "Who Is a Chicano? And What Is It the Chicanos Want?" in Salazar, *Border Correspondent*, pp. 235–37.

249 **"swimming-pool communists":** Domanick, *To Protect and to Serve*, p. 223.

249 **Kids demonstrating against:** Garcia, "Introduction," in Salazar, *Border Correspondent*, p. 25.

249 **one college counselor per four thousand students:** Mario T. García and Sal Castro, *Blowout! Sal Castro and the Chicano Struggle for Educational Justice* (Chapel Hill: University of North Carolina Press, 2011), p. 113.

250 **one of the most debated tragedies:** Contemporary and contradictory accounts of the slaying came on successive days: David Shaw and Richard Vasquez, "Contradictory Reports Given in Slaying of Columnist Salazar," *Los Angeles Times*, August 30, 1970, and Paul Houston and Richard Vasquez, "Salazar Was Killed by Tear-Gas Shell," *Los Angeles Times*, August 31, 1970. Three decades later, the city's paper of record, on the basis of further investigations and the release of formerly classified FBI files, would still not rule definitively: Robert J. Lopez, "FBI Files Shed Little Light on Rubén Salazar's Death," *Los Angeles Times*, November 18, 1999.

251 *The Wall That Speaks, Sings and Shouts*: LA mural painted by Paul Botello, Gerardo Herrera, Adalberto Ortiz, and Gustave Sanchez in 2001.

251 **"La Tragedia Del 29 De Agosto":** Lalo Guerrero and Sherilyn Mentes, *Lalo: My Life and Music* (Tucson: University of Arizona Press, 2002), p. 141.

251 **a member of Los Four:** Karen Mary Davalos, *Chicana/o Remix: Art and Errata Since the Sixties* (New York: New York University Press, 2017), p. 194.

251 **Self Help Graphics & Art:** Sister Boccalero founded Art, Inc. in 1970 but incorporated the organization under the name Self Help Graphics & Art in 1973.

252 **all to commemorate Rubén Salazar:** "We've got to do something to honor the people who died in this struggle. We've got to do something to honor Rubén Salazar, who tried to do something about it." Interview with Consuelo Flores, n.d., http://lahistoryarchive.socalstudio.org/resources/Boccalero/oral.html. Also see the narrative time line of SHG: "Flores . . . points to the killing of Salazar as catalyst for SHG's first Día de los Muertos, held twenty-five months later." http://www.lahistoryarchive.org/resources/SHG/essay.html#a42.

252 **"newsroom objectivity may result":** Garcia, "Introduction," in Salazar, *Border Correspondent*, p. 29.

252 **"THE . . . MURDER . . . AND RESURRECTION":** Hunter S. Thompson, "Strange Rumblings in Aztlan," in *Fear and Loathing in Las Vegas and Other American Stories* (1971; repr., New York: Modern Library, 1991), p. 217.

253 **"two bags of grass":** Thompson, *Fear and Loathing in Las Vegas and Other American Stories*, p. 4.

254 his "name mask": Ilan Stavans, *Bandido: The Death and Resurrection of Oscar "Zeta" Acosta* (1995; repr., Evanston, IL: Northwestern University Press, 2003), p. 61.

254 "the violent arm of the rich": Oscar Zeta Acosta, *The Revolt of the Cockroach People* (1973; repr., New York: Vintage, 1989), p. 136.

254 Zeta lost by over a million votes: Rubén Salazar, "To the Chicanos, It Is How Narrowly a Candidate Lost," *Los Angeles Times*, June 2, 1970, in Salazar, *Border Correspondent*, p. 258.

255 "only reason for describing him": Hunter S. Thompson, "The Banshee Screams for Buffalo Meat" (1979), in *The Great Shark Hunt: Strange Tales from a Strange Time* (New York: Simon & Schuster, 2011), p. 512.

255 "the writer must participate": Hunter S. Thompson, "Jacket Copy for *Fear and Loathing in Las Vegas*," in *Fear and Loathing in Las Vegas and Other American Stories*, p. 208.

256 "My God! Hunter has stolen my soul": Stavans, *Bandido*, p. 99.

256 a letter from Zeta: Oscar Zeta Acosta, *Oscar "Zeta" Acosta: The Uncollected Works*, ed. Ilan Stavans (Houston, TX: Arte Público Press / University of Houston, 1996), p. 109.

256 scuzzy descendant "gonzo porn": The genre has only grown since David Foster Wallace analyzed it in "Big Red Son" (1998), in *Consider the Lobster* (Boston: Little, Brown, 2005), pp. 25–27.

257 "the most detestable city on earth": Acosta, *Revolt of the Cockroach People*, p. 23.

257 The rumors are rife: Stavans, *Bandido*, pp. 117–23.

257 "Is he a hero, a myth?": Stavans, *Bandido*, p. 115.

258 For more than half a century: From Herbert Hoover's passing in 1964, seven of ten dead presidents have been interred in their libraries.

258 The first of those came out in 1978: Richard Nixon, *RN: The Memoirs of Richard Nixon* (New York: Simon & Schuster, 1978).

259 the new exhibits: Christine Mai-Duc, "The 'New' Nixon Library's Challenge: Fairly Depicting a 'Failed Presidency,'" *Los Angeles Times*, August 16, 2016, https://www.latimes.com/politics/la-pol-ca-nixon-library-reopening-20160816-snap-htmlstory.html.

259 embattled Nixon *Agonistes*: Garry Wills, *Nixon Agonistes: The Crisis of the Self-Made Man* (Boston: Houghton Mifflin, 1970).

261 they found an actor: Matthew Carey, "First Tupac, Then Roy Orbison, and now Ronald Reagan Comes Back as a Lifelike Hologram," *Los Angeles Daily News*, October 10, 2018, https://www.dailynews.com/2018/10/10/the-ronald-reagan-presidential-library-has-a-new-speaker-ronald-reagan-thanks-to-hollywood/.

261 version of a "Pepper's Ghost": Cyrus Farivar, "Tupac 'Hologram' Merely Pretty Cool Optical Illusion," *Ars Technica*, April 16, 2012, https://arstechnica.com/science/2012/04/tupac-hologram-merely-pretty-cool-optical-illusion/.

261 "under Ronald Reagan": Michael Eric Dyson, *Holler If You Hear Me: Searching for Tupac Shakur* (2001; repr., New York: Basic Civitas Books, 2006), p. 81.

263 The dilemma for *Plan 9*: Bill Warren, *Keep Watching the Skies! American Science Fiction Movies of the Fifties*, 21st century ed. (Jefferson, NC: McFarland, 2010), p. 663.

263 called "Fake Shemps": Bruce Campbell, *If Chins Could Kill: Confessions of a B Movie Actor* (New York: LA Weekly Books for Thomas Dunne/St. Martin's Press, 2002), pp. 111–12.

263 suffered a fatal heart attack: Jeff Lenburg, Joan Howard Maurer, and Greg Lenburg, *The Three Stooges Scrapbook*, updated ed. (Chicago: Chicago Review Press, 2012), p. 43.

264 CGI Bruce paces: Alexander Abad-Santos, "Johnnie Walker Offends by Using Bruce Lee in Chinese Ad," *The Atlantic*, July 12, 2013. https://www.theatlantic.com/business/archive/2013/07/heres-reason-fans-dont-johnnie-walker-using-bruce-lee-its-latest-ad/313391/.

265 "I shall endeavor": Lisa Colletta, *British Novelists in Hollywood, 1935–1965: Travelers, Exiles, and Expats* (New York: Palgrave Macmillan, 2013), p. 76.

265 English visitors including: See those two scabrous novels by Englishmen in Los Angeles, Aldous Huxley, *After Many a Summer Dies the Swan* (1939), and Evelyn Waugh, *The Loved One: An Anglo-American Tragedy* (1948).

266 the crematorium literally collapsed: Alice Bolin, "The Evergreen Dream," *LARB Quarterly Journal* no. 4 (Fall 2014), https://lareviewofbooks.org/article/evergreen-dream/.

266 "ultimate way in this town": Charlie Leduff, "Comeback for Resting Place of Movie Stars," *New York Times*, December 1, 2002, https://www.nytimes.com/2002/12/01/us/comeback-for-resting-place-of-movie-stars.html.

266 "more stars than there are": Tino Balio, *MGM* (London: Routledge, 2018), p. 1.

Conclusion: Tears in Rain

268 magicians of the aether: Vincent Brook, "Still an Empire of Their Own: How Jews Remain Atop a Reinvented Hollywood," in *From Shtetl to Stardom: Jews and Hollywood The Jewish Role in American Life*, eds. Michael Renov and Vincent Brook (West Lafayette, IN: Purdue University Press, 2017), p. 5.

269 "Connections need not": Robert Menasse, *The Capital*, trans. Jamie Bulloch (New York: Liveright/W. W. Norton, 2019), p. 9.

271 "the winds of the city": Harlan Ellison, "Bleeding Stones," in *Deathbird Stories* (New York: Harper and Row, 1975), p. 182.

272 Three of the central themes: These observations draw from conversations with science fiction author and futurist Bruce Sterling.

273 impossible interstellar journeys: Judith B. Kerman, "Technology and Politics in the Blade Runner Dystopia," in *Retrofitting Blade Runner: Issues in Ridley Scott's* Blade Runner *and Philip K. Dick's* Do Androids Dream of Electric Sheep?, 2nd ed. (Madison: University of Wisconsin Press, 1997), p. 20. In a commentary track on the 2007 DVD for *Blade Runner: The Final Cut*, director Ridley Scott says that *Blade Runner* takes place in the same fictional future as his 1979 film *Alien*, in which voyages between the stars are commonplace.

274 "Take the Bradbury Building": Esther McCoy, "A Vast Hall, Full of Light" (1953), in *Piecing Together Los Angeles: An Esther McCoy Reader*, ed. Susan Morgan (Los Angeles: East of Borneo Books, 2012), p. 255.

274 "a vast hall full of light": Edward Bellamy, *Looking Backward* (1888, under the title *Looking Backward: 2000–1887*; repr., Mineola, NY: Dover Thrift Editions, 1996), p. 49.

275 McCoy's primary sources: John Crandell, "Sumner, George & Esther: The Bradbury, Reconsidered," in *Homage to Downtown: In Search of Place and Memory in Ancient L.A.* (Sacramento, CA: Visions of L.A., 2007), pp. 205 and 214.

277 "like tears in rain": There is an extended analysis of Roy Batty's final scene, and Rutger Hauer's contributions to the dialogue, in Paul M. Sammon, *Future Noir: The Making of Blade Runner*, revised and updated ed. (New York: Dey Street/HarperCollins, 2017), pp. 229–31.

INDEX

Note: Page numbers in *italics* indicate photographs.